Mediatization of Politics

Mediatization of Politics

Understanding the Transformation of Western Democracies

Edited by

Frank Esser
University of Zurich, Switzerland

Jesper Strömbäck
Mid Sweden University, Sweden

First published 2014 by
PALGRAVE MACMILLAN

Palgrave Macmillan in the UK is an imprint of Macmillan Publishers Limited,
registered in England, company number 785998, of Houndmills, Basingstoke,
Hampshire RG21 6XS.

Palgrave Macmillan in the US is a division of St Martin's Press LLC,
175 Fifth Avenue, New York, NY 10010.

Palgrave Macmillan is the global academic imprint of the above companies
and has companies and representatives throughout the world.

Palgrave® and Macmillan® are registered trademarks in the United States,
the United Kingdom, Europe and other countries.

ISBN 978–1–137–27583–7 hardback
ISBN 978–1–137–42597–3 paperback

Contents

Part IV Conclusion

Figures and Tables

Figures

Tables

Acknowledgments

The idea behind this book originated in the fall of 2011 when Jesper was a visiting professor at the Institute of Mass Communication and Media Research at the University of Zurich (IPMZ) where Frank teaches and also co-directs the Swiss National Center of Competence in Research on Challenges to Democracy in the 21st Century (NCCR Democracy). We thank both institutions for their stimulating research environments.

Frank Esser, Jesper Strömbäck

Contributors

Jay G. Blumler is Emeritus Professor of Public Communication at the University of Leeds and Emeritus Professor of Journalism at the University of Maryland. His research has involved studies of political communication effects, observations of journalistic newsmaking during election campaigns, analysis of change over time in politician–journalist relationships and the comparative analysis of political communication systems. His books include *The Internet and Democratic Citizenship: Theory, Practice and Policy* (2009, with Stephen Coleman) and *The Crisis of Public Communication* (1995, with Michael Gurevitch).

Florin Büchel is a doctoral candidate and research assistant at the Institute of Mass Communication and Media Research, University of Zurich. His main research and teaching interests are international and comparative aspects of political communication, journalism cultures, political and media systems and cultural industries. His PhD project is a cross-country comparison of media interventionism as manifested in televised election news coverage.

Paul D'Angelo is Associate Professor of Mass Media and Political Communication at the College of New Jersey. He is the co-editor of *Doing News Framing Analysis: Empirical and Theoretical Perspectives* (2010). His research on theories and effects of news framing in political campaign settings, both within the United States and in comparative settings, has appeared in *American Behavioral Scientist*, the *Journal of Communication* and the *International Journal of Press/Politics*. His work on the historiography of the discipline of political communication in the United States has appeared in *Mass Communication and Society* and *Communication Yearbook*.

Claes H. de Vreese is Professor and Chair of Political Communication at ASCoR (Amsterdam School of Communication Research), University of Amsterdam. He has published widely on various topics on political communication, media effects and electoral behavior. He was the director of ASCoR from 2005–2013 and is the founding director of the Center for Politics and Communication.

Patrick Donges is Professor of Communication Science at the University of Greifswald. His research focuses on political communication, organizational communication, media structures and media policy and communication theory. More information can be found at www.phil.uni-greifswald.de/patrickdonges.html.

Frank Esser is Professor of International and Comparative Media Research at the University of Zurich. There he also co-directs an 80-person strong National Competence Center in Research on Challenges to Democracy in the 21st Century (NCCR Democracy). After studying in Mainz and London, he was assistant professor at the University of Missouri and visiting professor at the University of Oklahoma, of Texas (Austin) and of California (San Diego). His research focuses on cross-national studies of news journalism and political communication. His books include *Comparing Political Communication* (2004, with B. Pfetsch), *Handbook of Comparative Communication Research* (2012, with T. Hanitzsch) and *Democracy in the Age of Globalization and Mediatization* (2013, with H. Kriesi).

Otfried Jarren is Professor of Mass Communication and Media Research at the University of Zurich and Vice President for Arts and Social Sciences at the University of Zurich. His research focuses on the interface between media and society, especially the various connections between media and politics.

Jens Lucht is Senior Researcher at the Research Institute for Public Sphere and Society at the University of Zurich. His research focuses on media populism in political communication, identity building processes in the public sphere and political theory.

Frank Marcinkowski is Professor of Communication at the University of Münster, Germany, where he specializes in media theory, political communication and science communication. He holds a PhD in political science from Mercator University, Duisburg/Essen. He has written articles and book chapters on the role of the media in electoral politics and referenda, the mediatization of science, the role of the media in new forms of governance, and online campaigning. He is co-editor, together with Barbara Pfetsch, of *Politics in Media Democracy* (2009).

Gianpietro Mazzoleni is Professor of Sociology of Communication and of Political Communication at the University of Milan. He was visiting professor of political communication at the University of Innsbruck, George Mason University (Fairfax, VA) and Freie Universität Berlin. He is co-founder and editor of the peer-reviewed journal *Comunicazione Politica* and general editor of the forthcoming *International Encyclopedia of Political Communication*, and serves on the editorial boards of the *European Journal of Communication* and *Political Communication*. His main research interests are mass communication, media policy and political communication. His recent publications include *La comunicazione politica* (2012), and *La politica pop* (2009, with A. Sfardini).

Winfried Schulz is Professor Emeritus of Mass Communication and Political Science at the University of Erlangen-Nuremberg (Germany). He holds doctoral degrees from the University of Mainz and an honorary doctorate from the Charles University, Prague. His publications and his continuing research focus on political communication, mediatization and media effects, news analysis and election communication.

Adam Shehata is Assistant Professor in Media and Communication at the Department of Journalism, Media and Communication, University of Gothenburg. His research focuses on political communication, with a particular focus on patterns of media use and effects, socialization processes and public opinion formation.

Adrian Steiner is responsible for public affairs at the Association of Swiss Cantonal Banks. Previously, he was Head of Political Analysis and Communication in the Swiss Federal Department of Foreign Affairs and Research Associate at the Institute of Mass Communication and Media Research at the University of Zurich. His areas of expertise are political communication and public affairs.

Jesper Strömbäck is Professor in Political Communication and Ludvig Nordström Professor and Chair in Journalism at Mid Sweden University, where he is also research director at the research institute DEMICOM. He has published more than 150 books, book chapters and journal articles on political communication, political news journalism, political public relations and political marketing, public opinion formation and the mediatization of politics. Among his most recent books are *Opinion Polls and the Media: Reflecting and Shaping Public Opinion*, edited together with Christina Holtz-Bacha (2012), and *Political Public Relations: Principles and Applications*, edited together with Spiro Kiousis (2011).

Gunnar Thesen is Senior Researcher at the International Research Institute of Stavanger (IRIS), Norway and postdoctoral scholar at the Department of Political Science and Government, Aarhus University, Denmark. His research focuses on political agenda-setting, parties, media and organized interests.

Linards Udris is Senior Researcher at the Research Institute for Public Sphere and Society at the University of Zurich. His research focuses on the quality of the news media from a comparative perspective, and on populism and extremism in political communication.

Peter Van Aelst is Associate Professor of Political Science at the University of Antwerp and founding member of the research group "Media, Movements and Politics" (www.M2P.be). He also has a research position at Leiden University to coordinate the VIDI-project on media and politics in comparative perspective. His work in the fields of political communication and comparative politics is published in a wide range of international journals.

Rens Vliegenthart is a Professor of Communication Science in the Department of Communication Science and at the Amsterdam School of Communication Research (ASCoR), University of Amsterdam. His research focuses on political agenda-setting, media effects and social movements.

Stefaan Walgrave is Professor of Political Science at the University of Antwerp. He publishes on media and politics, political communication, public opinion and social movements. He is an advanced ERC grant holder with a project on information-processing of individual political actors.

Part I
Introduction

1
Mediatization of Politics: Towards a Theoretical Framework

Jesper Strömbäck and Frank Esser

During the last few decades, the world has witnessed a dual democratic transformation. On the one hand and beginning with the fall of communism, the number of electoral democracies worldwide almost doubled between 1989 and 2011 (Freedom House, 2012). The victory of democracy and capitalism may not have marked the "end of history" (Fukuyama, 1992), but today there is no alternative political system that enjoys the same worldwide support and legitimacy as democracy (Inglehart & Welzel, 2005; Inglehart, 2003). On the other hand, many established democracies have witnessed a transformation towards increasing complexity, less deferential and increasingly critical and dissatisfied citizens (Norris, 2011), lower electoral turnout and trust in politicians and political institutions (Franklin, 2004; Norris, 1999), and increasingly autonomous, market-driven and critical media (Hallin & Mancini, 2004; Hamilton, 2004; Patterson, 1993). National political institutions and actors thus find themselves under increasing pressure from both citizens and the media, while the need to find solutions to major challenges such as global warming, rising inequalities, weak growth and increasing deficits appears both more urgent and more difficult to tackle.

The paradox is that the global trend towards an expanding number of electoral democracies has occurred at roughly the same time as the trend *within* many established democracies towards an increasing gap between expectations and demands and what political institutions are able to deliver. The demand for political action to solve pressing problems may be stronger than ever, but the preconditions for political decision-making, public deliberation and political legitimacy have at the same time weakened.

In this context, and together with other large-scale processes such as individualization and globalization, the role of the media is key to understanding the transformation of established democracies (Kriesi et al., 2013). Due to the importance of the media as a source of information for citizens as well as a channel of communication between policymakers and the citizenry and between different parts of the political system, and due to the fact that the media hold the key to the public sphere and can have a major influence on public opinion formation, no political actor or institution can afford not to take the media into consideration. The media can thus have a major influence not only on public opinion, but also on the structure and processes of political decision-making and political communication (Koch-Baumgarten & Voltmer, 2010).

One key concept in understanding the role of the media in the transformation of established democracies is *mediatization*, which has also been described as a meta-process on a par with other transformative social change processes such as globalization and individualization (Hjarvard, 2013; Kriesi et al., 2013; Krotz, 2007, 2009). During the last decade, mediatization has also become an increasingly popular concept, applied not only in the context of politics and democracy (Asp, 1986; Kepplinger, 2002; Mazzoleni & Schulz, 1999; Esser, 2013; Meyer, 2002; Schillemans, 2012; Strömbäck, 2008, 2011a, 2011b; Strömbäck & Esser, 2009), but also in other areas ranging from the toy industry (Hjarvard, 2004) to consumption (Jansson, 2002) and culture and society in a wider sense (Hjarvard, 2013; Lundby, 2009a).

At heart, the term "mediatization" refers to a social change process in which media have become increasingly influential in and deeply integrated into different spheres of society (Asp, 1986; Strömbäck, 2008). Mazzoleni (2008a) thus defines the mediatization of society as indicating "the extension of the influence of the media (considered as both a cultural technology and as an organization) into all spheres of society and social life", while Hjarvard (2008, p. 113) defines mediatization as "the process whereby society to an increasing degree is submitted to, or becomes dependent on, the media and their logic". Asp and Esaiasson (1996, pp. 80–81) similarly define mediatization as a "development towards increasing media influence".

Mediatization is thus distinct from the related concept of mediation, which refers to the more neutral act of transmitting messages and communicating through different media (Mazzoleni, 2008b; Strömbäck, 2008). The fact that more messages and experiences than ever are transmitted and experienced through media – that is, mediated – is an important part of mediatization, but mediatization is a broader process, and these concepts should not be understood as synonymous. While mediation is a rather static and descriptive concept, mediatization is an inherently dynamic and process-oriented concept that cannot be reduced to the transmission of messages or communication through media (Esser, 2013; Hjarvard, 2013; Mazzoleni, 2008b; Schulz, 2004; Strömbäck & Esser, 2009).

Despite the increasing scholarly interest in mediatization, and broad consensus that mediatization refers to a process of increasing media influence, many unresolved issues and ambiguities remain. Thus far mediatization has the character of a theoretical perspective more than of a proper theory, and it remains more of a "sensitizing" than a "definitive" concept. Although the distinction between these types of concepts represents a continuum rather than a dichotomy, "sensitizing" concepts are more loosely defined than "definitive" ones, and more used as exploratory tools than as carefully defined concepts that lend themselves to precise operationalizations that can be used in empirical research (Hjarvard, 2013, pp. 4–5).

Partly this can be explained by the multifaceted and complex nature of mediatization. Other multidimensional meta-processes such as globalization also lack precise definitions, and the processes may manifest themselves differently in various spheres of society and at different levels of analysis. This may call for partly different and situational definitions and conceptualizations, depending on the subject under scrutiny and the level of analysis. Partly it can be explained by the multidisciplinary study of mediatization: communication scholars, political scientists, sociologists and others often tend to approach the field from somewhat different perspectives. The very ambiguity of the concept may also be part of why it has attracted increasing interest, as it has allowed scholars greater freedom to fill it with their own interpretations. In addition, there are some who seem to reject more precise definitions and operationalizations of mediatization, fearing that they would reduce the complexity of the concept and the phenomena it refers to.

The downside is that loosely defined concepts are difficult to operationalize and investigate empirically. To understand reality, we need theory and theoretical concepts, but we also need theories that can be assessed empirically and thereby help us understand the world around us. Otherwise a conceptual idea may too easily become a matter of belief rather than a proper theory that can be tested, refined and perhaps even refuted.

Against this background, the purpose of this book is twofold: first, to bring together state-of-the-art chapters on the mediatization of politics, and thereby to assess what we know and provide a framework for further research; second, to move theory and research on the mediatization of politics forward towards a more fully developed theory. Ultimately, we believe mediatization is key to understanding the transformation of Western democracies, but also that the mediatization of politics should be considered a theory under development that needs empirical analysis and verification, and not as a taken-for-granted fact or a loosely defined catch-all concept. This book thus aims at both assessing and furthering our theoretical as well as empirical understanding of the mediatization of politics.

As part of this aim, the purpose of this particular chapter is to move towards a theory on the mediatization of politics. We will do this by first explicating our conceptualization of the mediatization of politics as a four-dimensional concept and process, and then by addressing some key ambiguities in mediatization research related to the component concepts of media influence, media, political logic and media logic. At the outset, it should however be stressed that we do not think of mediatization as a replacement of other theories that deal with media influence or the politics–media relationship. The promise of mediatization is rather that it holds the potential to integrate different theoretical strands within one framework, linking micro-level with meso- and macro-level processes and phenomena, and thus contributing to a broader understanding of the role of the media in the transformation of established democracies.

Mediatization of politics as a four-dimensional concept

The essence of mediatization theory is that mediatization is a long-term process of increasing media importance and direct and indirect media influence in various spheres in society (Hjarvard, 2013; Lundby, 2009a; Mazzoleni, 2008a). Consequently and in the context of politics, *the mediatization of politics may be defined as a long-term process through which the importance of the media and their spill-over effects on political processes, institutions, organizations and actors have increased* (Asp, 1986; Mazzoleni, 2008b; Meyer, 2002; Strömbäck, 2008, 2011a, 2011b; Strömbäck & Esser, 2009). Mazzoleni and Schulz (1999) go one step further to argue that mediatization of politics describes a process in which politics has increasingly "lost its autonomy, has become dependent in its central functions on mass media, and is continuously shaped by interactions with mass media" (p. 250).

Following Strömbäck (2008, 2011a; Strömbäck & Esser, 2009), the mediatization of politics is a process where four distinct but highly related dimensions can be identified. *The first dimension* refers to the degree to which the media constitute the most important source of information about politics and society. This dimension thus refers to the extent to which politics has become mediated. *The second dimension* refers to the degree to which the media have become independent from other political and social institutions. Although all institutions should be perceived as interdependent, for the media to have an independent influence on politics they have to form an institution in their own right. *The third dimension* refers to the degree to which media content and the coverage of politics and current affairs is guided by media logic or political logic. In essence, this dimension deals with the extent to which the media's own needs and standards of newsworthiness, rather than those of political actors or institutions, are decisive for what the media cover and how they cover it. Finally, *the fourth dimension* refers to the extent to which political institutions, organizations and actors are guided by media logic or political logic. This dimension deals with the very essence of the mediatization of politics, that is, the ripple effects of media in political processes and on political actors and institutions (Figure 1.1).

What this framework highlights is not only that the mediatization of politics is a complex and multidimensional process but also that it is possible to break it down into discrete dimensions which can facilitate a greater understanding of the process of mediatization and empirical studies along different dimensions. For example, Strömbäck and Dimitrova (2011) and

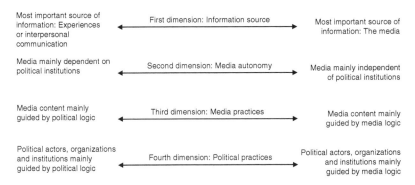

Figure 1.1   A four-dimensional conceptualization of the mediatization of politics

Esser (2008) investigated the extent to which the media in different countries intervene and shape their election news coverage to meet the media's own needs and standards of newsworthiness, that is, these studies focused on the third dimension of mediatization. As another example, Elmelund-Praestekaer et al. (2011) and Schillemans (2012) investigated the effects of mediatization on members of parliament and governmental organizations respectively, that is, they focused on the fourth dimension of mediatization.

It is important to note that mediatization along each of the dimensions is a matter of degree. The media can be *more* or *less* important as a source of information, and *more* or *less* independent from political institutions, and media content as well as political institutions and actors can be *more* or *less* guided by media logic as opposed to political logic. There might also be variations across different media and, not least importantly, different political actors, organizations and institutions, both within and across countries. The degree of mediatization along different dimensions is ultimately an empirical question and most often contextual.

The four dimensions of mediatization should at the same time be understood as strongly linked together. More precisely, the first phase of mediatization of politics takes place when the media have become the most important source of information and channel of communication (first dimension). As politics becomes increasingly mediated, it becomes more important for political actors and institutions to use the media to reach out to larger groups in society. It is however as media institutions become increasingly autonomous from political institutions that the process of mediatization gathers pace (second dimension). The more independent from political institutions the media become, the more important the media's needs and standards of newsworthiness – in short, media logic – will become for what the media cover and how they cover it (third dimension). When this happens, political institutions and actors will successively realize that in order

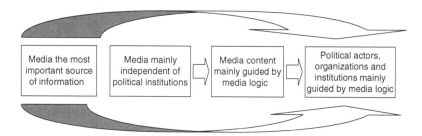

| Media the most important source of information | Media mainly independent of political institutions | Media content mainly guided by media logic | Political actors, organizations and institutions mainly guided by media logic |

Figure 1.2   Relationship between the four dimensions of the mediatization of politics

to influence the media, and through the media the public, they will have to adapt to the media and the media's logic (fourth dimension). Adapting to the media thus becomes a prime means of political actors and institutions trying to win the desired – or avoid undesirable – media coverage, and to use the media to their own advantage (Strömbäck & van Aelst, 2013).

What this suggests is that the degree of mediation forms the basis of the mediatization of politics, while mediatization along the second dimension functions as a prerequisite for the third and fourth dimensions. The degree of mediatization along the first, second and third dimensions furthermore contributes to the degree of mediatization along the fourth dimension (see Figure 1.2).

This is not to say that the mediatization of politics is a linear or unidirectional process or that political or other institutions and actors have all become media slaves. The extent to which politics has become mediatized is – as are all other aspects of the media–politics relationship – contingent on a host of factors at different levels of analysis that may vary both within and across countries (Blumler & Gurevitch, 1995; Esser & Hanitzsch, 2012; Hallin & Mancini, 2004; Strömbäck & Kaid, 2008), and the relationship between media and politics should always be understood as interactive (Wolfsfeld, 2011). If one important part of future research is to further operationalize the mediatization of politics to allow systematic empirical studies, another important part is hence to both theorize and empirically investigate the factors at different levels of analysis that shape the extent to which politics – along the different dimensions – has become mediatized.

For that to become possible, there is however a need to first define some of the key concepts within mediatization theory that are too often left vaguely defined or undefined. The most important of those concepts are media influence, media, political logic and media logic.

Mediatization of politics and media influence

The essence of mediatization is that it is a long-term process of increasing media importance and influence in various spheres in society. As the importance of the media has increased, and the media have become more embedded and integrated in all aspects of social and political life, so has the influence of media. One key question though is how the influence of the media should be conceptualized. What does it mean to state that the influence of the media has increased, and how does the concept of "media influence" relate to the concept of "media effects"?

Following Schulz (2004, pp. 88–90), at least four processes of social change arising from media-driven transformations can be identified: *extension, substitution, amalgamation* and *accommodation*. First, media extend human communication capabilities across time and space. No longer do people have to meet physically to communicate, and politicians do not have to travel across the country to meet their constituencies. First print media, and then radio, television and the Internet, have decoupled physical presence and the ability to communicate. Everything that is communicated through the media may in addition be stored, thus extending the content of communication across time. In this respect, the media have extended the reach of collective and easily accessible human memory.

Second, different media "partly or completely substitute social activities and institutions and thus change their character" (Schulz, 2004, p. 88). Activities that used to require face-to-face interaction or a physical presence can now be accomplished or experienced through media use. We do not have to go to the town square to listen to a politician, or to a bank to do banking, or to meet others to socialize. All these and endless other activities can be done through the media. In this process, not only do the media substitute traditional forms of communication; what were once non-media activities also assume media form. Television, for example, gave more importance to how politicians look and behave at the expense of the content of their speeches, giving rise to what has been labeled "intimate politics" (Hart, 1998; Stanyer, 2012) and contributing to the personalization of politics (Adam & Maier, 2010; Karvonen, 2012; van Aelst et al., 2012).

Third, media activities merge and mingle with non-media activities or processes, and in the process dissolve the boundaries between mediated and non-mediated activities. Today there are virtually no social or political processes where the media are not present and deeply woven into these processes. The media are virtually everywhere, and information gained from or through the media merges and mingles with information gained through interpersonal communication or personal experiences. As this happens, "the media's definition of reality amalgamates with the social definition of reality" (Schulz, 2004, p. 89). Although most of us have never met leading politicians, we may still feel that we know them and their personalities, and although most of us lack firsthand or deeper knowledge about most of the issues being on the political agenda, we may still feel knowledgeable.

Fourth, and most important, the increasing presence and importance of the media in all parts of social and political life induces social change and creates incentives for social and political actors to accommodate and adapt to the media (Altheide & Snow, 1979; Strömbäck & van Aelst, 2013). The more important the media have become, and the more independently they operate, the more important it has become for those actors that either want to communicate through the media or may find themselves in a spot where the media is interested in their activities to accommodate and adapt to the media and their logic. This holds particularly true in the case of mass media, but with the spread of mobile media it has become increasingly important to realize that there is virtually no place outside home where one is private. There can be a smartphone with a camera anywhere, ready to record and transmit what is said and done.

One key aspect of mediatization is thus that the media increasingly permeate all aspects of private, social, political, cultural and economic life, from the micro (individual) to the meso (organizational) and the macro (societal) level of analysis. This is not to say that the media equally influence all individuals, organizations, institutions or societal systems. It is also not to say that different political or social actors and institutions have lost all their autonomy and influence. The exact nature, extent and effects of media influence are always contextual and situational – and an empirical question. The key point is instead that there is no part of contemporary society unaffected by the media, and that it consequently has become increasingly difficult to distinguish between the media and other parts of society (Silverstone, 2007).

As a consequence, media influence should not be equated with media effects (Schulz, 2004; Strömbäck, 2008). The literature on public agenda-setting (McCombs, 2004), political agenda-setting (Walgrave & van Aelst, 2006), framing (Iyengar, 1991), priming (Roskos-Ewoldsen & Roskos-Ewoldsen, 2009) and cultivation (Morgan, 2009) – to mention just a few prominent media effect theories – is highly relevant for an understanding of mediatization in general and the mediatization of politics in particular, but several features of most effect theories set them apart from the larger form of media influence that mediatization involves. First, the main focus of most effect theories is on media effects on individual perceptions and opinions. Thus, they depend on a causal logic where it is possible to divide the world into dependent and independent variables, whereas a key aspect of mediatization is that the media increasingly permeate all social life, and this makes it difficult to treat the media as an exogenous and independent variable. Second, most media effect theories focus on the individual level of analysis, whereas mediatization is a process also involving the meso and macro levels of analysis. Third, most media effect theories assume that media effects follow from content, whereas mediatization also includes how the media through their very existence and semi-structural properties exert influence. Fourth, traditional media effect theories do not take the anticipatory effects of the media into account, that is, when effects occur because social actors anticipate how the media will behave. In essence, while important, most media effect theories largely fail to account for the interactions, interdependencies and transactions at the meso and macro levels of analysis, and with respect to how the media through their existence, formats and semi-structural properties as well as content shape, reshape and structure politics, culture and people's way of life and sense-making. In other words, media influence from the perspective of mediatization "both transcends and includes media effects" (Schulz, 2004, p. 90).

Hence, from the perspective of mediatization, media influence refers to all activities and processes that are altered, shaped or structured by the media and the perceived need of individuals, organizations and social systems to communicate with or through the media. Oftentimes, it may be the "presumed" influence of the media that induces political actors to act in a forward-looking manner.

Mediatization and the concept of media

Another key ambiguity in many accounts of mediatization is the concept of media. Literally speaking anything that communicates may count as media, ranging from our own voices and individual media such as cellphones to institutionalized media such as newspapers and TV, further on to the Internet and social media where individually produced content mingles with content professionally produced by political, commercial and traditional media organizations. Such a broad perspective is not very analytically useful, however. Something that refers to everything usually falls prey to meaning nothing. In addition, all media are not created equal. Some media are more important and significant than others.

From the perspective of the mediatization of politics – if not all forms of mediatization – the media that are most important are *news media as socio-technological organizations and institutions*. In essence, this means newspapers, radio, television and news magazines in their traditional or digital formats, or purely digital newspapers, radio and television channels to the extent that they are organized and operate as institutional news media.

The notion that these media are socio-technological highlights that each of these media have their particular formats and structural properties, but also that they are socially and culturally shaped. Although television is a technology, television news today is not the same as in the 1970s, and television news in different countries varies in both form and content (Esser, 2008; Aalberg & Curran, 2011; Dimitrova & Strömbäck, 2010). Technology matters, but how a particular media technology is used is not only a matter of technological properties. It is also a matter of sociocultural norms, values and expectations, and thus may change over time. The medium is not the only message, to paraphrase McLuhan (1964), and mediatization is not a theory of technological determinism.

Although digital media have created unprecedented opportunities for anyone to create their own web pages or blogs, or communicate through various social media, the media that dominate media environments and matter most are organizational news media, whether run as commercial or as public service media, and whether in their traditional or digital formats. These media are organized *institutional* actors, which pursue certain goals and act in the interest of reaching these goals, whether the aim is to make a profit or provide high-quality journalism (Allern & Blach-Ørsten, 2011; Cook, 2005; Esser, 2013; Sparrow, 1999). Like all institutions, they are also rather stable and predictable over time, and shaped by their own particular rules, routines, norms and values. These rules, routines, norms and values can be both formal and informal, but in either case they provide a framework through which those within the media act and interact, while at the same time affecting the behavior of others that in one way or another interact with the media.

Not only do single news media organizations constitute institutional actors: as noted by many scholars, there are great similarities across different news media in terms of how they operate and their rules, routines, norms, and values (Cook, 2005; Esser, 2013; Hjarvard, 2008; Sparrow, 1999), particularly within the confines of different national contexts and national media systems (Hallin & Mancini, 2004). Thus, different news media tend to follow similar news production practices and adhere to similar criteria of newsworthiness (Cook, 2005; O'Neill & Harcup, 2009; Shoemaker & Cohen, 2006), and journalists working within different news organizations tend to hold similar role conceptions (Weaver et al., 2007; Weaver & Willnat, 2012). Not least important is that different news media tend to follow similar news-related *media logic* (Altheide & Snow, 1979; Brants & Praag, 2006; Esser, 2013; Hjarvard, 2008, 2013; Mazzoleni, 2008c; Schrott, 2009; Strömbäck, 2008, 2011a).

Because of this "transorganizational agreement on news processes and content" (Cook, 2005, p. 64), and from the perspective of *neo-institutionalism*, different news media can be grouped together as an interorganizational field and be conceived of as a *singular institution*. Various news media constitute the building blocks of the news media as an institution, but the rules and norms that govern the news media as a whole are typically more important than what distinguishes one news media company, outlet, type, or format from another (Altheide & Snow, 1979; Cook, 2005; Hjarvard, 2013; Mazzoleni, 2008b; Sparrow, 1999; Strömbäck, 2008). Neo-institutionalism consequently conceptualizes the news media as exerting influence through overall rather *consistent operational behavior* and *consonant* and *cumulative* coverage of politics and current affairs (Cook, 2005; Esser, 2013).

This notion of the news media as a single institution is important, as it highlights the relative autonomy of the media from political institutions

(Hallin & Mancini, 2004). This constitutes another key feature and the second dimension of mediatization, as the idea of increasing media importance and influence presumes that the media are not subordinate to other institutions. It is through the functional and structural differentiation of the news media from other institutions that they have come to form an institution in their own right, and it is through becoming an institution in their own right that the news media have come to increase their weight. As noted by Hjarvard (2013, p. 3),

> A significant portion of the influence that the media exert arises out of the double-sided development in which they have become an *integral part* of other institutions' operations, while also achieving a degree of *self-determination and authority* that forces other institutions, to greater or lesser degrees, to submit to their logic.

Although no institution from a social systems perspective is fully independent of other institutions, without highly autonomous media institutions there would be no mediatization of politics.

Hence, from the perspective of the mediatization of politics, the concept of media primarily refers to the news media as an institution. This includes all those media that form part of the news media system in a particular country, primarily television, newspapers, radio and news magazines, regardless of whether they are published in their traditional or digital formats or whether they are only published online. What matters most is not the technical form of the media, but whether the organizations behind different individual media form part of the news media as an institution.

Mediatization of politics and the concepts of political logic and media logic

Two key concepts in virtually all accounts of the mediatization of politics are media logic and political logic (Esser, 2013; Mazzoleni, 1987; Meyer, 2002; Schillemans, 2012; Strömbäck, 2008; van Aelst et al., 2008), and media logic in particular has proved to be a popular and frequently invoked concept (Altheide & Snow, 1979, 1991; Brants & Praag, 2006; Hjarvard, 2008; Schrott, 2009). Hjarvard (2013, p. 17), for example, defines mediatization as the process "whereby culture and society to an increasing degree become dependent on media and their logic", while Schrott (2009, p. 42) defines mediatization as "the institutionalization of media logic in other societal subsystems. In these subsystems, media logic competes with established guidelines and influences on the actions of individuals." According to our own conceptualization of mediatization, the degree to which media content and political actors and institutions, respectively, are guided by media logic versus political logic also constitute the third and the fourth dimensions of the mediatization of politics (Strömbäck & Esser, 2009).

Both concepts have however been criticized, albeit for different reasons. Oftentimes the concept of political logic is left unspecified, while the concept of media logic has been criticized because it is too elusive and vague, because it suggests a linearity and singularity that is not there, because it lends itself to technological determinism, or because the concept may hide important patterns of social interaction (see, for example, Couldry, 2008; Lundby, 2009; Landerer, 2013). It is also unclear exactly what "logic" refers to.

The basic idea behind the concepts of media logic and political logic is that media and politics constitute two different institutional systems that serve different purposes and that each has its own set of actors, rules and procedures, as well as needs and interests. These institutional rules and procedures can be formal as well as informal, and are often "understood as the quasi-natural way to get things done" (Cook, 2005, p. 71) within each sphere. Thus, within each of these institutional systems, there is a certain "logic of appropriateness" that guides behavior and action and that is usually followed because it is perceived as "natural, rightful, expected, and legitimate" (March and Olsen, 2004, p. 3, 1989). To follow the logic of appropriateness within a certain sphere is thus to behave the way one is supposed to behave given the institutional structure, purposes, rules and routines within which the action is taking place, while not following the logic of appropriateness would violate legitimate expectations on how to behave. Thus, there are behaviors we expect from journalists or politicians – or from media institutions or political institutions – that are considered legitimate and normal, while there are others that we would consider out of bounds.

From this perspective, *logic* in the concepts of political logic and media logic should be understood as the specific logics of appropriateness within each institutional sphere, that is, the formal and informal rules, routines and principles for thinking and acting within the political and media spheres respectively. Neither media logic nor political logic is set in stone, and both may evolve in accordance with institutional as well as significant contextual changes, but neither is arbitrary. Both have evolved to serve as guidelines for appropriate thinking and acting within each institutional sphere and are based on each sphere's purposes, interests, needs and institutional structures.

The key question then becomes how media logic and political logic respectively should be conceptualized within the framework of the mediatization of politics.

Mediatization and the concept of political logic

At the heart of any conceptualization of political logic lies the fact that politics ultimately is about collective and authoritative decision-making as well as the implementation of political decisions. This includes the processes of winning public support and elections, of distributing political power, of deliberation, bargaining and decision-making, of implementing political decisions and of power as it relates to "who gets what, when, and how" (Lasswell, 1950). All these processes take place within a certain institutional structure, including the legal and administrative framework that different political actors must follow. Based on this, three major dimensions of politics together shape political logic: *polity*, *policy* and *politics* (Esser, 2013; see also Meyer, 2002; Pennings et al., 2006).

- *Polity* refers to the system of rules regulating the political process in any given country, including the institutional structure. This includes, for example, the type of political system (presidential, semi-presidential or parliamentary), the electoral system (proportional or majoritarian elections and whether people vote for parties or candidates), the party system (few-party system or multiparty system), the judicial system (degree of judicial independence and right to challenge laws), and the bureaucratic system (degree to which administrative bodies are autonomous from central government). At an overall level of analysis, the polity forms the basis of the political logic of appropriateness within any given country.
- *Policy* refers to the processes of defining problems and forming and implementing policies within a certain institutional framework. This includes processes of coordinating, balancing and aggregating interests, organizing negotiations and bargaining, debating alternative policy choices, devising programs through deliberation and collective decisions, finding enough support for taking political decisions, and finally implementing political decisions. It is in these processes that political parties and other political actors try to make sure that their preferred policies prevail and that solutions can be found that address what are perceived as important and substantial issues.
- *Politics* refers to the processes of garnering support for one's candidacy, party or political program. These processes can take place either before elections when the short-term goal is to make electoral progress and increase the vote share, or between elections when the goal might be to increase the standing in opinion polls or increase public or political support in different processes of problem definition and framing, agenda-setting, policy formation and political negotiations. In contrast to *policy*, which often takes place backstage and focuses on the content of policies and substantial issues, *politics* always has a public face and focuses more on tactics and strategies for winning public support and publicity, symbolic politics, image projections and branding, and on the presentational side of politics.

Thus, the political logic of appropriateness in any given country is shaped by the overall institutional framework of politics, the need to form, take

Political logic		
Polity	Policy	Politics
The institutional and formal framework of politics	Policy- and decision-based production of politics	Power- and publicity-gaining presentational politics

Figure 1.3   The three constituents of political logic

decisions on and implement policies, and the need to be successful in different processes of winning support in elections or in the battle for publicity, public opinion, and influence in negotiations and bargaining (Figure 1.3). It is important to note that politics cannot be reduced to only one or two of these dimensions. Political processes are about power as well as about policies and issues, and always take place within and are conditioned by the institutional framework.

One implication of this is that the exact nature of political logic will vary across countries with different institutional frameworks *and* across political institutions within countries with different roles and purposes within the overall polity (see also Schillemans, 2012). Another implication is that political logic has a situational character, as different aspects of political logic will be more important depending on, for example, closeness to an election. A third implication is that the likelihood that politics becomes mediatized depends on what aspect of political logic is at the forefront, as media logic can be assumed to affect the front-stage part of political processes (*politics*) more easily and forcefully than the backstage part (*policy*), and have less, if any, influence on the institutional framework (*polity*; see Esser, 2013). This reinforces the notion that mediatization is always a matter of degree, and that the degree of mediatization can vary across time as well as countries and processes and institutions within countries. We thus fully agree with Marcinkowski (2005) that a democratic system will never be mediatized in full but rather distinguished by islands of higher and lower mediatization.

Mediatization and the concept of media logic

In contrast to political logic, there is a large literature discussing the concept of media logic, and it is often perceived as the engine of mediatization (Mazzoleni, 2008c; Schrott, 2009). The term was first introduced by Altheide and Snow (1979, p. 10), according to whom media logic

> consists of a form of communication; the process through which media present and transmit information. Elements of this form include the various media and the formats used by this media. Format consists, in part, of how material is organized, the style in which it is presented, the focus

or emphasis on particular characteristics of behavior, and the grammar of media communication. Format becomes a framework or a perspective that is used to present as well as interpret phenomena.

Although influential, this understanding of media logic has been criticized, perhaps most forcefully by Lundby (2009b), who questions whether media logic can constitute a "form" or a "format" and argues that it is "not viable to speak of an overall media logic" (p. 117). The original definition of media logic also suggests a linearity and singularity that simply does not exist, while at the same time being elusive and vague. Oftentimes media logic is also used as shorthand to describe "the whole of such processes that eventually shape and frame media content" (Mazzoleni, 2008c, p. 2930). Hjarvard (2013, p. 17) thus understands media logic "as a conceptual shorthand for the various institutional, aesthetic, and technological modus operandi of the media, including the ways in which the media distribute material and symbolic resources, and operate with the help of formal and informal rules". Following a similar approach, but focusing on the news media, Strömbäck (2011a, p. 373) defined *news media logic* as "the institutional, technological, and sociological characteristics of the news media, including their format characteristics, production and dissemination routines, norms and needs, standards of newsworthiness, and to the formal and informal rules that govern news media".

None of these definitions escapes the criticism of being vague and lacking conceptual precision, however (Landerer, 2013), and none clearly explicates the mechanisms and logic of appropriateness behind media logic. To address this, Esser (2013, pp. 166–174) suggested that media logic, similar to political logic, should be conceived as combining three sub-concepts, which all influence the culture of news production in individual media organizations as well as in media institutions as a whole. Following Esser (2013), and focusing specifically on news media logic, the three dimensions that together shape news media logic are *professionalism*, *commercialism* and *media technology*.

- *Professionalism* refers to the extent to which journalism is differentiated as an occupation and institution from other social institutions, in particular politics. Following Hallin and Mancini (2004), journalistic professionalism presupposes first and foremost a growing *autonomy* from outside influences and outside control over one's work. Second, journalistic professionalism means that there is a distinct set of professional *norms and values* among journalists. The most important set of norms and values relate to journalists' news values and news selection criteria, that is, a broadly shared understanding of what constitutes news and what should be important when selecting news. Among important and more or less universally accepted criteria for determining newsworthiness are, for example, timeliness, proximity, surprise, negativity, elite involvement, conflict and personalization (Galtung & Ruge, 1965; Harcup & O'Neill, 2009; Shoemaker & Cohen, 2006; Strömbäck et al., 2012). Third, a key aspect of professionalism is the claim to serve the public interest by, for example, providing people with the kind of information they need to be free and self-governing and by acting as a fourth estate and watchdog (Kovach & Rosenstiel, 2007). In essence, professionalism thus refers to a broadly shared understanding among journalists that they are and should be independent, that standards of newsworthiness should be maintained and that their work serves the public interest.

- *Commercialism* refers to the persistent fact that most media are commercial organizations, which has significant implications for all processes of news production, news selection and news presentation. McManus (1994, p. 85) has most clearly spelled out what this means, namely, that rational news departments "should compete with each other to offer the least expensive mix of content that protects the interests of sponsors and investors while garnering the largest audience advertisers will pay to reach". Hamilton (2004) has similarly suggested that the most important questions for commercial media are: (a) who cares about a particular piece of information? (b) what are they willing to pay to find it, or what are others willing to pay to reach them? (c) where can media or advertisers reach these people? (d) when is it profitable to provide the information? and (e) why is it profitable? If professionalism creates incentives for the media to provide people with the kind of information they need as citizens, commercialism creates incentives for the media to provide any kind of content that is economically efficient, that is, relatively cheap to produce and report in relation to how successful it might be in garnering the largest possible audience among those groups that advertisers are interested in reaching.

- *Media technology* refers to how the applied communication technologies shape content in production and reproduction processes, and the processes of finding news or reshaping news to fit the socio-technological format of different media. This is the part that comes closest to the definition of media logic by Altheide and Snow (1979) and their focus on format, and highlights that each media technology has certain affordances or inherent characteristics, that both enable and restrict news organizations in their production, processing and presentation of news (Hjarvard, 2013, pp. 27–29). Each media technology thus pressures the news media to adapt to and take advantage of the particular format of that medium, whether it is television with its emphasis on visuals, radio with its emphasis on audio, newspapers with their emphasis on print or digital media with their emphasis on interactivity and instantaneousness. Media technology is never the only message, but it is always an important part of the message.

News media logic		
Professionalism	Commercialism	Media technology
News production according to distinctively journalistic norms and criteria	News production according to economically motivated rationales	News production according to different media technologies' affordances

Figure 1.4   The three constituents of news media logic

Thus, the combinatory forces of professionalism, commercialism and technology shape news media logic at any time and for any media (Figure 1.4). From this perspective, there is no singular news media logic, set in stone and consistent across time or media, and news media logic cannot be reduced to either professional, commercial, or technological imperatives. All three dimensions of news media logic have a dynamic component to them and have developed differently in different countries and across time. There is also tension between them and most often a strained relationship between professionalism and commercialism. Professionalism might thus have a greater impact on the logic of some news media, while commercialism might have a greater impact on that of other news media.

In essence, the exact nature of news media logic will vary across countries *and* across media within countries. Hallin and Mancini's influential comparative analysis (2004) thus suggests that commercialism is stronger in countries belonging to the liberal model of media and politics – for example, the United States – than in the democratic corporatist model – for example, Sweden – or the polarized pluralist model – for example, France. Supporting this, comparative research on the degree of media interventionism and mediatization along the third dimension suggests that election news coverage is more strongly governed by news media logic than political logic in the United States than in, for example, France or Sweden (Esser, 2008; Strömbäck & Dimitrova, 2011). There is also some evidence that commercial media such as private television and tabloids have a stronger tendency to frame politics as a strategic game – often used as an indicator of commercialism and media logic rather than political logic – than public service media or broadsheets (Strömbäck & van Aelst, 2010).

The situational character of political logic and news media logic

The above analysis suggests that neither political logic nor news media logic is fixed and consistent across time, countries, or political or media institutions within countries. Rather, both political logic and news media logic have a situational and partly dynamic character. This has several important implications for the overall theory of the mediatization of politics.

First, it highlights that the tension between political logic and news media logic must be understood within the context of particular processes. For example, when studying the extent to which the media coverage is guided by political logic or news media logic – the third dimension of mediatization – there is a need to specify which elements of the news media coverage follow from political logic and news media logic respectively. The basic question should be whether a particular feature of news media coverage – for example, the length of soundbites, or the framing of politics – follows from the news media's interests or from the interests and logic of political actors or institutions. Similarly, when studying the behavior of political actors, organizations or institutions, there is a need to specify whether a particular behavior follows from political logic or whether it is adapted to accommodate the news media and the news media's logic. The basic question should be whether a particular behavior (or non-behavior) on part of a political actor, organization or institution should (or should not) have taken place in the absence of news media, or if the political actor, organization or institution could decide what the news media covered or how they covered it. To the extent that political actors, organizations and institutions act in a certain way – or abstain from some actions – because they need or want to win favorable media coverage or because they are afraid of non-favorable media coverage, it can be perceived as an adaption to news media logic and hence of mediatization along the fourth dimension. This suggests that one key aspect of mediatization is the news media's and news media logic's structure-forming quality, and how mediatization affects the decision criteria and action rationales of political actors and institutions (Esser, 2013; Hjarvard, 2013; Mazzoleni & Schulz, 1999; Schillemans, 2012; Strömbäck, 2011a).

Second, the notion that political logic and news media logic have a situational and partly dynamic character highlights that mediatization is not a linear and unidirectional process with a uniform influence across political actors and institutions within or across countries. The degree to which political actors and institutions are governed by – or adapt to – news media logic will depend on such things as whether, for example, a political process or issue is mostly related to *polity*, *policies* or *politics*, with the likelihood of mediatization being greatest with respect to *politics* and processes of electioneering or winning public support and least with respect to *polity*. Political institutions or organizations that are more likely to be the subject of media interest, or that have a greater need of public support or decide as a strategy to try to use the media to win some kind of benefits, are also more likely to be mediatized than political institutions and organizations that operate outside of the media spotlight and with a lesser need of public support (Schillemans, 2012). Hence, the strategies of political parties or governmental organizations also matter, with vote-seeking parties and public organizations with a need for public support more likely to adapt to news media logic than policy-seeking parties and public organizations that do not see a great need to influence public opinion (Landerer, 2013; Schillemans, 2012; Strömbäck & van Aelst, 2013; for the distinction between party types, see Strøm, 1990).

Third, the situational and partly dynamic character of political logic and news media logic, and hence mediatization in general, may help account for one of the controversies in the literature on the mediatization of politics and the politics–media relationship. This controversy centers on the issue of power. While virtually everyone agrees that the relationship between politics and media is interdependent and interactional, some scholars argue that political actors and institutions hold the upper hand and are more influential (Bennett, 2012; Wolfsfeld, 2004, 2011), whereas others argue that the media have the upper hand (Meyer, 2002; Patterson, 1993). What mediatization suggests is that at a macro level, the media have increased their status significantly at the expense of political actors and institutions, but also that media influence is not unconditional and that it might be indirect as well as direct. First, media influence is greater with respect to *politics* than *policies* and *polity*. Second, and at the meso and micro level, political institutions and actors can try to increase their influence over the media by, for example, increasing the resources devoted to and skills in news management, agenda-building and frame-building (Lieber & Golan, 2011; Tedesco, 2011; Zoch & Molleda, 2006). The key to success in such efforts, however, is to adjust to the media and news media logic, which entails both anticipating how the media will act or react and adapting to the (presumed) influence of the media.

A key concept in understanding this process is *self-mediatization* (Meyer, 2002), which captures the process through which political actors have internalized and adapted to the media's attention rules, production routines and selection criteria – that is, news media logic – and try to exploit this knowledge to reach different strategic goals. The fact that political institutions and actors allocate ever more time, energy and resources to news management, media agenda-building, media frame-building, stage management and other marketing and political public relations strategies and tactics (McNair, 2003; Strömbäck & Kiousis, 2011) should thus be understood as self-mediatization and an expression of the increasing influence of the news media and news media logic.

The paradox is thus that political actors can increase their influence through adapting to news media logic, while at the same time confirming the influence of the media. As noted by Cook (2005, p. 163), by adapting to the media "politicians may then win the daily battles with the news media, by getting into the news as they wish, but end up losing the war, as standards of newsworthiness begin to become prime criteria to evaluate issues, policies, and politics".

Media actors, on the other hand, might experience political actors' efforts at influencing the media as evidence of increasing political clout, and try to counteract that through more interpretive and critical coverage, focused more on the strategic game than on the substance of issues and by trying to deconstruct the political came (Esser & D'Angelo, 2006; Aalberg et al., 2012; Lengauer et al., 2012; Patterson, 1993; Salgado & Strömbäck, 2012). By doing this, the media reaffirm their leverage and the fact that the rules, in everyday political communication processes, are set by the media. What political institutions and actors can do is to become better at applying the rules, which may again trigger media efforts to counteract political attempts to influence them. Such actions and reactions playing out in the politics–media relationship may together create what Asp (1986, p. 361) has labeled a *spiral of mediatization*.

What this illustrates is that media influence is broader than media effects, and that media influence should be understood as all activities and processes that are altered, shaped or structured by the media and the perceived need of individuals, organizations and social systems to communicate with or through the media. Mediatization does not rule out that political institutions, organizations and actors can be successful in influencing the media, but it strongly suggests that the key means of doing this is to internalize media logic.

Towards a theory on the mediatization of politics

To sum up the analysis in this chapter, the mediatization of politics describes a long-term process through which the importance of the news media as an institution, and their spill-over effects on political processes and political institutions, has increased. It is a process where macro-level changes in the interaction between politics and media have tipped the balance to favor ripple effects of the media within politics, and where the news media as an institution and news media logic to an increasing degree form the incentive structure and framework in which the politics–media relationship takes place.

A key precondition for the mediatization of politics is the notion that the media constitute the most important source of information about politics and society, and hence that the news media through consonant and cumulative coverage can influence public opinion and that those political institutions and actors that are dependent on public support must communicate through the news media. The next step in this process of mediatization is when the news media become increasingly independent from political institutions and actors and form an institution in their own right. As the news media become increasingly independent, their coverage of politics and society becomes increasingly guided by news media logic, shaped by the combinatory forces of media professionalism, media commercialism and media technology, and less guided by political logic, which is shaped by the combinatory forces of polity, policy and politics. In this process, political institutions and actors find themselves under increasing expectation to adapt to the news media and news media logic, a process that ends by increasing the relevance of media considerations in political processes and political institutions.

Although political institutions and actors can become more skilled, through self-mediatization, at influencing and using the media for their own purposes, it is by adapting to the news media and news media logic – and thereby reaffirming the perceived influence of the news media – that they can become successful. Such successes are usually short-term, however. Through processes of mediatization, changes in the political logic of appropriateness may arise to align more with the news media logic of appropriateness. The more political activities and processes are altered, shaped or structured by the news media as an institution and the perceived need of political actors and institutions to communicate with or through the news media, the more politics has become mediatized.

This is in essence the first draft of a theory of mediatization of politics – a draft that will be revisited in the concluding chapter in light of the chapters of this book. As noted throughout this introductory chapter, this outline summary is not to say that politics everywhere has become equally mediatized. Mediatization is always a matter of degree. This holds true for the independence of the news media as an institution from politics. It holds true for the extent to which the media coverage of politics and society is guided by news media logic. And it holds true for the extent to which political actors and institutions adapt to news media logic. Some political institutions, actors and processes are more likely to become mediatized than others, both within and across countries, and media influence is more likely in some situational contexts than in others.

If this is the general theory of the mediatization of politics, there is a great need for further empirical research on the extent to which politics in its different facets has become mediatized; what structural, semi-structural and situational factors contribute to or inhibit the mediatization of politics; how, in more detail, political institutions and actors adapt to the news media and news media logic; how changes in media technologies and digitalization influence the mediatization of politics; and the consequences for democracy and different processes of democratic governance. These are some of the relevant questions that we have asked our contributors to address in the succeeding chapters. We are convinced that such a collaborative approach is most suitable to advance cumulative theory-building in mediatization research.

Taking all chapters together, our hope is that this volume will contribute to further research in these and other related areas. There should be little doubt that democracies worldwide have been transformed during the last decades, and to understand the transformation of contemporary democracies and its consequences for democratic governance, we need to understand not only processes such as globalization and individualization. It is equally important to understand the mediatization of politics and democracy. We will return to these issues in the concluding chapter.

References

Aalberg, T. & Curran, J. (2011). *How Media Inform Democracy: A Comparative Approach.* London: Routledge.

Aalberg, T., Strömbäck, J., & de Vreese, C. H. (2012). The Framing of Politics as Strategy and Game: A Review of Concepts, Operationalizations, and Key Findings. *Journalism,* 13(2), 162–178.

Adam, S., & Maier, M. (2010). Personalization of Politics: A Critical Review and Agenda for Research. In C. Salmon (Ed.), *Communication Yearbook 34* (pp. 213–257). New York, NY: Routledge.

Allern, S., & Blach-Ørsten, M. (2011). The News Media as a Political Institution: A Scandinavian Perspective. *Journalism Studies,* 12(1), 92–105.

Altheide, D. L., & Snow, R. (1991). *Media Worlds in the Post-Journalism Era.* New York, NY: DeGruyter.

Altheide, D. L., & Snow, R. P. (1979). *Media Logic.* Beverly Hills: Sage.

Asp, K. (1986). *Mäktiga massmedier: Studier i politisk opinionsbildning.* Stockholm: Akademilitteratur.

Asp, K., & Esaiasson, P. (1996). The Modernization of Swedish Campaigns: Individualization, Professionalization, and Medialization. In D. L. Swanson & P. Mancini (Eds.), *Politics, Media, and Modern Democracy: An International Study of Innovations in Electoral Campaigning and Their Consequences* (pp. 73–90). Westport: Praeger.

Bennett, W. L. (2012). *News: The Politics of Illusion.* 9th Edition. New York: Longman.

Blumler, J. G., & Gurevitch, M. (1995). *The Crisis of Public Communication.* London: Routledge.

Brants, K., & van Praag, P. (2006). Signs of Media Logic: Half a Century of Political Communication in the Netherlands. *Javnost–The Public,* 13(1), 25–40.

Cook, T. E. (2005). *Governing with the News: The News Media as a Political Institution.* 2nd Edition. Chicago, IL: University of Chicago Press.

Couldry, N. (2008). Mediatization or Mediation? Alternative Understandings of the Emergent Space of Digital Storytelling. *New Media & Society,* 10(3), 373–391.

Dimitrova, D. V., & Strömbäck, J. (2010). Exploring Semi-Structural Differences in Television News between the United States and Sweden. *International Communication Gazette,* 72(6), 487–502.

Elmelund-Praestekaer, C., Hopmann, D. N., & Nørgaard, A. S. (2011). Does Mediatization Change MP–Media Interaction and MP Attitudes toward the Media? Evidence from a Longitudinal Study of Danish MPs. *International Journal of Press/Politics,* 16(3), 382–403.

Esser, F. (2008). Dimensions of Political News Cultures: Sound Bite and Image Bite News in France, Germany, Great Britain, and the United States. *International Journal of Press/Politics,* 13(4), 401–428.

Esser, F. (2013). Mediatization as a Challenge: Media Logic versus Political Logic. In H. Kriesi, S. Lavenex, F. Esser, J. Matthes, M. Bühlmann & D. Bochsler (Eds.), *Democracy in the Age of Globalization and Mediatization* (pp. 155–176). Basingstoke: Palgrave Macmillan.

Esser, F., & D'Angelo, P. (2006). Framing the Press and Publicity Process in U.S., British, and German General Election Campaigns: A Comparative Study of Metacoverage. *Harvard International Journal of Press/Politics,* 11(3), 44–66.

Esser, F., & Hanitzsch, T. (Eds.) (2012). *The Handbook of Comparative Communication Research*. New York, NY: Routledge.

Freedom House (2012). *Freedom in the World 2012: The Arab Uprisings and Their Global Repercussions. Selected Data from Freedom House's Annual Survey of Political Rights*. Washington, DC: Freedom House.

Franklin, M. N. (2004).*Voter Turnout and the Dynamics of Electoral Competition in Established Democracies since 1945*. New York, NY: Cambridge University Press.

Fukuyama, F. (1992). *The End of History and the Last Man*. New York, NY: Free Press.

Galtung, J., & Ruge, M. H. (1965). The Structure of Foreign News. *Journal of Peace Research*, 2(1), 64–91.

Hallin, D. C., & Mancini, P. (2004). *Comparing Media Systems: Three Models of Media and Politics*. New York, NY: Cambridge University Press.

Hamilton, J. T. (2004) *All the News That's Fit to Sell: How the Market Transforms Information Into News*. Princeton, NJ: Princeton University Press.

Hart, R. P. (1998). *Seducing America: How Television Charms the Modern Voter*. Thousand Oaks: Sage.

Hjarvard, S. (2004). From Bricks to Bytes: The Mediatization of a Global Toy Industry. In I. Bondebjerg & P. Golding (Eds.), *European Culture and the Media* (pp. 43–63). Bristol: Intellect Books.

Hjarvard, S. (2008). The Mediatization of Society: A Theory of the Media as Agents of Social and Cultural Change. *Nordicom Review*, 29(2), 105–134.

Hjarvard, S. (2013). *The Mediatization of Culture and Society*. London: Routledge.

Inglehart, R. (2003). How Solid Is Mass Support for Democracy – and How Can We Measure It? *PS: Political Science & Politics*, 36(1), 51–57.

Inglehart, R., & Welzel, C. (2005). *Modernization, Cultural Change, and Democracy: The Human Development Sequence*. New York: Cambridge University Press.

Iyengar, S. (1991). *Is Anyone Responsible? How Television Frames Political Issues*. Chicago, IL: University of Chicago Press.

Jansson, A. (2002). The Mediatization of Consumption: Towards an Analytical Framework of Image Culture. *Journal of Consumer Culture*, 2(1), 5–31.

Karvonen, L. (2012). *The Personalisation of Politics: A Study of Parliamentary Democracies*. Colchester: ECPR Press.

Kepplinger, H. M. (2002). Mediatization of Politics: Theory and Data. *Journal of Communication*, 52(4), 972–986.

Koch-Baumgarten, S., & Voltmer, K. (Eds.) (2010). *Public Policy and Mass Media: The Interplay of Mass Communication and Political Decision Making*. London: Routledge.

Kovach, Bill & Rosenstiel, Tom (2007). *The Elements of Journalism: What Newspeople Should Know and the Public Should Expect*. 2nd Edition. New York, NY: Crown Publishers.

Kriesi, H., Lavenex, S., Esser, F., Matthes, J., Bühlmann, M., & Bochsler, D. (2013). *Democracy in the Age of Globalization and Mediatization*. Basingstoke: Palgrave Macmillan.

Krotz, F. (2007). The Meta-Process of "Mediatization" as a Conceptual Frame. *Global Media and Communication*, 3(3), 256–260.

Krotz, F. (2009). Mediatization: A Concept with Which to Grasp Media and Societal Change. In K. Lundby (Ed.), *Mediatization. Concept, Changes, Consequences* (pp. 21–40). New York, NY: Peter Lang.

Landerer, N. (2013). Rethinking the Logics: A Conceptual Framework for the Mediatization of Politics. *Communication Theory*, 23(3), 239–258.

Lasswell, H. D. (1950). *Politics: Who Gets What, When and How*. New York: Peter Smith.

Lengauer, G., Esser, F., & Berganza, R. (2012). Negativity in Political News: A Review of Concepts, Operationalizations and Key Findings. *Journalism*, 13(2), 179–202.

Lieber, P. S., & Golan, G. (2011). Political Public Relations, News Management, and Agenda Indexing. In J. Strömbäck & S. Kiousis (Eds.), *Political Public Relations: Principles and Applications* (pp. 54–74). New York, NY: Routledge.

Lundby, K. (2009a). Introduction: "Mediatization" as Key. In K. Lundby (Ed.), *Mediatization: Concept, Changes, Consequences* (pp. 1–18). New York, NY: Peter Lang.

Lundby, K. (2009b). Media Logic: Looking for Social Interaction. In K. Lundby (Ed.), *Mediatization: Concept, Changes, Consequences* (pp. 101–119). New York: Peter Lang.

March, J. G., & Olsen, J. P. (1989). *Rediscovering Institutions*. New York, NY: Free Press.

March, J. G., & Olsen, J. P. (2004). *The Logic of Appropriateness*. Arena Working Paper 04/09. Oslo: Arena. Centre for European Studies.

Marcinkowski, F. (2005). De Medialisierbarkeit politischer Institutionen. In P. Roessler & F. Krotz (Eds.), *Mythen der Mediengesellschaft – The Media Society and its Myths* (pp. 341–367). Konstanz: UVK Verlagsgesellschaft.

Mazzoleni, G. (2008a). Mediatization of Society. In W. Donsbach (Ed.), *The International Encyclopedia of Communication*, vol. VII (pp. 3052–3055). Malden, MA: Blackwell.

Mazzoleni, G. (2008b). Mediatization of Politics. In W. Donsbach (Ed.), *The International Encyclopedia of Communication*, vol. VII (pp. 3047–3051). Malden, MA: Blackwell.

Mazzoleni, G. (2008c). Media Logic. In W. Donsbach (Ed.), *The International Encyclopedia of Communication*, vol. VII (pp. 2930–2932). Malden, MA: Blackwell.

Mazzoleni, G. (1987). Media Logic and Party Logic in Campaign Coverage: The Italian General Election of 1983. *European Journal of Communication*, 2(1): 81–103.

Mazzoleni, G., & Schulz, W. (1999). Mediatization of Politics: A Challenge for Democracy? *Political Communication*, 16(3), 247–261.

McCombs, M. (2004). *Setting the Agenda: The Mass Media and Public Opinion*. Cambridge, MA: Polity Press.

McLuhan, M (1964). *Understanding Media: The Extensions of Man*. New York, NY: Mentor.

McManus, J. H. (1994). *Market-Driven Journalism: Let the Citizen Beware?* Thousand Oaks: Sage.

McNair, Brian (2003). *An Introduction to Political Communication*. 3rd Edition. London: Routledge.

Meyer, T. (2002). *Media Democracy: How the Media Colonize Politics*. Cambridge: Polity.

Morgan, M. (2009). Cultivation Analysis and Media Effects. In: R. L. Nabi & M. B. Oliver (Eds.), *The SAGE Handbook of Media Processes and Effects* (pp. 69–82). Thousand Oaks: Sage.

Norris, P. (2011). *Democratic Deficit: Critical Citizens Revisited*. New York, NY: Cambridge University Press.

Norris, P. (Ed.) (1999). *Critical Citizens: Global Support for Democratic Government*. New York, NY: Cambridge University Press.

O'Neill, D., & Harcup T. (2009). News Values and Selectivity. In K. Wahl-Jorgensen & T. Hanitzsch (Eds.), *Handbook of Journalism Studies* (pp. 161–174). New York, NY: Routledge.

Patterson, T. E. (1993). *Out of Order*. New York, NY: Vintage.

Pennings, P., Keman, H., & Kleinnijenhuis, J. (2006). *Doing Research in Political Science: An Introduction to Comparative Methods and Statistics*. London: Sage.

Roskos-Ewoldsen, D. R., & Roskos-Ewoldsen, B. (2009). Current Research in Media Priming. In R. L. Nabi & M. B. Oliver (Eds.), *The SAGE Handbook of Media Processes and Effects* (pp. 177–192). Thousand Oaks: Sage.

Salgado, S., & Strömbäck, J. (2012). Interpretive Journalism: A Review of Concepts, Operationalizations and Key Findings. *Journalism*, 13(2), 144–161.

Schillemans, T. (2012). *Mediatization of Public Services: How Organizations Adapt to News Media*. Frankfurt am Main: Peter Lang.

Schrott, A. (2009). Dimensions: Catch-All Label or Technical Term. In K. Lundby (Ed.), *Mediatization. Concept, Changes, Consequences* (pp. 41–62). New York, NY: Peter Lang.

Schulz, W. (2004). Reconstructing Mediatization as an Analytical Concept. *European Journal of Communication*, 19(1), 87–101.

Shoemaker, P. J., & Cohen, A. (2006). *News around the World: Content, Practitioners, and the Public*. New York, NY: Routledge.

Silverstone, R. (2007). *Media and Morality: On the Rise of the Mediapolis*. Cambridge, MA: Polity.

Sparrow, B. H. (1999). *Uncertain Guardians: The News Media as a Political Institution*. Baltimore, MD: John Hopkins University Press.

Stanyer, J. (2012). *Intimate Politics: Publicity, Privacy and the Personal Lives of Politicians in Media Saturated Democracies*. Cambridge, MA: Polity.

Strøm, K. (1990). A Behavioral Theory of Competitive Political Parties. *American Journal of Political Science*, 34(2), 565–598.

Strömbäck, J. (2008). Four Phases of Mediatization: An Analysis of the Mediatization of Politics. *The International Journal of Press/Politics*, 13(3), 228–246.

Strömbäck J. (2011a). Mediatization of Politics: Toward a Conceptual Framework for Comparative Research. In E. P. Bucy & R. L. Holber (Eds.), *Sourcebook for Political Communication Research: Methods, Measures, and Analytical Techniques* (pp. 367–382). New York, NY: Routledge.

Strömbäck, J. (2011b). Mediatization and Perceptions of the Media's Political Influence. *Journalism Studies*, 12(4), 423–439.

Strömbäck, J., & Dimitrova, D. V. (2011). Mediatization and Media Interventionism: A Comparative Analysis of Sweden and the United States. *International Journal of Press/Politics*, 16(1), 30–49.

Strömbäck, J., & Esser, F. (2009). Shaping Politics: Mediatization and Media Interventionism. In K. Lundby (Ed.), *Mediatization. Concept, Changes, Consequences* (pp. 205–224). New York, NY: Peter Lang.

Strömbäck, J., & Kaid, L. L. (Eds.) (2008). *The Handbook of Election News Coverage Around the World*. New York, NY: Routledge.

Strömbäck, J., & Kiousis, S. (Eds.) (2011). *Political Public Relations: Principles and Applications*. New York, NY: Routledge.

Strömbäck, J., & van Aelst, P. (2010). Exploring Some Antecedents of the Media's Framing of Election News: A Comparison of Swedish and Belgian Election News. *International Journal of Press/Politics*, 15(1), 41–59.

Strömbäck, J., & van Aelst, P. (2013). Why Political Parties Adapt to the Media: Exploring the Fourth Dimension of Mediatization. *International Communication Gazette*, 75(4), 341–358.

Strömbäck, J., Karlsson, M., & Hopmann, D. N. (2012). Determinants of News Content: Comparing Journalists' Perceptions of the Normative and Actual Impact of Different Event Properties When Deciding What's News. *Journalism Studies*, 13(5–6), 718–728.

Tedesco, J. (2011). Political Public Relations and Agenda Building. In J. Strömbäck & S. Kiousis (Eds.), *Political Public Relations. Principles and Applications* (pp. 75–94). New York, NY: Routledge.

van Aelst, P., Maddens, B., Noppe, J., & Fiers, S. (2008). Politicians in the News: Media or Party Logic? Media Attention and Electoral Success in the Belgian Election Campaign of 2003. *European Journal of Communication,* 23(2), 193–210.

Walgrave, S., & van Aelst, P. (2006). The Contingency of the Mass Media's Political Agenda Setting Power: Toward a Preliminary Theory. *Journal of Communication,* 56(1), 88–109.

Weaver, D. H., Beam, R. A., Brownlee, B. J., Voakes, P. S., & Wilhoit, G. C. (2007). *The American Journalist in the 21st Century: U.S. News People at the Dawn of a New Millennium.* Mahwah, NJ: Erlbaum.

Weaver, D. H., & Willnat, L. (Eds.) (2012). *The Global Journalist in the 21st Century.* New York, NY: Routledge.

Wolfsfeld, G. (2004). *Media and the Path to Peace.* Cambridge: Cambridge University Press.

Wolfsfeld, G. (2011). *Making Sense of Media & Politics: Five Principles in Political Communication.* New York, NY: Routledge.

Zoch, L. M., & Molleda, J. C. (2006). Building a Theoretical Model of Media Relations Using Framing, Information Subsidies, and Agenda-Building. In C. H. Botan & V. Hazleton (Eds.), *Public Relations Theory II.* New York, NY: Lawrence Erlbaum.

Part II
Foundations

2
Mediatization and Democracy

Jay G. Blumler

The concept of "mediatization" is doing heavy duty these days at several levels of communication analysis, many spheres of communication organization and various facets of political communication. A burgeoning literature of "mediatization-in-politics" has produced well-defined, well-analyzed and research-serviceable versions of the concept (see especially Chapter 1 of this volume; Strömbäck, 2008; Strömbäck & Esser, 2009; Schulz, 2004). Major works have treated mediatization as a prime axis on which the modern political communication process revolves (Brants & Voltmer, 2011; Kriesi et al., 2013).

If mediatization is political communication's rising tide, then it is supremely important to consider its implications for democracy. This is not easily done, nor has it often been attempted (but see Kriesi, 2013). However, the authors of a pioneering and seminal commentary on mediatization did discuss the relationship at some length, subtitling their article "A Challenge for Democracy?" (Mazzoleni & Schulz, 1999). Interestingly, they weren't all that alarmed. Although they fully acknowledged the workings and transforming impacts of the mediatization process and spelled out in some detail the societal, political and media trends which were propelling it, they denied (at the systemic level) "that we are heading toward a media-driven democracy" and concluded (at the practical level) that we are witnessing "an intense yet harmless mediatization of politics".

But that was relatively early days in experience of, thought about and scholarship on mediatization. How does its relationship to democracy look now, almost a decade and a half after Mazzoleni and Schulz produced their audit?

I will seek illumination in a sequence of steps: first, by placing mediatization in a historical background of past understandings of politician–media relationships (the mediatization literature is somewhat thin on this aspect); next, by briefly describing my analytical approach, centering on the notion of "self-mediatization"; then, by asking how mediatization may be influencing the content of political communications; next, by addressing the issue

31

of its effects on democracy; and finally, by identifying two main ways in which the systemic foundations of mediatization may be changing, leaving open the question of how democracy might fare in the wake of those developments in the future.

The background of politician–journalist relationships

The mediatization hypothesis was a late-coming contributor – though a creative and inventive one – to an ever-building corpus of understandings of politics–media relationships in liberal democracies. In Swanson's (1999) words, "From the 1960s forward [...] political communication has been created by practitioners and explained by scholars essentially as the product of a well-understood dynamic between political actors on the one hand, and mainstream news media on the other hand, with both soliciting the attention and consideration of the public."

It has often been noted that the operative relationships between the politicians and journalists involved in this dynamic have always been to some extent entangled – due basically to a combination of mutual dependency and conflicts of interest among them. Also important, however, and less remarked upon, is how over time these relationships have been in a condition of what might be thought of as a structured flux. If so, it should be instructive to consider where "mediatization" fits in that development, which the following potted history of politician–journalist relations in the postwar period will try to show.

First, in the early postwar years something like a division of labor could be said to have prevailed between the two political communicating sides. For example, Katz (1971), drawing on a metaphor that had been coined by the editor of Britain's ITN News, depicted the political communication process of his day in terms of "Platforms and Windows". The idea was that through their election broadcasts (and advertising in some countries), political parties had a platform from which to address the voting public, while through its news and current affairs programs television was becoming a window through which the elector could observe the activities of the politicians and the reactions of informed individuals to the policies and claims of party spokespeople.

Several forces conspired to smudge this distinction. The most important were, on the one hand, a diminishing party-mindedness in the political psyches of electorates, weakening the parties' support bases and lessening the credibility of their (platform-disseminated) messages, and on the other hand, the growing strength and appeal of television news, both in general and as a source of political coverage (with its attractive anchors, knowledgeable reporters and ever more sophisticated presentation techniques). From the need to cope with this "double whammy", political parties more or less throughout the democratic world eventually adopted what has variously been termed a "professionalised advocacy" model of political communication (Blumler & Gurevitch, 1995), or "strategic communication" via "the scientific engineering and targeting of messages" for "the achievement of narrow political goals" (Bennett & Manheim, 2001) or a "Going Public" model (Kernell, 1993). Whatever the label, central was the assumption that the priorities of a polity's short-term and long-term agendas were often lodged in daily news reports and that from there they could be passed on to audience member-voters with follow-on implications for how those voters would regard governments and their rivals. This seemed to necessitate the adoption by major political parties of determined, high-profile and well-resourced approaches and tactics to project their own agendas to the public through the news media (and to do this more effectively than their similarly active opponents might manage to achieve) rather than simply to respond after the fact to whatever agendas the media, fuelled by journalistic drives, would be putting forward.

Many journalists were disturbed by this development. According to their occupational ideology, they should be in charge, setting news agendas in line with their judgments, not politicians' priorities. As Zaller (2001) explained, the "strategy of aggressive news management attempts to force journalists into a role they detest, that of mechanically conveying politicians' words and actions to the public." There ensued, according to Zaller, something of a journalistic fight-back, in which reporters substituted more of their own product in place of politicians' offerings, including more provision of negative news (e.g., about policy failures), coverage of the ups, downs and foibles of political personalities, revelation of scandals and a pejorative underlining of politicians' publicity maneuvers, terming them "spin-doctoring", for example (Esser et al., 2001 provide a cross-national analysis of this practice).

And this is where "mediatization" may have stepped into the picture of politician–journalist relations. If trying to dominate political journalism could be counter-productive, a more fruitful alternative for politicians to follow might be to harness and exploit its propensities – less a matter of battering their way into the news, then, than one of riding on its coat-tails. It is true that this approach retains many of the organizational features which the political parties had previously adopted: very high publicity priorities; ample communication resources (of funds, staffing and reliance on expert consultants and advisors); and a detailed and assiduous, round-the-clock attention to political news flows (Strömbäck & Van Aelst, 2013). But instead of pushing their messages at journalists in ways that could be construed as news management, politicians would try more often to present them with events, initiatives, statements, reactions, etc., that would chime with their news values – riding the waves with them, as it were – rather than striving to overcome them. From this standpoint, then, mediatization may be defined (Esser, 2013, calls this "self-mediatization") as *a process whereby politicians (and by extension other opinion advocates) tailor their message offerings to the perceived news values, newsroom routines and journalism cultures prevalent in their societies.*

The basis of analysis

Readers of the Introduction by Strömbäck and Esser (Chapter 1 of this volume) will recognize the above as an elaborated version of the fourth dimension of the mediatization dynamic, which concerns the influence and importance of media *within* political processes and *over* political actors and institutions (Strömbäck, 2008). It is true that all four of their dimensions are probably implicated to some extent in the workings of democracy. (The others are: the degree to which media have become the most important information source in politics and society; the degree to which media have become independent from other political and social institutions; and the extent to which media coverage of politics is governed by media logic rather than political logic.) But of these, the fourth dimension is most suited to examination of the mediatization–democracy nexus because (a) it lends itself more readily to an identification of specific phenomena with possible implications for democracy, (b) it is the phase in which politicians are most in danger of losing their autonomy and (c) it is also the phase in which politicians and journalists are most likely to concur in their perspectives on reality, potentially narrowing citizens' ways of regarding that reality. Strömbäck and Esser are unlikely to disagree with this approach, since they do say of the fourth dimension that it "deals with the very essence of the mediatization of politics".

If (self-)mediatization, then what?

What consequences might ensue the more that politicians and their advisors deliberately shape their communications to suit what they perceive to be the news values, workways and prevailing narratives of journalists in the hope of winning favorable coverage thereby? The following tendencies seem likely to result:

- *Increased complicity* with politicians as courtiers and journalists willing to be seduced. If politicians manage to stroke journalists' news values and other predilections, when putting forward their initiatives, claims and pronouncements, why shouldn't editors and reporters just pass them on to their consumers without, or with little, question? (Davis, 2010 provides a graphic case study of this process, centering on the rise to power of David Cameron in Britain.) In handling stories, journalists may have a choice between processing them – e.g., accepting them at more or less face value, as Davies (2008) has documented – or probing them – e.g., to get at the truth, to learn more, to check claims or to tap other views. But probing would normally require an expenditure of extra time and effort that may not always be affordable in those conditions of newsroom stringency that prevail today. Mediatization might tend to favor processing over probing routines.

- *The "here today and gone tomorrow" rhythm of much news production.* Since news feasts on "the new", all involved in its making are drenched in the fluid immediacy of events and their coverage. For their part, politicians and their advisors often seem impelled to keep up with and respond to the news on its terms and in its time. This may result in ill-considered ploys, sloganizing and news-steered gimmickry (publicity dressed up as policy!). The fact that what is highlighted in the news at one time is off the radar at others may be consequential in other ways. Attention to even important issues, such as climate change, may follow a "now you see it, now you don't" pattern. Politicians who have made policy commitments in response to a propitious news environment at a particular time may disregard or flout them when the agenda has switched gear, moving to different topics and concerns later on. Coleman and Blumler (2011), for example, present striking examples of such behavior by the Conservative and Liberal Democratic Parties before and after the British General Election of 2010.
- *Predominant "framing".* In addition to the multiplicity of events eligible for reporting, there are often one or two more abiding issues of contemporary politics that the news continually reverts to and on which politicians are expected to comment. But these may be presented through the lens of a singular, albeit broadly shaping and more or less enduring frame of reference. According to Entman's (1993) analysis, such frames typically include a particular problem definition, a causal interpretation, a moral evaluation and a treatment recommendation. An example in our period might be the dominance of a "deficit reduction by austerity" frame throughout most West European political communication systems after the onset of the financial crisis in 2008. It seems that even journalists employed in different types of news outlets can share a common overarching frame, although their approaches within it might differ. It also seems that the news media can only work within one overarching frame at a time. As Entman (1993) has pointed out in a telling comment, framing functions "as much through what it shuts out as what it includes" and "sets the boundaries of discourse over an issue". If so, self-mediatizing politicians could feel constrained to ensure that their own comments stay within, rather than break out of, the bounds of a prevailing frame.
- *The portrayal of dramatic incidents of institutional failure.* The news often reports dramatic and shocking incidents in the conduct of public institutions. The occurrence of a single happening in a particular institution is quite different, however, from a spread or a representative sample of

such cases throughout an institution. The question is (or should be) whether the incident that makes the headlines was a "one-off" or the tip of a systemic iceberg. The news media do not always observe such a distinction, however, and may imply that the fault must be extensive even if evidence of same is lacking. Of course the reporting of even a single case or a small number of cases may have a positive outcome, especially if further abuses come to light as a result or expert and judicious enquiries are established to determine what went wrong, how widespread the problems actually are and what options for improvement might be available. But politicians may be tempted to exploit news of this kind for their own partisan purposes, to denounce roundly what has happened, to sound systemic alarm bells prematurely and to rush in with supposed remedies "on the hoof", hoping to garner media praise for their decisive actions. But an unfortunate by-product of such a storyline can be the wholesale and unjustified smearing of dedicated workers in the institution concerned, whose morale may suffer as a result. In Britain in recent years, some social workers, nurses and teachers may have felt that they had been on the receiving end of just such unwarranted treatment.

- *Ratcheting up the tone of political rhetoric.* The depiction of conflict is of course a central news value for journalists (Lengauer et al., 2012). Although this has always included extensive reporting of political conflict, in the past journalists have also occasionally served as guardians of minimal standards of rhetorical propriety. More recently, that role seems to have been relinquished. Consequently, when catering for journalists' appetites for conflict, politicians' contributions to debate may become sharper, less temperate and more abusive. The defining of issues, the presentation of policies on them, the rejection of opponents' stands on them – all may be expressed in more strident terms. Faced with such a barrage, citizens may be hard pressed to discern the substantive pros and cons of the issues at stake beneath the heated argumentation.
- *Certain abiding imperfections of the news media.* Like politics itself, mainstream coverage of politics is something of a rough trade. Although it enables and lubricates democracy in many ways (see McQuail, 2013 for an excellent elaboration), research has established a number of its inbuilt limitations. Examples might include the stereotyping of minorities and other vulnerable groups in society (such as the depiction of welfare benefit recipients, immigrants and asylum seekers in Britain at present); distorted depictions of social reality (as in overestimations of the incidence of crime and violence in society); a predominant portrayal of politics as a power game, neglecting its role as a sphere of policy consideration; reporting strikes and demonstrations chiefly in terms of the occurrence (or not) of violence and disorder with little mention of the

participants' policy demands and ideas; and a marked elitist bias in the views, experiences and problems that are regularly aired in the media (compared with the all-too common silencing of underdogs). For their part, politicians may have to take such features of media reality as givens and relate their rhetoric and even their policy proposals to them rather than challenge them or enunciate alternative views about them.

Mediatization and democracy: What's the charge sheet?

However the above may read, it should not be taken as an unqualified condemnation of the role of news values in political communication. For all their faults, the media do perform an indispensable bridging function between happenings in remote arenas and ordinary people's awareness of whatever in that wider world could matter or be of interest to them. As Schulz (1983) has put it, "In order to make politics comprehensible to the citizen, it must first be reduced by journalists to a few simple structural patterns." Trouble arises, however – democracy may be threatened or perverted – when, through mediatization, the tension between political leadership and journalistic commentary is adulterated, when, in other words, political logic is converted into or displaced by media logic.

Specifically, mediatized political communication may be "bad news" (pardon the wordplay) for democracy in several ways. First, it may sustain what can only be called communication injustices – when "out-groups" are shut out (so, doubly "outed") of the national conversation. Second, it may entail the neglect of or pay only erratic attention to society's major, long-term challenges, due to the mediatized partners' continual focus on more immediate short-term ones. Third, due especially to the perpetration of monolithic framing and stereotyping, it may limit, sometimes perhaps drastically limit, citizens' awareness of the choices available for tackling important issues and their ability to make informed choices when acting politically themselves. If the main mediatizing actors repeatedly present the same impressions of the civic world, materials for genuine and meaningful choice will be in short supply. Fourth, policy proposals, decisions and outcomes, to the degree that politicians and journalist are in cahoots over them, may be subjected less often to informed scrutiny. Fifth, the possibility that citizens can gain something worthwhile from the voicing of political differences – such as a clarification of what is at stake – may be reduced if those exchanges are little more than slanging matches. Sixth, and most seriously perhaps, mediatization seems to confuse, perhaps even fracture, the chain of accountability that is supposed to operate in a democracy. The empirical observation that politicians have adapted their game to fit in with the logic of the media raises the question of whether unaccountable media institutions should determine the roles of accountable politicians.

Yet more structured flux?

But is mediatization as actualized and understood so far the terminus of politician–journalist relationships? Possibly not; further stages of "structured flux" may change them yet again in the future. Two prospective developments of this kind merit consideration.

One of these concerns the systemic foundations of mediatization. Mediatization in theory and practice belonged to a certain underlying model of the political communication process. This was essentially pyramidal: tripartite (politicians, journalists, audience-voters); linear and top-down in transmission (politicians and reporters actively disseminating communications to receivers); and pivotally based on close and complex inter-institutional relationships between politicians and journalists.

But today this model, though still applicable to much elite-driven and official communication, is in some paradigmatic disrepair (Blumler & Coleman, 2013). Its locked-in and all-embracing qualities no longer seem quite so impregnable. They have been weakened by the expansion, segmentation and fragmentation of communication practices, including the ever-increasing generation and utilization of Internet-based facilities. In the new, still emerging dispensation, politicians may have more targets to aim their messages at than before; journalists may have access to a greater variety of sources than before; and "ordinary people" may be able to transmit more communications of their own making to whomever and wherever they like than before. Those who formerly spoke from the top of the pyramid virtually unchallenged must now attend more closely to what is being said and exchanged at the grassroots level and consider how best to intervene there. Whether all this will appreciably dent the involvement of journalists and politicians in mediatizing relationships and practices is unclear. One possibility is that the production of a great deal of civic communication will continue to be shaped by the mediatization process for a while but that this will gradually be supplemented, surrounded and even infiltrated by a number of other sources of political communication. If so, though still important, mediatization might no longer be the only political communication game in town.

What might some of those other sources be? The answer points to a second form of structured flux that mediatization researchers might wish to take into account. If we were to think of present-day political communication as a large lake, then its waters do seem to be continually fed by the following:

- *A rationalization stream* – a flooding of the public sphere by a great deal of systematically gathered evidence, some of it quantitative, on social trends, social problems, institutional performances, policy effects and publics' views, published by sundry bodies, such as think tanks, public interest organizations, numerous cause and campaigning groups, other interest and pressure groups, international agencies, parliamentary committees and academic researchers.

- *A large and varied single issue or single cause stream* – as indicated in some of the above, the undertaking of much political activity outside party ranks, including the production of materials intended for media consumption, by a large and varied number of campaigning organizations, interest groups, charities, etc., some with large memberships and support bases, with carefully tended websites and in some cases with sizable treasure chests.
- *A grassroots stream* – the proliferating, variegating and vigorous supplies of comments of many kinds about current events, issues and personalities, emanating from non-official communicators, sent and exchanged through popular social media and other channels, rhetorically very different from mainstream communications, facilitating exertions of pressure and opening new avenues of mobilization, and attracting the ever closer attention of mainstream politicians and journalists.
- *A popularizing stream* – politicians' projections of themselves in vehicles of entertainment and popular drama, plus the readiness of some of those vehicles to address politics from more off-beat angles of comment, amusement and satire.
- *A party faithfuls stream* – the efforts of some political party members to bind their leaders to policies reflective of a more authentic faith than the conduct of pragmatic politics and the adoption of PR strategies can, in their view, realize.

But what might all this have to say about mediatization? It's not at all evident, since mediatization thinking itself has so far had little to say about it. From the start, political communications have been conceived as products of politicians and journalists – full stop! I plead guilty to having promulgated such a perspective myself, when many years ago I defined the very notion of a political communication system as pivoting on

> two sets of institutions – political and media organizations – which are involved in the course of message preparation in much "horizontal" interaction with each other while on a "vertical" axis, they are separately and jointly engaged in disseminating and processing information and ideas to and from the mass citizenry.
>
> (Gurevitch & Blumler, 1977)

Of course that focus was natural and can never be treated as peripheral. But neither should it be left that way, for in contemporary democracy there are many other sources of views and concerns with communication axes to grind and with motivations and resources to wield them. Are those forces mainly outside or inside the mediatization process? And if the latter, is their relationship to it similar to that of politicians or different and, for that matter, are their relationships to it significantly different from each other? Speculation suggests a few points on this, but more research and analysis will be needed to clarify them (and others). For example, all groups that are concerned about their standing in public opinion could be enmeshed in mediatization – the more so, the more they consider that realization of their goals could depend on how, through communications, they are regarded in society at large. But if their aim is chiefly that of influence on public affairs, they may be better able to pick and choose prospectively favorable moments of attempted publicity intervention than politicians can, whose ultimate aim, being that of power, must be to man the publicity barricades unceasingly. What non-party groups have to say may sometimes be received by journalists with less automatic suspicion than they accord politicians' ploys. It is also possible that some non-party groups will be more protective of the integrity of their policy positions than some politicians are and less willing to compromise them by resorting to media logic.

In order to address questions like these and other related ones, aiming to establish how, comparatively across a broad spectrum of politically minded groups, mediatization works, differs or is even set aside in the course of sundry source–journalist interactions, perhaps the field of our analysis and research should be broadened from "the mediatization of politics" to "the mediatization of the public sphere".

Acknowledgments

I am grateful for valuable comments on a previous draft of this chapter received from Lance Bennett, Stephen Coleman, Sonia Livingstone, Winfried Schulz – and the editors.

References

Bennett, W. L., & Manheim, J. (2001). The Big Spin: Strategic Communication and the Transformation of Pluralist Democracy. In W. L. Bennett & R. M. Entman (Eds.), *Mediated Politics: Communication in the Future of Democracy* (pp. 279–298). Cambridge: Cambridge University Press.

Blumler, J. G., & Coleman, S. (2013). Paradigms of Civic Communication. *International Journal of Communication*, 7, 173–187.

Blumler, J. G., & Gurevitch, M. (1995). *The Crisis of Public Communication*. London: Routledge.

Brants, K., & Voltmer, K. (2011). *Political Communication in Postmodern Democracy: Challenging the Primacy of Politics*. Houndmills Basingstoke: Palgrave Macmillan.

Coleman, S., & Blumler, J. G. (2011). The Wisdom of Which Crowd? On the Pathology of a Listening Government. *The Political Quarterly*, 82(3), 355–364.

Davies, N. (2008). *Flat Earth News*. London: Vintage Publishing.

Davis, A. (2010). *Political Communication and Social Theory*. Abingdon Oxon: Routledge.

Entman, R. M. (1993). Framing: Towards Clarification of a Fractured Paradigm. *Journal of Communication*, 32(4), 51–58.

Esser, F. (2013). Mediatization as a Challenge: Media Logic versus Political Logic. In H. Kriesi, S. Lavanex, F. Esser, J. Matthes, M. Bühlmann & D. Bochsler (Eds.), *Democracy in the Age of Globalization and Mediatization* (pp. 155–176). Houndmills Basingstoke: Palgrave Macmillan.

Esser, F., Reinemann, C., & Fan, D. P. (2001). Spin Doctors in the United States, Great Britain and Germany: Metacommunication of Media Manipulation. *The Harvard International Journal of Press/Politics*, 6(1), 16–45.

Gurevitch, M., & Blumler, J. G. (1977). Linkages between the Mass Media and Politics: A Model for the Analysis of Political Communication Systems. In J. Currran, M. Gurevitch & J. Wollacott (Eds.), *Mass Communication and Society* (pp. 270–290). London: Edward Arnold.

Katz, E. (1971). Platforms and Windows: Broadcasting's Role in Election Campaigns. *Journalism Quarterly*, 38(3), 304–314.

Kernell, S. (1993). *Going Public*. Washington, DC: Congressional Quarterly.

Kriesi, H. (2013). Conclusion: An Assessment of the State of Democracy Given the Challenges of Globalization and Mediatization. In H. Kriesi, S. Lavanex, F. Esser, J. Matthes, M. Bühlmann & D. Bochsler (Eds.), *Democracy in the Age of Globalization and Mediatization* (pp. 202–215). Houndsmill Basingstoke: Palgrave Macmillan.

Kriesi, H., Lavanex, S., Esser, F., Matthes, J., Bühlmann, M., & Bochsler, D. (2013). *Democracy in the Age of Globalization and Mediatization*. Houndsmill Basingstoke: Palgrave Macmillan.

Lengauer, G., Esser, F., & Berganza, R. (2012). Negativity in Political News: A Review of Concepts, Operationalizations and Key Findings. *Journalism*, 13(2), 179–202.

Mazzoleni, G., & Schulz, W. (1999). "Mediatization" of Politics: A Challenge for Democracy? *Political Communication*, 16(3), 247–262.

McQuail, D. (2013). *Journalism and Society*. London: Sage Publications.

Schulz, W. (1983). One Campaign or Nine? In J. G. Blumler (Ed.), *Communicating to Voters: Television in the First European Parliamentary Elections* (pp. 337–344). London: Sage Publications.

Schulz, W. (2004). Reconstructing Mediatization as an Analytical Concept. *European Journal of Communication*, 19(1), 87–101.

Strömbäck, J. (2008). Four Phases of Mediatization: An Analysis of the Mediatization of Politics. *The International Journal of Press/Politics*, 13(3), 228–246.

Strömbäck, J., & Esser, F. (2009). Shaping Politics: Mediatization and Media Interventionism. In K. Lundby (Ed.), *Mediatization. Concept, Changes, Consequences* (pp. 205–224). New York, NY: Peter Lang.

Strömbäck, J., & van Aelst, P. (2013). Why Political Parties Adapt to the Media: Exploring the Fourth Dimension of Mediatization. *International Communication Gazette*, 75(4), 341–358.

Swanson, D. L. (1999). About This Issue. *Political Communication*, 16(3), 203–207.

Zaller, J. (2001). The Rule of Product Substitution in Presidential Campaign News. In E. Katz & Y.Warshel (Eds.), *Election Studies: What's Their Use?* (pp. 247–270). Boulder, CO: Westview Press.

3
Mediatization and Political Populism

Gianpietro Mazzoleni

The rapid development of communication technology and of the products of the culture industry has brought about a worldwide phenomenon that has taken shape particularly in the decades after World War II. Known as "mediatization", this phenomenon involves various processes, such as (a) extending human communication beyond their natural limits, (b) replacing several social activities and institutions and above all (c) obliging social actors and organizations to accommodate themselves to the logic of the media (Schulz, 2004).

Mediatized environments

Mediatization affects "all spheres of society, from the structure of the family to the aging process, from gender relationships to power, from the political apparatus to economic structures" (Mazzoleni, 2008c, p. 3052). This phenomenon has reached an unprecedented intensity with the advent of the new media and the global diffusion of personal communication tools that allow people to connect easily and ceaselessly with their surrounding social environment, and to access, consume and even produce a wide variety of contents. The traditional mass media, such as the press, television, cinema and the new instruments of "self-mass communication" (Castells, 2009), namely, the social media, have penetrated so deeply into all human activities that it is impossible to imagine individuals and social groups existing outside the dense web of media influences. In brief, the media and society have grown together into a mutually indispensable and interdependent entity.

The mediatized society can also be seen as an ecosystem that allows the circulation and exchange of ideas on a large scale and at high speed. Fads, fandoms, beliefs and rumors originate within society and spread via the media, thanks to the platforms it offers. There are several dynamics via which the classical mass media and the new media combine to pervade and mold our "mediatized society": from private to formal relationships, from creation to consumption, from religion to art, from local to global, from journalism to politics, and many more.

While the contribution of mediatization in most of these domains has been largely disregarded by scholarly reflection, it has gained wide attention in the political sphere, as shown and illustrated in this book (see also Kepplinger, 2002; Strömbäck & Esser, 2009). Accordingly, this chapter focuses on the political dimensions of the mediatization process and on its links to populist manifestations in contemporary politics.

The mediatization of politics is clearly part of the larger process of mediatization of society, but it assumes special importance wherever the exercise of power and related relationships are involved. It can be defined as the result of media-driven influences in the political domain: "[t]he media have gained a central position in most political routines, such as election campaigns, government communication, public diplomacy and image building" (Mazzoleni, 2008b, p. 3048). This shows how the logic of the political sphere – or a good part of it – is yielding to the supremacy of the logic and imperatives of the media in contemporary societies. Politics and communication have of course always been interlaced, and the former has tended to use the latter to achieve its aims. Only in the age of the mass media, and especially since the birth of television, has politics had to face the challenge of powerful new players in the public sphere that competed in addressing the same audiences but used more effective means and more appealing narratives. Politics itself has been treated by the media like any other subject, ultimately being created and presented on the basis of the "news values" of the media industry and often of show business too. The most tangible result has been a conversion and adaptation of the traditional stylistic features of political communication to typical media formats (Altheide & Snow, 1979, 1991). Strömbäck (2008) places this transformation in what he labels the "third phase of mediatization" where the media emancipate themselves more strongly from the political actors and succeed in making their formats, content, grammar and rhythm so pervasive that "no social actors requiring interaction with the public or influence on public opinion can ignore the media or can afford not to adapt to its logic" (p. 238). Politicians have increasingly understood that they have to take heed of the inescapable demands of the (commercial) media, lest they are ignored or other, non-political contents be preferred by mass audiences. The media-driven pressure on politics to adopt discursive strategies that have proved to be successful in the commercial domain has been so strong that mediatized discourse has become the accepted way for politics to address the citizenry.

Different labels have been used by researchers to designate the forms and implications of the mediatization of politics: the "spectacularization" of political discourse, "personalization" involving a focus on personal aspects at the expense of policies, the "agenda shaping" power of the media to launch issues for public debate, the "fragmentation" and "simplification" of political speeches – the "sound-bite" effect – and the "winnowing" of political actors according to their mediagenic presentation (Mazzoleni, 2008b, pp. 3048–3051).

In much the same way as has happened in society at large, new media are joining the "old" media in radicalizing the mediatization of politics and political communication. Thus, Williams and Delli Carpini (2011) list a number of important effects of the advent of the "New Information Environment": a dramatic increase in the volume and range of the information available to and about citizens; the faster rate at which this information is gathered, retrieved and transmitted; the decentralization of sources of information; greater control by individuals over the information they receive; an increased ability to target specific contents to specific audiences; an increase in both vertical and horizontal communication between citizens and elites of the one-to-one, one-to-many, many-to-one, and many-to-many kinds (p. 286). The massive utilization of social networks in recent election campaigns worldwide and in the rise and diffusion of political movements (such as the Piraten Partei, the Indignados, Beppe Grillo's M5S, Occupy Wall Street (OWS), and the upheavals in the Arab world) epitomize the way in which politics, political communication and political information are changing towards a "Mediatization 2.0" situation in which the logic of the traditional media blends with interactive modes of communication to make the political system more dependent than ever on the media. This transition from the former "centripetal" forms of communication to "centrifugal" ones envisaged by Blumler and Kavanagh (1999) takes the form of a "multi-axial" ecosystem (Williams & Delli Carpini, 2011) in which political communicators have lost their central position in favor of a plurality of communicators who join the established players in the competition for power.

This chapter deals with the effects of political mediatization on contemporary populism, and analyses the media impact on this phenomenon. We will first define what is meant by "political populism", then examine how and to what extent "populist" outlooks and behaviors in the media link up to populist phenomena. The section thereafter will discuss the mediatization of populist leadership and discourse in more detail. Finally, the concluding section examines the idea of complicity and partnership between the media's own brand of populism and its political counterpart.

Political populism

The phenomenon of political populism has been present in all ages and diverse national contexts. Populist movements arose in the fast-changing society of 19th-century America, or were spun off from the socialist-oriented struggles of the European countries in the early 20th century. Some ultimately developed into the Fascist parties that came to power in Italy, Spain, Germany and Portugal, whereas others popped up here and there in the electoral turmoil of the immediate postwar age (such as *Poujadism* in France and *Qualunquismo* in Italy). In more recent times, populism has thrived in many mature democracies, often as a reaction to the dramatic transformations wrought by globalization which challenge existing power balances, prosperity levels, economic indices and labor models.

Political scientists have made various attempts to define the concept of populism, but its ever-shifting nature, manifold national varieties and unexpected electoral trajectories have all prompted them to be cautious in providing a definition applicable to all political latitudes. Indeed, various authors emphasize its "constitutional ambiguity" (Taguieff, 1997), its "vagueness" (Canovan, 1999), its "chameleonic quality" or its "impalpability and slipperiness" (Taggart, 2000). However, the efforts made to characterize populist attitudes and related behaviors have yielded an extremely interesting catalogue of the distinctive features of populism as a social and political phenomenon. Thus, Mudde (2004) sees populism "as an ideology that considers society to be ultimately separated into two homogenous and antagonistic groups, 'the pure people' versus 'the corrupt elite', and which argues that politics should be an expression of the general will of the people" (p. 562). Mény and Surel (2000) speak of it as the offspring of a "democratic malaise" (p. 21), something that has now also been identified as an "antipolitical" resentment of the privileges and corruption of the political classes (Albertazzi & McDonnell, 2008).

While most populist movements are undoubtedly right-wing in their ideology (with different degrees of extremism), such as Le Pen's Front National, the Vlaams Blok, Haider's FPÖ and Bossi's Lega Nord, populism in itself is not a prerogative of the far right. Several claims by populists to be the "government of the people" can be found in many constitutional charters of democratic regimes. When such claims are accompanied by anti-elitist slogans and dissatisfaction with mainstream politics, such as OWS, the Spanish Indignados and Grillo's M5S,[1] they display clear liberal, left-wing features, especially if they recoil from nationalist, anti-immigration platforms.

Most populist movements are initiated by charismatic figures that tend to become absolutist leaders and authority figures. They are often media-savvy and exhibit remarkable public rhetoric skills. Theirs is usually a highly emotional, vehement, slogan-based, tabloid-style language spiced up by theatrical performances, all traits that guarantee media attention and wide visibility (Stewart et al., 2003).

Citizens of the advanced democracies tend to be well educated and keen to employ peaceful and civil means to further their political aims. This makes extremist politics the province of a vociferous minority in society. Whereas populist movements have sometimes won substantial electoral support, they have rarely succeeded in seizing power, and when they do, they have to join coalitions with more moderate parties and tone down their fiery rhetoric. But, as Mudde notes in introducing the concept of a "populist zeitgeist", "populist discourse has gone mainstream in the politics of contemporary western democracies" (2004, p. 562). This means that many leaders of established and government parties do not recoil from striking sensitive popular chords and use populist slogans, while avoiding the rudeness of extremist populist speech, to please and coax their traditional electorates who may be tempted by outsider or challenger parties.

Scholars in political communication have thus far paid scant attention to political populism, and really only began to do so in the last decade of the new century. Thus, Jagers and Walgrave (2007), in their seminal reflection on the concept of "populism", have moved away from definitions that reflect the diverse manifestations and institutional forms of this phenomenon in national contexts and argue that populism is above all a "communication style" with two facets, namely, "thick" and "thin": "In the thin conceptualization, populism is totally stripped of all pejorative and authoritarian connotations [...] It is a normal political style adopted by all kinds of politicians in all times" (p. 323). Hence, we can find elements of populism wherever and whenever a political leader speaks about the people. It becomes "thick" populism "[w]hen political actors talk about the people *and* combine this with an explicit anti-establishment tone *and* exclude certain population categories" (p. 323).

Cranmer (2011) builds on the idea of populism as a style of communication and attempts to operationalize it by introducing some elements that may be used to measure populist manifestations (movements and parties) in their real contexts. She considers references to "the people" to be "populist if a political actor claims that he or she defends the will of 'the people' (advocacy), is accountable to 'the people' (accountability), and/or legitimizes his or her claim by referring to 'the people' (legitimacy)" (p. 92).

However, the argument that populism is primarily a rhetorical phenomenon seems a bit simplistic, vis-à-vis the "thickness" of certain cases of populism and the aggressive nature of their creed. Indeed, Pauwels (2011) notes that not all academics espouse this view, and claims that the ideological framework of a party or movement must be considered in any definition of this phenomenon, especially if certain parties include "a normative dimension in their populist discourse, making it more of an ideology than a style" (p. 99).

The academic debate about the proper definition of such a "slippery" phenomenon is bound to continue, as each school emphasizes either its institutional or cultural dimension. Our approach considers populism from a culturalist perspective, because this ties in with the specific nature of the media and their effects, most notably the process of mediatization.

The example of populist leadership helps us to understand how it links up with the cultural and media dimensions of populism. As in other widely studied political phenomena, such as election campaigns, populist movements and parties are headed by leaders whose personality traits cannot fail to attract the attention of the media and are crucial in building up a public image that can determine their fortunes or failure. Populist leaders are engaged in political activities that can be considered primarily as modes of communication: this applies to their discourse(s), the issues they raise, the content of their speeches in rallies and television shows or press interviews, and the communication strategies they pursue in chasing the popular consensus. All populist leaders are controversial politicians who bully the established parties. They target domestic audiences who can be resistant or receptive to discourses that harp on issues varying from nationalism and revanchism, to an outspoken defense of ethnic identities, anti-immigration platforms and (in the European Union) hostility towards the euro and similar targets. In an age of "audience democracy" (Manin, 1995), public opinion is increasingly shaped by communication channels and networks. So the creed generated by populist leaders can be given a boost by the media, who give their "communication style" substance and a specific format.

The sender (populist leaders), the message (populist speech), the channel (the mass and new media) and the receiver (the potential supporters) are the classical ingredients of communication explored by research into political communication.

Media populism

If the "thick" and "thin" versions of political populism depend so much on their communication channels and media representations, a closer look at the media dynamics involved will cast further light on this phenomenon.

The overarching concept that embraces both the process and impact of mediatization on the rise of political populism is once again that of media logic. The concept of "media populism" then comes into the picture and points to the connections and nexus of influences that exist between the workings of this logic and the phenomenon of populism.

A due distinction should be made before discussing this concept further. Two conceptions of "media populism" are current today: the first has to do with the inner character of contemporary mass communication as a whole, including news and entertainment, while the other relates to the ideological outlook and conduct of certain news channels which can be identified as "populist media". The first type is illustrated in Blumler and Kavanagh's (1999) enumeration of the features of the "third age of political communication" which provide the phenomenological setting for media populism, namely, "the proliferation of the main means of communication, media abundance, ubiquity, reach, and celerity" (p. 213), but also the undermining of political journalism by a strong market orientation, an infotainment approach to politics, the popularization of broadcast programming and the pick-and-choose culture of the audiences (pp. 223–224). The move towards a market orientation and a more audience-focused culture also effects established media institutions (such as the BBC in the UK).

> Communicators who wish to inform, persuade, or simply keep the attention of their auditors must [...] adapt more closely than in the past to what ordinary people find interesting, engaging, relevant, and accessible. Politicians are impelled to speak in a more popular idiom and to court popular support more assiduously. Media organizations are driven to seek ways of making politics more palatable and acceptable to audience members. (p. 220)

Although Blumler and Kavanagh do not talk about media logic, its influences are omnipresent. However, media logic and media populism appear to be somewhat overlapping concepts insofar as the media pursue popular ends to stay in the market and make a profit.

As regards the specific embodiments of media populism, the examples of infotainment and politainment can be seen in several highly mediatized political contexts. While infotainment applies to the entire news business, and not only to its political contents, as it "denote[s] the decline of hard news [...] programs and the corresponding development of a variety of entertainment shows that mimic the style of news" (Baym, 2008), politainment is "symbiotic" with politics, as it "denotes [...] the entangling of political actors, topics, and processes with the entertainment culture" (Nieland, 2008).

Infotainment flourishes wherever journalists and news outlets cover political figures, leaders, issues and events: the features it displays contribute greatly to acquiring an understanding of how populism can become mediatized. In fact, it is well known that the news media promote news values and implement production routines that favor persons rather than abstract entities, celebrities rather than anonymous people, scandals rather than approved behaviors, accidents rather than ordinary events – whatever is newsworthy is what breaks the routine, in other words, "bad news". So, whenever the news-making machine processes politics, politicians are imbued with an aura of celebrity: only those who adopt a mediagenic style of communication become media darlings. If they are involved in scandalous stories, they will be scrutinized and given wide coverage; controversial figures make the headlines; political speeches are reported only in the form of "sound-bites". As well described by Richardson et al. (2013),

> Political news does not just cover [...] the serious "hard news" of governance, or reasoned debate between political elites, but gaffes, trivia and revelations about politicians' behavior and character "behind closed doors". The ever-shifting professional values and presumptions of "what counts" as political news, with its serious "hard" subjects as well as tabloid

treatments, make any definition prone to certain strains and fuzziness around the borders. (p. 6)

The mass media, which respond primarily to commercial imperatives, thus produce content that caters to the tastes and needs of vast and largely undefined audiences. The close connection between media populism and the popular content spread by the media industry in its various forms supports the idea that the media's own brand of populism can provide a platform that, intentionally or unintentionally, is conducive to political populism. It couples perfectly with Jagers and Walgrave's idea of populism as a communication style ("thin" populism).

The second concept of media populism broadens our view onto how political populism relates to media activities that assume its "thick" character. In fact, popular media contents may carry ideologically sensitive elements such as anti-elitist stances, anti-political accents and the like, thus creating a climate of opinion favorable to political populism. Krämer (2014) sees this type of media populism as combining stylistic *and* ideological elements, namely, in the construction and favoritism of in-groups, hostility towards elites, circumvention of the institutions of representative democracy, a reliance on charisma and common sense, and an appeal to moral sentiments (i.e., an emotionalizing and personalizing approach). As we will show, some news as well as entertainment media not only play an indirect instrumental role but also act as primary players in promoting a populist agenda.

To sum up, we can conclude that populism is largely a communicative phenomenon and that political populism ("thick" and "thin") is strongly correlated with media populism (with its popular and ideological bias), and can now examine the features of "mediatized populism". That is the focus of the next section.

Mediatized populism

This description of the mediatization of politics highlighted several features that perfectly illustrate the relation between populist actors (leaders and movements) and the diversified worlds of the media: the tug-of-war between political and media logic, politicians' messages adjusting to news values when carried by media channels, the adaptation of party or party leader communication strategies to media styles and demands and, in the context of "Mediatization 2.0", politicians facing a fragmented, reactive and largely uncontrollable audience.

Accordingly, we can question whether, how and to what extent media populism may be related to political populism, and whether there exists some sort of causal effect analogous to the changes in politics and political communication induced by media logic. In other words, is there anything like a "mediatized populism"? The many examples of populist movements or flamboyant populist leaders all show how strongly they are intertwined with the modes of communication of both the mass and social kinds.

The tabloid media in particular have often appeared to legitimize the slogans and actions of populist leaders. The existence of "newsroom populism" in the Austrian tabloids of the 1990s appears to have created a climate of opinion favorable to the FPÖ (Plasser & Ulram, 2003). In Switzerland, "the tabloid press and 'tabloidized' Sunday papers devote more attention to issues of identity politics and law and order than the populist radical right itself. [...] It is precisely these media types that have been finding a larger audience in Switzerland in recent decades" (Udris, 2012, p. 21). In Italy, the rise of the Lega Nord in the 1990s and its latest tumble, as well as the unexpected electoral successes of Grillo's M5S in 2013, owe much to the heavy coverage (and reprimand) by the popular media (such as TV satire and talk shows) and the mainstream press of scandals, misbehavior and squandering of public funds by the ruling political classes. In the case of M5S, "Grillo has identified political themes that tap into the concerns of many Italians – and made them mainstream: corruption, bribery, sexual scandals and the politics of privileges and favors that he argues has created the 'Casta' (caste)" (Bartlett et al., 2013, p. 14). The dramatic rise of UKIP (the United Kingdom Independence Party) in the 2013 British local elections has been explained with reference to the contribution of the media, blamed by critics to have given it "disproportionate, unchallenging coverage".[2] UKIP's leader, Nigel Farage, has succeeded in attracting media attention thanks to his engaging personality: "He is an anti-politician who embodies many of the characteristics that people feel are absent from his mainstream rivals: he appears blunt, forthright, authentic, patriotic, principled and charismatic."[3] David Cameron tried to tune in into the "populist zeitgeist" by mimicking UKIP's propaganda and promising to call a referendum on Great Britain's EU membership, but was evidently unable to halt the popular drift to Farage's party.

Across the Atlantic, the pro-conservative mass media, especially the tabloid style of TV programs favored by Rupert Murdoch's Fox News and press outlets, were instrumental in stirring dissent against Obama's healthcare reforms via their sympathetic reporting of the "Tea Party revolution" and their typical themes (Di Maggio, 2011). On the opposite side, the OWS movement enjoyed strong support in the editorials of elite papers such as the *New York Times* and *Washington Post*. OWS is an interesting case in which the non-tabloid pro-system media end up bolstering a populist movement.

Recent research has questioned the argument that the popular or tabloid media are keener than the quality media to give greater prominence to populists than to mainstream leaders, and found that there are "no differences between the various media outlets" (Bos et al., 2010, p. 157), and that "there is no ground for the idea that popular newspapers are more sympathetic toward populist parties than quality newspapers" (Akkerman, 2011, p. 942).

However, the cases investigated are very limited and the authors themselves warn: "as long as more extensive comparative research is lacking, it seems wise to hold on to a distinction between the tabloids and the serious press based solely on style" (p. 943). Clearly, the styles of both the tabloid and quality media differ enormously between diverse national contexts, so what may be true in Austria and Switzerland or in India may not apply in the Netherlands and the United Kingdom. That said, it is undeniable that a "tabloidization" of the information industry as a whole is under way on a global scale, induced by new ICT and online news media. Sensationalism, the salacious coverage of scandals, a focus on personal details and an abundance of "soft news" and lifestyle stories, are just a few features of the news-making style that several quality newspapers, as well as public service broadcasting companies, adopt in their news and current affairs sections (including domestic and international politics). Most mainstream media regularly carry political cartoons of a satirical character. The online editions offer further scope for this trend towards "tabloidization" by soliciting the active participation of their readers and viewers via the social media. The latter have demonstrated a lively capacity to remix the offerings of the traditional media and to reshape their content according to popular tastes and expectations.

More cases from other democratic political contexts can be cited to show the key role played by the media in the various phases of the life cycle of old and new populist movements. In fact, *all the media* – tabloid and quality, independent and partisan – can be "accomplices" in one or all four of the phases identified by academic research (Stewart et al., 2003; Mazzoleni, 2008a). In the "ground-laying phase", which is by far the most crucial, the mass media can prime the public mood by harping on about sensitive issues, political scandals and social ills to respond readily to tub-thumping leaders who tap into the widespread discontent. However, the social media, especially Facebook, Twitter, YouTube and the blogosphere, have acquired a very special function in this phase, namely, of picking up the populist output of the mass media and relaunching it in the wider context of the electronic public sphere, thus generating a favorable climate of opinion.

In the "insurgent phase", when populists become "outsiders" who challenge the existing political balance in elections or parliaments, the media are more likely to show a differentiated response to the political game. The tabloid outlets, with their commercial orientation or overt support for the populists, tend to cover controversial actions, incendiary rhetoric and the theatre staged by populist leaders to satisfy the public appetite for catchy stories, thus providing valuable visibility on which populists can capitalize. In contrast, the mainstream media cannot help lifting the lid on the misdemeanors of the ruling classes and tend to be more cautious in distinguishing their ongoing criticism from that of the populists. This is also the phase in which populist movements resort massively to the social media in their efforts to mobilize support.

In the "established phase", when populists take up governing responsibilities or have simply become an established feature of the political landscape (like many parties founded decades ago), they may have to adopt more responsible behaviors to acquire full political legitimization, thus losing the transgressive aura that had initially attracted media attention. They may also come under the fire of intense criticism by the mainstream parties and media, and indeed by those of their own supporters who are unhappy with their governing performance. Thus, both the political support of the sympathetic media and the unintentional complicity of the media's own populism may fade, so that populist leaders and parties may lose the attention and the free publicity they had enjoyed in the previous stages. Finally, the "decline phase" can be triggered by internal conflicts, by the death of their founders (as in the cases of Pym Fortuyn and Jörg Haider) or by scandals involving the party's higher circles. The role played by the media can be as crucial here as in the initial phase. After all, the crisis of a movement that has been an important player in the domestic arena, and the fall of a formerly newsworthy leader, can be objects of juicy media coverage. Such events may even be triggered by a general hostile bombardment by the media, as happened in Umberto Bossi's scandal-ridden Lega Nord in 2012. Social media once again appear to accompany and boost the actions of the mainstream public and commercial media rather than take the lead in causing the decline.

If the media undeniably appear to be key players in the rise and the fall of populist movements, the mediatized contours of the populist agenda still remain to be examined.

The effects of the mediatization of politics outlined in this chapter and in the academic literature apply equally to populist phenomena and figures. Political leaders, parties and governments have all long sought the attention of the media and tried to give it their spin, even when nothing really newsworthy is involved. Media management has simply become a feature of modern politics. It reveals how intimately entangled politics has become with the media. Populist leaders are no exception: they do not hesitate to apply clever strategies to secure media attention, and wherever possible to bend it to their movement's own purposes. They have often shown themselves to be truly media-savvy, to perfectly understand the imperatives of the media, what is newsworthy and what is not. And, accordingly, their public actions tap easily into the media's hunger for entertaining events, human-interest stories, caustic language and the like. And if populists attract hostility from the elite-aligned media, they can turn this into an opportunity to fuel greater visibility by responding in ways that both the hostile and friendly media cannot ignore. Grillo might appear an exception in this respect, but, with due reservations, his is an exemplary case. A former TV comedian who is very familiar with the laws of show business, he has responded nimbly to the cut-and-thrust of competing parties and candidates. He has staged mini-shows in public squares, used tough talk and satire to pillory corruption in politics, as well as politicians, ministers and journalists (who he dubbed "servants of the powerful"), and, not least, high officials of public TV and Silvio Berlusconi's channels. At the same time, he managed to avoid appearing on any TV show during the entire election campaign. Yet, he was among the most widely covered leaders in TV newscasts, hitting the headlines every day. His controversial performances were shown and dissected in current events programs and electoral talk shows. All this assured him huge popularity that eventually turned into real political success. His is a paradigmatic example of just how mediatized populist communication has become: dramatization and personalization are its key ingredients, and that is equally true of Grillo's campaign as well as of those waged by most old and new populist leaders, at least in the established democracies.

The Grillo case also illustrates a variety of populism that, besides cunningly exploiting the populist character of commercial mass communication, bases its *élan vital* on an impressive use of the new social media. He launched his creed almost a decade ago through his blog, voted by *Time* magazine as one of the ten best blogs in the world,[4] and then organized a movement using the Meetup.com platform, gathering growing support from young voters angry at the country's corrupt politics. Many movements, populist or not, have notoriously relied on the powerful communication resources offered by the Internet: "The Pirate Party in Germany and the Occupy movement are examples of movements that have employed social media to grow rapidly and create a significant political and social impact" (Bartlett et al., 2013, p. 11).

Conclusion and discussion: Towards "Mediatization 2.0"

In this chapter, we have illustrated the concept of the mediatization of politics and analyzed its specific application to the phenomenon of political populism. The dual concept of media populism is the theoretical tool that has allowed us to understand how, when and where populism is affected by mediatization. It refers to the "natural" output of the media directed by commercial and popular interests coupled with the pro-populist editorial line of some influential news channels. We have seen that media populism is the "engine" of political populism, at least in its thin conceptualization of the "political communication style of political actors that refers to the people" (Jagers & Walgrave, 2007).

The discussion of this chapter has an underlying theme that still needs to be addressed, namely, whether and to what extent media populism is conducive to its political counterpart. We start from an empirical observation of very diverse national cases within a comparative framework. In the four phases of the life cycle of populism, the causal relationship between media output and the rise of populism has been assumed but not proven. Further empirical research is needed to advance our present knowledge of this phenomenon significantly.

Nevertheless, if we wish to measure this causality empirically, we must attempt to interpret the interaction between the media and political populism by observing the various national cases. What we can see is a significant correspondence between the purposes and conduct of the media and the goals and communication strategies of the populists, to the point that we really can speak of "complicity" (Mazzoleni, 2008a). When the logical framework of the media caters to popular needs, this complicity is largely unintentional, simply a matter of fact. This view is dominant in international academic reflection. However, we cannot ignore the fact that, in many countries, media outlets are overtly allied with populists and support the political aims of their leaders and movements. We can then envisage a kind of "ideological partnership" in which the media do not respond primarily to the sirens of commercial imperatives but are either active players in the political fray or act as tools at the service of political players, be they populists or otherwise. Hallin and Mancini (2004) have defined this collaboration in terms of "political parallelism", where "each news organization is aligned with a particular party, whose views it represents in the public sphere" (p. 27). Although this parallelism, once exemplified by the existence of the party press, has declined in recent decades in the Western democracies, an unmistakable ideological bias remains a distinctive feature of many tabloid and quality newspapers.

The proposition of a partnership of complicity best illustrates the transformation of political populism in terms of mediatization: populism can only be fully understood (or investigated) within the framework of the media-driven influences that shape its contemporary features.

Lastly, the "new media environment" which has settled within, around and outside the realms of the established media initiates processes that boost the impact of "traditional" mediatization. Several new movements are telling examples of a momentous development in the domain of political activism, of which political populism – chiefly in its early stages – is an expression, which relies greatly on the Internet without disdaining the alliance and/or complicity of the mass media.

All political subjects operating in such a media ecosystem necessarily undergo some adaptation to the logic of the old media and to the formats of the new. "Mediatization 2.0" would consequently seem to offer us the most appropriate theoretical framework for understanding the drive towards mass and self-communication adopted by populist movements of the present age.

Notes

1. A survey by Demos (Bartlett et al., 2013) on 1,865 Facebook fans of Grillo's movement M5S shows that its supporters are center-left, educated, young, tech-savvy, pro-immigration and pro-business. Definitely not a right-wing profile.

2. See http://averypublicsociologist.blogspot.it/2013/03/ukip-and-labour.html (seen 4 May 2013).
3. http://www.telegraph.co.uk/comment/telegraph-view/10035707/The-establish ment-feels-the-power-of-the-people.html (seen 4 May 2013).
4. http://www.time.com/time/specials/2007/article/0,28804,1725323_1727246,00 .html.

References

Akkerman, T. (2011). Friend or Foe? Right-Wing Populism and the Popular Press in Britain and the Netherlands. *Journalism*, 12, 931–945.
Albertazzi, D., & McDonnell, D. (Eds.) (2008). *Twenty-First Century Populism: The Spectre of Western European Democracy*. Basingstoke and New York, NY: Palgrave Macmillan.
Altheide, D. L., & Snow, R. P. (1979). *Media Logic*. Beverly Hills, CA: Sage.
Altheide, D. L., & Snow, R. P. (1991). *Media Worlds in the Postjournalism Era*. New York, NY: Aldine de Gruyter.
Bartlett, J., Froio, C., Littler, M., & McDonnell, D. (2013). *New Political Actors in Europe: Beppe Grillo and the M5S*. London: Demos.
Baym, G. (2008). Infotainment. In W. Donsbach (Ed.) *The International Encyclopedia of Communication*. Malden, MA: Blackwell Publishing (Blackwell Reference Online. 22 April 2013, http://www.communicationencyclopedia.com).
Blumler, J. G., & Kavanagh, D. (1999). The Third Age of Political Communication: Influences and features. *Political Communication*, 16, 209–230.
Bos, L., Van Der Brug, W., & De Vreese, C. (2010). Media Coverage of Right-Wing Populist Leaders. *Communications*, 35, 141–163.
Canovan, M. (1999). Trust the People! Populism and the Two Faces of Democracy. *Political Studies*, 47, 2–16.
Castells, M. (2009). *Communication Power*. Oxford: Oxford University Press.
Cranmer, M. (2011). Populist Communication and Publicity: An Empirical Study of Contextual Differences in Switzerland. *Swiss Political Science Review*, 17, 286–307.
Di Maggio, A. (2011). *The Rise of the Tea Party: Political Discontent and Corporate Media in the Age of Obama*. New York: Monthly Review Press.
Hallin, D., & Mancini, P. (2004). *Comparing Media Systems*. Cambridge, MA: Cambridge University Press.
Jagers, J., & Walgrave, S. (2007). Populism as Political Communication Style: An Empirical Study of Political Parties' Discourse in Belgium. *European Journal of Political Research*, 46, 319–345.
Krämer, B. (2014). Media Populism: A Conceptual Clarification and Some Theses on Its Effects. *Communication Theory*, 24 (1), 42–60.
Manin, B. (1995). *Principes du gouvernement représentatif*. Paris: Calman-Lévy.
Mazzoleni, G. (2008a). Populism and the Media. In D. Albertazzi & D. McDonnell (Eds.), *Twenty-First Century Populism: The Spectre of Western European Democracy* (pp. 49–64). Basingstoke and New York, NY: Palgrave Macmillan.
Mazzoleni, G. (2008b). Mediatization of Politics. In W. Donsbach (Ed.), *The International Encyclopedia of Communication* (pp. 3047–3051). Malden, MA: Blackwell Publishing.
Mazzoleni, G. (2008c). Mediatization of Society. In W. Donsbach (Ed.), *The International Encyclopedia of Communication* (pp. 3052–3055). Malden, MA: Blackwell Publishing.

56 *Foundations*

Mény, Y., & Surel, Y. (2000). *Par le people, pour le people: Le populisme et les democracies.* Paris: Fayard.

Mudde, C. (2004). The Populist Zeitgeist. *Government & Opposition,* 39, 541–563.

Nieland, J.-U. (2008). Politainment. In W. Donsbach (Ed.), *The International Encyclopedia of Communication.* Malden, MA: Blackwell Publishing. [Blackwell Reference Online. 22 April 2013, http://www.communicationencyclopedia.com].

Pauwels, T. (2011). Measuring Populism: A Quantitative Text Analysis of Party Literature in Belgium. *Journal of Elections, Public Opinion and Parties,* 21, 97–119.

Plasser, F., & Ulram, P. A. (2003). Striking a Responsive Chord: Mass Media and Right-Wing Populism in Austria. In G. Mazzoleni, J. Stewart & B. Horsfield (Eds.), *The Media and Neo-Populism: A Contemporary Comparative Analysis* (pp. 21–43). Westport, CT: Praeger.

Richardson, K., Parry, K., & Corner, J. (2013). *Political Culture and Media Genre: Beyond the News.* Basingstoke and New York, NY: Palgrave Macmillan.

Schulz, W. (2004). Reconstructing Mediatization as an Analytical Concept. *European Journal of Communication,* 19(1): 87–101.

Stewart, J., Mazzoleni, G., & Horsfield, B. (2003). Power to the Media Managers. In G. Mazzoleni, J. Stewart & B. Horsfield (Eds.), *The Media and Neo-Populism: A Contemporary Comparative Analysis* (pp. 217–237). Westport, CT: Praeger.

Strömbäck, J. (2008). Four Phases of Mediatization: An Analysis of the Mediatization of Politics. *The International Journal of Press/Politics,* 13, 228–246.

Strömbäck, J., & Esser, F. (2009). Shaping Politics: Mediatization and Media Interventionism. In K. Lundby (Ed.), *Mediatization. Concept, Changes, Consequences* (pp. 205–224). New York, NY: Peter Lang.

Taggart, P. (2000). *Populism.* Buckingham: Open University Press.

Taguieff, P.-A. (1997). Le populisme et la science politique: Du mirage conceptuel aux vrais problems. *Vingtième Siècle. Revue d'histoire.* 56, 4–33.

Udris, L. (2012). *Is the Populist Radical Right (Still) Shaping the News? Media Attention, Issue Ownership and Party Strategies in Switzerland.* Zurich: Working Paper of the NCCR Democracy.

Williams, B. A., & Delli Carpini, M. X. (2011). *After Broadcast News: Media Regimes, Democracy, and the New Information Environment.* Cambridge and New York, NY: Cambridge University Press.

4
Mediatization and New Media
Winfried Schulz

New media is not a new phenomenon. Printed publications, the mass press, radio and television were new media at the time when they emerged. However, what currently is new is that the *new* new media is referred to by a summary term instead of a proper name as was the case with the newspaper, the radio or television.[1] The established practice of referring to new media in the plural takes into account that recent innovations brought about diverse new communication means varying with respect to their modes of production, distribution, reception and utilization. New media are characterized by "underdetermination" (Poster, 1999). Symptomatic of this situation is the plurality of terms trying to capture new media developments: "digital media", "information and communication technology" (ICT), "computer-mediated communication", "Internet", "social media", even "new new media" (Levinson, 2013). "The Internet" often serves as a term for new media, although it is in itself a "bundle of different media and modalities" with various communication characteristics and manifold conditions of use (Lievrouw & Livingstone, 2002, p. 6).

Likewise, the mediatization of politics is not a new phenomenon. Mediatization as a distinctive perspective on politics rests on two premises. First, the advent of new media always gives rise to both new opportunities and new constraints to which political actors and organizations have to adapt. Second, political actors are always eager to employ new media functions and services. Corporate actors – such as interest groups, political parties, executive and legislative bodies – accommodate to the changing media environment and allocate an increasing share of their resources to utilizing new media for their strategic purposes. By the same token, actors on the political periphery take advantage of new media opportunities for engaging in politics. Individual citizens, social movements and opposition groups are drawing on new media for their empowerment, but also for subversive purposes. In this process, all types of actors have become increasingly independent of political journalism as a mediating agency.

This chapter begins by identifying key features of recently emerging new media. Against this backdrop it will discuss the idea of mediatization as well as the somewhat mysterious notion of "media logic". The sections that follow will then outline mediatization processes linked with new media developments and illustrate potentialities the utilization of new media involve. This will be specified with regard to different types of political actors. The final section discusses the obvious question of how mediatization and its consequences are to be assessed.

New media capabilities

Media revolutions in the historic past affected – and usually improved – one or more of the basic elements of communication: the encoding, storage, transmission and reception of messages or the organization, distribution and financing of message production. By contrast, the most recent media revolution has affected all of these features, though primarily the encoding of messages. While traditional media operate on different systems of analog coding the new media employ digital coding. Digital coding allows all kinds of signs and messages – including spoken language, texts, sounds and music, pictures and videos – to be expressed in the same universal language. Most importantly, digital messages can be managed by computers, and with the help of easy-to-handle software anybody can engage in processing, editing, amplifying, storing and distributing media content. Digitization has induced a number of new media capabilities with major advantages for political communication:

- A prime advantage of digitally coded messages is that they can be represented, transmitted and distributed electronically, thus conforming to the potential of the Internet. The Internet's huge processing and storage capacities together with its multiplex interconnections allows political *networking*, *collaboration* and *co-creation* on a global scale, thus outdoing by far conventional telecommunication services.
- Due to their digital nature new media allow an unprecedented degree of *interactivity* which is beneficial to a mode of political participation that "entails *active* civic involvement, not just passive surveillance" (Bucy & Gregson, 2001, p. 375).
- Digitally coded messages are amenable to compression technologies so they can be stored and transmitted in huge quantities, exceeding by far the capacities of conventional analog storage techniques like gramophone discs, audio and video tapes. This turns media use into a "pull" activity and, above all, allows *time-shifting* which makes the users less dependent on "pushed" messages of conventional mass media.
- Digitization allows *transcoding*, i.e., translating messages formatted according to the rules of one medium into the format of another medium

without altering the message content (Manovich, 2001, p. 47). Digital files can also be recombined to create *mash-ups* merging different media modalities and genres into multimedia formats.

- Since digital messages can be multiplied infinitely without any loss of quality conventional techniques of copying, reproducing and multiplying messages have become obsolete. Digital technologies give users the ability to easily *replicate, redistribute* and *share* political messages with others.
- The universal language and malleability of digital media spurs the *convergence* of old and new media. This allows adapting and distributing content on different media platforms. All major offline news outlets, for example, are now offering online editions enriched with digital media formats.

In addition to new modes of message encoding, storing and transmitting the new media brought about new ways of message production and reception. The computer terminal and more recently developed mobile devices such as laptops, smartphones, tablets and e-book readers have become the universal user interfaces for receiving, sending and also producing messages. Software for handling these interfaces enables users to design and publish on the Internet, especially on social media platforms, complex messages that compete with professional journalistic and entertainment media. Professional political communicators are benefiting from these capacities of new media to an even greater extent than are private citizens.

As it is often the case with emerging new media, the whole political communication system including the distribution of media power is affected. Citizens increasingly prefer online media as their most important source of political information. This has spurred a scholarly debate about whether the news media's influence on public opinion – especially their agenda-setting function – might be dwindling. Bennet and Iyengar (2008) envisage the dawning of "a new era of minimal effects" since people in the new media environment can easily find political content that conforms to their existing ideological orientations. As a consequence they expect the media to reinforce rather than change audiences' world views. The authors developed their thesis against the backdrop of a polarizing political culture and media system in the United States. However, Shehata and Strömbäck (2013), who have put these assumptions to the test in a European context, still find strong evidence for agenda-setting effects of traditional news media. At the same time, they demonstrate with a sophisticated study design that citizens using multiple online news sources are less susceptible to agenda-setting effects of the traditional media.

In spite of ongoing changes – and in accordance with Riepl's law – old and new media will coexist. Most conventional media, even if forfeiting some of their significance, survive by specializing on communication functions they still can serve in a changing environment. Adaptation processes are leading to "mutual domestication of and convergence between" old and new media (Fortunati, 2005, p. 28). On the one hand, many conventional mass media supplement their offline editions with background material, podcasts and videos on the Internet. Journalists regularly draw on the Internet as an information resource, even directly take up and redistribute material from web pages and social networking sites. Media users play their part in integrating old and new media by sharing breaking news with friends and followers on social networking sites. In addition, users are transmuting conventional television into "social TV" when they, while watching the program, post their comments on social media or give feedback to programmers. On the other hand, news sites on the web as the most widespread type of online journalism are committed to the conventions and styles of classical political journalism (Deuze, 2003). Also, news aggregators are transferring to the online world the logic of selecting and constructing news as practiced by conventional mass media.

Reconsidering mediatization

In a very general sense mediatization denotes communication media's spreading and penetrating all areas of society. Scholarly interests usually focus on the social transformations and especially the political consequences of these processes (see, e.g., Asp, 1990; Schulz, 2004). New media with their specific operational conditions offer new political opportunities, but also impose new constraints on political actors and institutions. The mediatization perspective draws special attention to "indirect effects" resulting from political actors responding to the operational conditions of communication media (Kepplinger, 2008). This resembles a phenomenon for which Kurt and Gladys Lang (1953) coined the term "reciprocity effect" (see also Kepplinger, 2007).

"Media logic" is an often used shortcut for the operational conditions of mass media. Altheide and Snow (1979) introduced this concept and explained its meaning by referring to synonyms like "format", "framework", "grammar" and "perspective". Media logic, in their view, is a specific quality of mass media with a far-reaching impact on society. Their basic thesis "that social reality is constituted, recognized, and celebrated with media" (Altheide & Snow, 1979, p. 12) implies that all mass media are committed to a unique and universal media logic determining the media user's – and ultimately the society's – definition of reality.[2] Altheide and Snow (1979) illustrate this by referring to specific selection criteria and presentation formats of mass media, especially of television. In elaborating the concept other authors are emphasizing that the mass media have become emancipated as an autonomous institution dominating other social institutions and, above all, wielding power over political actors and organizations (Hjarvard, 2008;

Mazzoleni, 2008; Strömbäck & Esser, 2009). The notion of media logic which has been governing much of the mediatization discourse in the television era implies large-scale, centralized production of political content and its distribution to a mass audience.

However, new media call into question the idea of universal media logic resulting in all-embracing media dependence of politics. New media not only brought about a variety of presentation formats and content genres which were completely unknown in the pre-Internet era. Most new media also operate on organizational principles, content production and distribution procedures which have little in common with conventional mass media. Above all, the assumption of audience dependence which is central to the notion of media logic became disputable in view of the empowering of users in the new media environment. The enormous proliferation and diversification of messages has led to a situation where media users – notably political actors – can bypass the filtering and gatekeeping of mass media, thus evading media powers. In principle, users are no longer reliant on prefabricated content delivered according to a heteronomous media production schedule. They can rather choose at their own pace among a broad supply and take advantage of new media for actively producing content or modifying prefabricated media messages. Even though up to now only a minority of citizens have exploited these opportunities, they may in the long run diminish the mass media's institutional autonomy and interventionist potential. As a result the theoretical idea of media logic is losing its explanatory potential and may at best be maintained in a specific sense referring to the conventional news media, as suggested by Esser (2013) and Strömbäck (2011, p. 373).

Following this line of reasoning, conceptual analogies like the "logic of the database" or the "grammar" of new media (see, e.g., Finnemann, 2011; Kluver, 2002; Manovich, 2001) which transfer to new media the assumption of a coherent media logic seem to be inapt. It also appears questionable whether the operational conditions of new media – their digital nature, data base structure, or "textual" grammar, originating from the media's technological base – can be expected to impact on political actors and processes in a way that is comparable to the logic of mass media, as was assumed by Altheide and Snow (1979). Lundby (2009, p. 117) concludes: "That's the thinking of the past, the age of mass communication when gatekeepers or editors did indeed control, frame, and format almost all media communication."

In essence, this argument against an overstated media-centric perspective accords with a recurrent theme of the new media discourse emphasizing the "underdetermination" and the "social shaping" (Poster, 1999) of new media. According to Lievrouw and Livingstone (2002) it is the social shaping which distinguishes new media from conventional mass media. One aspect of social shaping is the "recombination" and "continuous hybridization" of existing technologies and innovations. The other aspect is captured by the "network metaphor" contrasting the one-to-one and many-to-many configuration of new media with the one-to-many frames of conventional mass media. Social shaping takes place in the process of interacting with media "affordances". Among the specific affordances of new media are potentials of, for example, networking, time-shifting, sharing content, co-creating media products, and mashing-up messages (see, e.g., italicized features of digital media in the section above).

Looking at new media in terms of their social shaping while users interact with new media affordances is hardly compatible with core assumptions of the media logic concept. But it is very consistent with an *actor-centric* mediatization perspective. Referring especially to publicity -seeking political actors, Marcinkowski and Steiner (in this volume, Chapter 5) point out that the process of mediatization is not forced by the media. It is rather a "pull-process" which results from the need for public attention and the various ways to meet that demand. In this sense some authors speak of "self-mediatization" (e.g., Meyer, 2002). The actor-centric perspective implies two propositions: first, political actors and organizations anticipate that the media will operate in a specific way and adapt to the opportunities and constraints media usage entails; and second, political actors and organizations proactively take account of the media and try to capitalize on media performances for their political purposes. Following this rationale it seems promising to focus on responses to new media affordances and to examine the consequences for diverse political actors and political institutions.

Mediatization in the new media environment

In what follows, these arguments will be illustrated by first looking at citizens' utilization of new media for enacting their political roles and for engaging in political processes. Secondly, it will be demonstrated how political organizations accommodate to media affordances which are instrumental in pursuing organizational goals. The third part of this section considers new media performances from a systems perspective taking into account normative expectations of representative democracies. It is apparent at all three levels that the adoption of and adaptation to new media not only has immediate political effects, but also leads to long-term changes of citizens' political behavior, to lasting transformations of political organizations and to a transmutation of political systems.

Citizens wielding new media

An obvious result of transforming media systems is that people are changing their media use habits. Emerging new media increasingly alter the existing media's position as a source of information and political influence. In the

United States, for example, online media already rank second among citizens' sources of daily news, thus displacing the newspaper and the radio
(Pew Research Center, 2012a). Also, over the past two election cycles the
online political news audience "has grown dramatically" (Pew Research Center, 2012b). Other countries are rapidly catching up with this development.
However, the empirical evidence so far does not provide a clear picture of the
political consequences of the changing audience behavior (Michelstein &
Boczkowski, 2010). It is an open question whether online news consumption will in the long run complement or displace the traditional news
media. By the same token, the effects of online news consumption on political knowledge are still a matter of debate. And there are also conflicting
empirical findings on whether online news consumption contributes to civic
participation.

The picture becomes clearer if web-based activities as such are seen as a
form of political participation. Most remarkable in this respect is the worldwide spreading of social networking (Pew Research Center, 2012c). Although
Web 2.0 applications are primarily used for non political purposes, they nevertheless serve political functions such as expressing opinions, mobilizing
protest and organizing collective action (see, e.g., Loader & Mercea, 2012).
The uses of new media in the Arab Spring have provided impressive examples (see, e.g., Howard et al., 2011). While in general drawing on new media
expanded the repertoire of political engagement, this resulted particularly in
amplifying unconventional forms of participation, of political protest and
political consumerism (e.g., boycotting products).

What motivates citizens to draw on new media functions for engaging
in politics may be explained with reference to specific gratifications of web
applications (see, e.g., Kaye & Johnson, 2002; Shao, 2009). This is in accord
with normative expectations regarding citizens' communication behavior
as well as the media's role as an intermediate connecting the center and
the periphery of the political system. However, this relationship is fundamentally changing. On the one hand, the intermediation function has been
greatly extended due to an unprecedented wealth of information provided
by online versions of mass media, by the Internet presence of diverse political organizations, by knowledge bases such as Wikipedia and, not least, by a
plethora of expert and lay bloggers.

On the other hand, while the classical mass media distribute messages
journalists deem relevant according to news value criteria, the new media
concede users more control over the selection of political messages. Citizens no longer are confined to being passive consumers of standard political
journalism, of statements by party and government officials, but can react
to official sources and voice alternative positions in various new media
spaces. Web 2.0 applications allow citizens to engage in collaboration and
co-creation activities, sharing facts and opinions, commenting on blogs
and videos, contributing to wikis, to picture and video platforms, and in

organizing collective action (Harrison & Barthel, 2009). Especially during election campaigns, citizens may benefit from new opportunities of political participation the Internet and social media are providing (Kruikemeier et al., 2013; Tolbert & Mcneal, 2003).

Political organizations responding to new media

For political organizations communication media are relevant in at least three ways. First, media constitute significant environmental conditions to which they have to respond. Second, media are a means of intra-organizational communication. Third, organizations employ the media for connecting with the environment and pursuing their goals. This corresponds to a familiar perspective of organizational analysis distinguishing inputs, throughputs and outputs, which Schillemans (2012) has adopted for his study of public service organizations. New media may amalgamate with organizational input, throughput and output activities or may substitute these activities all together. Most importantly, adapting to and utilizing new media has the potential to extend the organizational reach, for example by serving as a recruitment tool, attracting new types of supporters and expanding activities geographically (Ward & Gibson, 2009). Especially, membership organizations, such as political parties, unions and NGOs, take advantage of these functions. Likewise, other types of political organizations, including parliaments and governments, have been adopting new media to improve their internal operations and their external links, e.g., to improve their services and their engagement with supporters and the general public.

Political parties have a vital interest in employing communication media for key political functions such as organizing participation, aggregating preferences and recruiting personnel for political offices. Media innovations brought about a number of new tools that extended the parties' communication repertoire, thus strengthening their output function, particularly in election campaigns. Meanwhile all political parties are using diverse Internet outlets for providing information about policy options and candidates, directed at party members and supporters as well as journalists and a wider public. New media serve to improve intra-organizational communication, both top-down, e.g., by distributing campaign material to party activists, and bottom-up, by engaging members in deciding on the election manifesto and on candidates for the ticket. There are also new modes and channels of organizational input, e.g., for raising funds and for monitoring the online behavior of supporters and target groups.

As Negrine (2008) demonstrates for the United Kingdom, these developments have been transforming party organizations, particularly by spurring the professionalization of party communication. Römmele (2003), who explores party changes from a cross-national perspective, shows that the parties' utilization of new media varies depending on political system factors, on the specific character of the party and the party's prevailing goal orientation. Referring to prevalent party typologies the author compares the strategies, audience approaches and message characteristics of new media adoption, particularly for election campaigns. She concludes from a number of studies that in less democratized contexts the new media are "able to operate as a real force of change", whereas in liberal democracies the new media, though strengthening communication pluralism, "are generally not leading to any far-reaching redress of existing power relations" (Römmele, 2003, p. 16).

In like manner parliaments and their members have an interest in connecting with their constituencies and the general public. It is already common practice in almost all representative democracies to employ the whole range of communication media for information delivery services and for facilitating public input to decision-making processes. New media seem to be especially suited as a channel connecting representatives and the represented, e.g., for making legislative decisions more responsive to the needs of citizens and the interests of stakeholder groups. In this spirit, the British Parliament as early as 1998 launched a series of online consultations involving selected citizens in parliamentary inquiries (Coleman, 2004; Coleman & Blumler, 2009, pp. 91–102). However, e-consultation and other interactive applications have not yet succeeded in becoming very widespread, as shown by the results of a global survey to which 134 parliaments responded in 2009, whereas webcasting of parliamentary activities is now a frequently used practice (Griffith & Leston-Bandeira, 2012).

The implementation and utilization of new communication technologies by governments and public agencies gave rise to what Dunleavy, Margetts, Bastow and Tinkler (2006) label "digital-era governance". This stage of e-democracy is considered to have succeeded the "new public management" movement of the late 20th century, with its focus on bureaucratic reforms making government service provision more efficient and less costly. More recently, many countries have been implementing digital technologies transforming agency-centered into citizen-centered processes. New electronic services are connecting citizens directly to state systems without any gatekeeping by service personnel. The ongoing shift towards self-government "implies a move away from 'closed' files government to a more 'open book' model" so that citizens "are 'co-producing' or even 'co-creating' public services" (Margetts, 2009, p. 125). Government initiatives under the headings "open government" and "open data" claim to be committed to principles as they are laid down in an OECD handbook:

(1) Respond to calls for greater transparency and accountability;
(2) meet citizens' expectations that their views be considered; and
(3) counter declining public support (Gramberger, 2001, pp. 19–20).

These principles, although already debated much earlier (Wojcik, 2012), have gained political momentum since Barack Obama presented his memorandum on "Transparency and Open Government" in 2009.[3] Meanwhile, governing bodies all around Europe and beyond draw on new media for launching open government strategies at national, regional and local levels (Huijboom & Van den Broek, 2011).

For non-governmental organizations and social movements, especially for those operating globally like, for example, Attac, Oxfam, Friends of the Earth, the Internet and social media have become the key instruments for political action. The availability and services of new media compensate for the scarce resources of these organizations. Examining the 100 largest non-educational US non-profit organizations, Nah and Saxton (2013) specified how capacities and resources as well as organizational strategies, governance features and external pressures determine the adoption and utilization of social media. Most notably, protest movements greatly benefit from the communication infrastructure of the Internet by spreading messages virally, creating networks and organizing collective action (see, e.g., van de Donk et al., 2004). A new organizational form which is constituted solely by communication networks, called "connective action" by Bennett and Segerberg (2012) in their analysis of protest movements in the context of the recent financial crisis, seems to be typical for late modern societies in which citizens are increasingly de-aligning from formal organizations.

System-level performances of new media

There is a long tradition of normative expectations regarding media performances in serving the democratic system.[4] Gurevitch and Blumler (1990), for example, proposed a catalogue of media functions and services which may be condensed into four points: first, as a mediating agent the mass media are expected to report on relevant events and issues and present a true picture of the political reality. Second, in their capacity to offer a public forum mass media are supposed to give access to relevant political actors and to represent major currents of public opinion and discourse. Third, media should scrutinize power holders and, by investigative reporting, expose power abuses, corruptions and scandals. And fourth, mass media are expected to voice the citizens' political interests and to support institutionalized forms of political participation.

Although these performance expectations refer primarily to the "old order" of media professionals producing political news and current affairs for a mostly passive mass audience they are in essence still valid in the "new order" where, on the one hand, mass media are better equipped to serve these functions, e.g., by drawing on new technologies for their investigations, for selecting, producing and distributing information, and where, on the other hand, new media have been greatly extending and supplementing political communication capabilities:

- New media have widened the citizens' window on the world of politics by an abundance of reports and comments by bloggers, citizen journalists and web pages of various organizations, bypassing the filter of professional journalism.
- New media compete with the conventional mass media in defining the relevance of political issues and actors; even creating a new breed of celebrities. As a consequence, established power holders may benefit from their public visibility online. But it has also become easier to challenge power holders by online activities of protesters and social movements.
- The Internet has considerably enlarged media constructed public spaces. These public spaces may not only span globally. Compared to the public sphere constructed by conventional mass media they are also more inclusive since weakly organized groups and individual citizens have much easier access.
- While the classical mass media apply news value criteria in filtering political messages according to what the media define as citizen interests, new media add to this the interests and preferences which citizens themselves – as well as diverse interest groups – voice online.
- The media's watchdog role has become much more effective due to the Internet's capacity to pillory misbehavior and leak information that power holders would rather keep secret.

These potentialities have inspired manifold reflections on new media as a remedy for the supposed crisis of democracy (see, e.g., Kersting, 2012). "E-words" like e-democracy, e-participation and e-governance are emblematic of the optimistic vision of media developments. Coleman (2005), for example, suggests rethinking the idea of democratic representation. In his conception of "digitally-mediated representation" the relationships between citizens and the political elite may be improved by three elements: by a more interactive kind of accountability, by a pluralistic network of representation, and "by creating new spaces of public self-representation and experiential reflexivity" (Coleman, 2005, p. 190). In collaboration with Blumler he launched the idea of a "civic commons in cyberspace" organized by a publicly funded body and independent of both the state and the market (Coleman & Blumler, 2009). A more skeptical position is taken by Ward and Vedel (2006) who concede that the new media provide ("for some") increased openness and access, but at the same time put pressure on the democratic system with the result of, among others, distancing the informal network style of politics from the formal system of representative democracy.

Mediatization ambivalence

In the search for explanations of an alleged crisis of democracy the mass media are an obvious candidate. This may be one reason why in the pre-Internet era a dismal view of mediatization prevailed, as expressed by the definition of Mazzoleni and Schulz (1999, p. 249): "The term mediatization denotes problematic concomitants or consequences of the development of modern mass media." This view implies a major impact of the news media on political processes and on political actors and institutions. The mediatization perspective of the pre-Internet era presupposes that the media have become an autonomous institution committed to highly similar operational conditions, selection criteria and presentation formats. Since the news media serve as the most important – and often exclusive – source of political information audiences and politicians have become media dependent. They have little choice but to adapt to the media's operational conditions, so that political processes in the long run are governed by the media logic.

As new media developments arise to challenge all these assumptions there is a need to modify the mediatization perspective. Particularly the premise of an autonomous media institution committed to homogeneous media logic has become disputable. New digital media defy the institutional autonomy of mainstream news media. Hence even proponents of an institutional approach to the news media have become critical of the "homogeneity hypothesis" (Cook, 2006, p. 163). The new media environment offers not only a wide variety of alternative information sources but even new ways of participating in public discourses. Political actors are becoming less dependent on the classical news media and their media logic. But this does not necessarily result in diminishing political media influence.

If political actors appropriate new media and adapt to their communication opportunities they have to face the specific constraints new media impose, even dysfunctional and disruptive consequences. Davis (2011) identifies, based on observations in Britain, a number of political expectations which new media developments have left unfulfilled and presents evidence for a widening gap between the center and the periphery of the political system. Due to the "pull character" of new media their political information is attracting the already engaged more than the disinterested, thus deepening participation gaps in society (Lusoli et al., 2006; Norris, 2012). The growing volume of user-generated content calls the reliability of political information on the Internet into question, even though a major share of online news is produced by professional journalists. Moreover, the open space of the Internet is often misused for offenses, hate speech and "hacktivism", and for criminal or extremist and terrorist activities. Other problematic consequences may result from the abundant entertaining material on the web that is absorbing people's media use budget, at the expense of political content online and offline. Fears that this will impair informed political deliberation and engagement seem to be justified.

A growing body of research is trying to assess whether positive or negative consequences of new media prevail. Based on a meta-analysis of pertinent studies Boulianne (2009) concludes that Internet use has a positive, though small, effect on political engagement while there is little evidence of a significant negative effect. Groshek (2010), who monitored 152 countries, shows that Internet diffusion has a democratizing effect, though primarily in developed countries that were at least partially democratic. Loader and Mercea (2012) in their summary of a number of studies admit that there are good reasons, even empirical support, for acknowledging the democratic potential of new media, but that it would also be advisable to not lose sight of their risks and disruptive capacities.

These and other attempts at weighing the political consequences of mediatization are posing the archetypical question fueling communication research for decades: How do we evaluate communication media's impact on society? The question might be ill-defined if it aims at an unequivocal answer, as Lazarsfeld and Merton (1948) warned us in the early days of communication research. New media, like all technologies may give rise to both beneficial and detrimental consequences, depending on how they are used. This is part of the fundamental ambivalence which marks media–society relationships in general (see, especially McQuail, 2010, pp. 80–91). Consequently, analyses of political mediatization have to be aware of the ambivalence of new media affordances. An actor-centric approach is open to beneficial aspects of mediatization, but it can neglect neither concerns nor empirical facts challenging the euphemistic visions sometimes associated with political "e-words".

Notes

1. "New media" appeared in 2001 for the first time as an entry to the cumulative index of the review journal *Communication Abstracts*. Also, the appearance of the first issue of the journal *New Media & Society* in 1999 may be taken as indicating the establishment of "new media" as a key term.
2. In this respect the idea of a universal media logic parallels key presumptions of the dependency model of Ball-Rokeach (1976) and of the spiral of silence (Noelle-Neumann, 1984).
3. See http://www.whitehouse.gov/open.
4. For a comprehensive analysis of media functions and performances, see McQuail (1992).

References

Altheide, D. L., & Snow, R. P. (1979). *Media Logic*. Beverly Hills, CA: Sage.
Asp, K. (1990). Medialization, Media Logic and Mediarchy. *Nordicom Review*, 11(2), 47–50.

Ball-Rokeach, S. J., & DeFleur, M. L. (1976). A Dependency Model of Mass-Media Effects. *Communication Research*, 3, 3–21.

Bennett, W. L., & Iyengar, S. (2008). A New Era of Minimal Effects? The Changing Foundations of Political Communication. *Journal of Communication*, 58(4), 707–731.

Bennett, W. L., & Segerberg, A. (2012). The Logic of Connective Action. Digital Media and the Personalization of Contentious Politics. *Information, Communication & Society*, 15, 739–768.

Boulianne, S. (2009). Does Internet Use Affect Engagement? A Meta-Analysis of Research. *Political Communication*, 26, 193–211.

Bucy, E. P., & Gregson, K. S. (2001). Media Participation: A Legitimizing Mechanism of Mass Democracy. *New Media & Society*, 3, 357–380.

Coleman, S. (2004). Connecting Parliament to the Public via the Internet. *Information, Communication & Society*, 7, 1–22.

Coleman, S. (2005). New Mediation and Direct Representation: Reconceptualizing Representation in the Digital Age. *New Media & Society*, 7, 177–198.

Coleman, S., & Blumler, J. G. (2009). *The Internet and Democratic Citizenship: Theory, Practice and Policy*. Cambridge, MA: Cambridge University Press.

Cook, T. E. (2006). The News Media as a Political Institution: Looking Backward and Looking Forward. *Political Communication*, 23(2), 159–171.

Davis, A. (2011). New Media and Fat Democracy: The Paradox of Online Participation. *New Media & Society*, 12, 745–761.

Deuze, M. (2003). The Web and Its Journalisms: Considering the Consequences of Different Types of News Media Online. *New Media & Society*, 5(2), 203–230.

Dunleavy, P., Margetts, H., Bastow, S., & Tinkler, J. (2006). New Public Management Is Dead – Long Live Digital-Era Governance. *Journal of Public Administration Research and Theory*, 16, 467–494.

Esser, F. (2013). Mediatization as a Challenge: Media Logic versus Political Logic. In H. Kriesi, D. Bochsler, J. Matthes, S. Lavenex, M. Bühlmann & F. Esser (Eds.), *Democracy in the Age of Globalization and Mediatization* (pp. 155–176). Basingstoke: Palgrave Macmillan.

Finnemann, N. O. (2011). Mediatization Theory and Digital Media. *Communications*, 11, 67–89.

Fortunati, L. (2005). Mediatization of the Net and Internetization of the Mass Media. *Gazette*, 67, 27–44.

Gramberger, M. (2001). *Citizens as Partners: OECD Handbook on Information, Consultation and Public Participation in Policy-Making*. Paris: OECD.

Griffith, J., & Leston-Bandeira, C. (2012). How Are Parliaments Using New Media to Engage with Citizens? *Journal of Legislative Studies*, 18, 496–513.

Groshek, J. (2010). A Time-Series, Multinational Analysis of Democratic Forecasts and Internet Diffusion. *International Journal of Communication*, 4, 142–174.

Gurevitch, M., & Blumler, J. G. (1990). Political Communication Systems and Democratic Values. In J. Lichtenberg (Ed.), *Democracy and the Mass Media: A Collection of Essays* (pp. 269–289). Cambridge, MA: Cambridge University Press.

Harrison, T. M., & Barthel, B. (2009). Wielding New Media in Web 2.0: Exploring the History of Engagement with the Collaborative Construction of Media Products. *New Media & Society*, 11, 155–178.

Hjarvard, S. (2008). The Mediatization of Religion: A Theory of the Media as Agents of Religious Change. *Northern Lights: Film & Media Studies Yearbook* (Vol. 6, pp. 9–26). Bristol: Intellect.

Howard, P. N., Duffy, A., Freelon, D., Hussain, M., Mari, W., & Mazaid, M. (2011). Opening Closed Regimes: What Was the Role of Social Media during the Arab Spring? Project on Information Technology & Political Islam. Department of Communication, University of Washington, Working Paper 2011.1. Retrieved from www .pitpi.org

Huijboom, N., & Van den Broek, T. (2011). Open Data: An International Comparison of Strategies. *European Journal of* e Practice, 12, 1–13.

Kaye, B. K., & Johnson, T. J. (2002). Online and in the Know: Uses and Gratifications of the Web for Political Information. *Journal of Broadcasting & Electronic Media*, 46, 54–71.

Kepplinger, H. M. (2007). Reciprocal Effects: Toward a Theory of Mass Media Effects on Decision Makers. *Press/Politics*, 12(2), 3–23.

Kepplinger, H. M. (2008). Media Effects: Direct and Indirect Effects. In W. Donsbach (Ed.), *International Encyclopedia of Communication* (Vol. 7, pp. 2883–2885). Malden, MA: Blackwell.

Kersting, N. (2012). The Future of Electronic Democracy. In N. Kersting (Ed.), *Electronic Democracy* (pp. 11–54). Opladen: Barbara Budrich Publishers.

Kluver, A. R. (2002). The Logic of New Media in International Affairs. *New Media & Society*, 4, 499–517.

Kruikemeier, S., van Noort, G., Vliegenthart, R., & de Vreese, C. H. (2013). Getting Closer: The Effects of Personalized and Interactive Online Political Communication. *European Journal of Communication*, 28, 53–66.

Lang, K., & Lang, G. E. (1953). The Unique Perspective of Television and Its Effect: A Pilot Study. *American Sociological Review*, 18, 2–12.

Lazarsfeld, P. F., & Merton, R. K. (1948). Mass Communication, Popular Taste and Organized Social Action. In L. Bryson (Ed.), *The Communication of Ideas: A Series of Addresses* (pp. 95–118). New York, NY: Harper & Row.

Levinson, P. (2013). *New New Media*. 2nd Edition. Boston, MA: Pearson.

Lievrouw, L. A., & Livingstone, S. (2002). The Social Shaping and Consequences of ICT. In L. A. Lievrouw & S. Livingstone (Eds.), *Handbook of New Media* (pp. 1–16). London: Sage.

Loader, B. D., & Mercea, D. (2012). Networking Democracy? Social Media Innovations in Participatory Politics. In B. D. Loader & D. Mercea (Eds.), *Social Media and Democracy: Innovations in Participatory* Politcs (pp. 1–10). London: Routledge.

Lundby, K. (2009). Media Logic: Looking for Social Interaction. In K. Lundby (Ed.), *Mediatization: Concepts, Changes, Consequences* (pp. 101–119). New York, NY: Peter Lang.

Lusoli, W., Ward, S., & Gibson, R. (2006). (Re)connecting Politics? Parliament, the Public and the Internet. *Parliamentary Affairs*, 59, 24–42.

Manovich, L. (2001). *The Language of New Media*. Cambridge, MA: Massachusetts Institute of Technology.

Margetts, H. (2009). Public Management Change and E-government: The Emergence of Digital-Era Governance. In A. Chadwick & P. N. Howard (Eds.), *Routledge Handbook of Internet Politics* (pp. 114–127). London: Routledge.

Mazzoleni, G. (2008). Media Logic. In W. Donsbach (Ed.), *International Encyclopedia of Communication* (Vol. 7, pp. 2930–2932). Malden, MA: Blackwell.

Mazzoleni, G., & Schulz, W. (1999). "Mediatization" of Politics: A Challenge for Democracy? *Political Communication*, 16, 247–261.

McQuail, D. (1992). *Media Performance: Mass Communication and the Public Interest*. London: Sage.

72   *Foundations*

McQuail, D. (2010). *McQuail's Mass Communication Theory.* 6th Edition. London: Sage.

Meyer, T. (2002). *Media Democracy: How the Media Colonize Politics.* Cambridge, MA: Politiy Press.

Mitchelstein, E., & Boczkowski, P. J. (2009) Between Tradition and Change: A Review of Recent Research on Online News Production. *Journalism*, 10(5), 562–586.

Nah, S., & Saxton, G. D. (2013). Modeling the Adoption and Use of Social Media by Nonprofit Organizations. *New Media & Society*, 15(2), 294–313.

Negrine, R. (2008). *The Transformation of Political Communication: Continuities and Changes in Media and Politics.* Houndmills: Palgrave Macmillan.

Noelle-Neumann, E. (1984). *The Spiral of Silence: Public Opinion – Our Social Skin.* Chicago, IL: University of Chicago Press.

Norris, P. (2012). "To them that hath ... ". News Media and Knowledge Gaps. *Zeitschrift für vergleichende Politikwissenschaft*, 6, 71–98.

Pew Research Center. (2012a). In Changing News Landscape, Even Television is Vulnerable. Trends in News Consumption: 1991–2012. Retrieved from http://www.people-press.org/2012/09/27/in-changing-news-landscape-even -television-is-vulnerable/

Pew Research Center. (2012b). The Internet's Role in Campaign 2008. Retrieved from http://www.pewinternet.org/Reports/2009/6--The-Internets -Role-in-Campaign-2008/3--The-Internet-as-a-Source-of-Political-News/2--Online -news-audience.aspx

Pew Research Center. (2012c). Social Networking Popular Across Globe. Arab Publics Most Likely to Express Political Views Online. Retrieved from http://www .pewglobal.org/2012/12/12/social-networking-popular-across-globe/

Poster, M. (1999). Underdetermination. *New Media & Society*, 1, 12–17.

Römmele, A. (2003). Political Parties, Party Communication and New Information and Communication Technologies. *Party Politics*, 9, 7–20.

Schillemans, T. (2012). *Mediatization of Public Services. How Organizations Adapt to News Media.* Frankfurt am Main: Peter Lang.

Schulz, W. (2004). Reconstructing Mediatization as an Analytical Concept. *European Journal of Communication*, 19, 87–101.

Shao, G. (2009). Understanding the Appeal of User-Generated Media: A Uses and Gratification Perspective. *Internet Research*, 19, 7–25.

Shehata, A., & Strömbäck, J. (2013). Not (Yet) a New Era of Minimal Effects: A Study of Agenda Setting at the Aggregate and Individual Levels. *International Journal of Press/Politics*, 18(2), 234–255.

Strömbäck, J. (2011). Mediatization of Politics: Toward a Conceptual Framework for Comparative Research. In E. P. Bucy & R. L. Holbert (Eds.), *The Sourcebook for Political Communication Reasearch: Methods, Measures, and Analytical Techniques* (pp. 367–382). New York, NY: Routledge.

Strömbäck, J., & Esser, F. (2009). Shaping Politics: Mediatization and Media Interventionism. In K. Lundby (Ed.), *Mediatization. Concepts, Changes, Consequences* (pp. 205–223). New York, NY: Peter Lang.

Tolbert, C. J., & Mcneal, R. S. (2003). Unraveling the Effects of the Internet on Political Participation? *Political Research Quarterly*, 56, 175–185.

Van de Donk, W., Loader, B. D., Nixon, P. G., & Rucht, D. (Eds.) (2004). *Cyberprotest: New Media, Citizens and Social Movements.* London: Routledge.

Ward, S., & Gibson, R. (2009). European Political Organizations and the Internet: Mobilization, Participation, and Change. In A. Chadwick & P. N. Howard (Eds.), *Routledge Handbook of Internet Politics* (pp. 25–39). London: Routledge.

Ward, S., & Vedel, T. (2006). Introduction: The Potential of the Internet Revisited. *Parliamentary Affairs*, 59, 210–225.

Wojcik, S. (2012). Open Government and Open Data. In N. Kersting (Ed.), *Electronic Democracy* (pp. 125–151). Opladen: Barbara Budrich Publishers.

5
Mediatization and Political Autonomy: A Systems Approach

Frank Marcinkowski and Adrian Steiner

This chapter aims to analyze "mediatization" as a societal phenomenon. In particular it deals with the question of what triggers the process of mediatization, what drives the process, and what consequences result from the process. Socio-theoretical contributions to the discourse on mediatization are few and far between. For example, American sociologist John B. Thompson (1995) sees the transformation of premodern agrarian societies into the functionally differentiated social formations of the modern era as the result of capacities for accumulating, communicating and storing information. For Thompson, these capacities were (initially) provided by the printed and (later) by the electronic mass media, and it is a process he calls "mediazation" (Thompson, 1995, p. 46). Building on Thompson's work, Hjarvard (2008) conceives of "mediatization" as a process of modernization, at the center of which the organizational, technological, and aesthetic operating mode of the media (media logic) is shaping the forms of interactions between social institutions. In this paper, we adopt a systems theory perspective to supplement some of the socio-theoretical work that has been carried out in relation to the causes and consequences of mediatization. We understand mediatization here as a supra-individual phenomenon that occurs within non-media social systems. It results from the differentiation of a media system containing its own intrinsic logic and the need for public attention expressed in other social systems. The term "mediatization" denotes not so much the passive submission of other systems to media forces but the *active* utilization of media services. The structural consequences of accessing these services are conceived as "consequences of mediatization". We therefore understand mediatization not in terms of a linear, media-induced influence but as resulting from a complex interaction of manifold media and non-media causes.

Drawing on a theory of functional differentiation, we first show which socio-structural conditions must be met in the first place to observe a phenomenon such as mediatization. Then we draw on the "theory of self-referential social systems" to demonstrate the meaning of mediatization from this specific perspective as well as looking at what other relationships – in addition to those between media and politics – must be distinguished, what levels of analysis have to be observed, and what conditions must be met in the surrounding systems of the media for their mediatization to occur. Following this, we use the example of the mediatization of politics to specify further these basic ideas and use our systems approach to deduce a number of fundamental theorems, which in turn may serve to guide empirical research on mediatization in the future. Finally, we briefly summarize the conceptual proposals made in this chapter.

Mediatization and the functional differentiation of modern societies

The distinction between politics and media, which underlies the notion of the "mediatization of politics", represents a contingent analytical perspective. The distinction could also be drawn differently – for example, as a distinction between politics and economics, media and education or science and business. The scientific validity of where to draw the distinction depends on what the distinction can help us reveal and, where appropriate, explain. In this case, it not only enables us to determine more accurately what is to be understood by "media phenomenon" or "political phenomenon", but it is also a necessary condition for allowing us to observe reciprocal performance relations between politics and media in the first place. Here, we assume that this difference is not a purely analytical distinction but an empirical category which denotes the corresponding phenomena of empirical reality. This "realistic" view of the term appears logical because the distinction between media and politics is also made in areas outside of academia and has practical value beyond academic research because people generally know whether they are voting or watching television.

Politics and media are therefore two distinguishable and dissimilar empirical phenomena in an overarching whole that we call society. They are dissimilar because they perform different functions for society: the production of collectively binding decisions on the one hand and the creation of a public space for issues and opinions on the other. Because functions of social systems cannot be placed in a transitive hierarchy – both functions are equally indispensable – the exclusive function of each system also represents the fundamental equality of both parts. To think simultaneously in terms of dissimilarity (systems perform different functions) and equality (systems cannot replace each other) is, in our opinion, necessary if we wish to have a meaningful discussion of mediatization or politicization. In other words, the functionally differentiated society is the categorical and empirical background against which processes of mediatization can become visible.

What does this mean for the socio-theoretical importance of the concept of mediatization? First, the theory of functional differentiation treats politics and media as two social subsystems among others. We can identify other function-systems such as economics, science, law, education and religion. What we have said above applies to all these subsystems: i.e., in their exclusive function-area, they too are both dissimilar and fundamentally equal. Under these conditions society takes a paradoxical form, which we can call the unity of differents. Each system constitutes, through its borders, a different relation to society and develops its own image of society. The society of economics is different from the society of politics and from the society of media, etc. (cf. Luhmann, 1997). Therefore, the social system as a whole appears to be the sum of multiple perspectives. In other words, the functionally differentiated society recognizes no preferred perspective from which a generally accepted "true" description of society can be gained (cf. Luhmann, 1997, p. 598).

For the discipline of communication science, this means that, despite their political importance, the terms "media society" and "mediatization" actually spring from a contingent perspective the significance of which is dramatically relativized when we draw distinctions differently. For example, the perspective of economics brings phenomena of economization (be it of politics, media or science) into view, the perspective of law makes us attend to the judicialization of social subsystems, and the perspective of science illuminates the scientification of society and its subsystems (cf. Nassehi, 2000). These processes must be thought of as being similar, equal and simultaneous, while everything else is simply a matter of analytical perspective.

The "theory of functional differentiation" that we use here allows mediatization to be observable and opens a perspective to other function-systems and other interdependencies. The loss of uniqueness is thereby compensated for by the opportunities it offers for comparisons. We can ask, for example: how does the mediatization of politics differ from the mediatization of science or economics? What is the relation between the economization and politicization of media? How does the economization of science affect the mediatization of universities? Given these questions, it is wrong to understand mediatization as a "meta-process" in the sense of being the most important one, as the dominant or somehow superordinate process of social change, one which leads inevitably to a social formation dominated by mass media. Rather, a proper understanding of mediatization is only possible when we take a differentiated look at other subsystems, other interdependencies, and other ways of describing society.

Mass media, public attention and the mediatization process

Here we propose understanding the functionally differentiated society according to a "theory of self-referential communication systems" (Luhmann, 1995). We therefore presuppose a social order where primary differentiation occurs along a multitude of subsystems. Each subsystem is tailored specifically to deal with different functional needs of society. Assigning exclusive functions to subsystems constitutes their identity and autonomy. Functions are performed using a binary code to which all operations refer in the last instance. The functional differentiation of systems corresponds in this sense to a "technization" of the reference to the world, with the help of a binary schematization (cf. Luhmann, 1982). The code – for example, the distinction between right and wrong in law, true and false in science, beautiful and ugly in art, or healthy and ill in healthcare – defines the primary rule of information processing in the system, in each case displaying a built-in preference for the positive value of the code (right, true, beautiful, healthy). Events in the system's environment only gain relevance for a social system when they can be related to its code, while everything else is disregarded. The code as a general selection rule thus reduces the complexity of the world to a level that is workable for the system (reduction of complexity). At the same time, the general character of the code ensures that many things can potentially become relevant for the system (enabling complexity). The interaction of both mechanisms allows for the high degree of specialization and efficiency that modern societies have developed in the course of their transition towards functional differentiation.

However, the abstract distinction does not provide sufficient selectivity to enable communication. It must be further specified through secondary and tertiary selection structures and, as it were, "operationalized" at a deeper structural level. Secondary and tertiary selection structures are called "programs" in systems theory, and, in the case of organizations, for example, known as internal decision-making structures in the form of programs of purpose and programs of conditionality. At this level, the abstract codes are "translated" into "productive" structural guidelines that enable the formation of processes and structures. The functional differentiation of a system coincides with the establishment of a function-specific selection structure (code and programs) which guides all processes within the system. All of a system's processes are geared exclusively to system-inherent structures and cannot be directly determined by conditions of the environment. This self-referentiality constitutes the autonomy of systems (cf. Luhmann, 1982).

The functional differentiation of a system of mass media (Marcinkowski, 1993; Luhmann, 1996) is a necessary condition of mediatization. According to this reading, the "increased importance" of mass media, which the majority of writers see as being the primary cause of mediatization processes (e.g., Schulz, 2004), can therefore be regarded as a corollary of the functional differentiation of society and, in particular, of the functional autonomization of the mass-media system. This can be illustrated by three determining factors of functional differentiation:

- *Universality*: Functional autonomization of mass media is a key requirement for their continued internal differentiation and increasing complexity. Differentiation and complexity of the media tend to grow quickly and without opposing internal stopping mechanisms, as social systems tend inevitably to absolutize the fulfillment of their primary goal. This can be seen empirically, for example, in the multiplication of new technical channels of communication, the diversification of organizational forms of mass media, the universalization of media operating structures, the expansion and acceleration of public communication – and ultimately in the ubiquity of mass media and their communication within society.

- *Exclusivity*: Functional autonomization is necessary for mass media to retain their monopoly status for creating and disseminating descriptions of reality, and to make them widely shared and accepted. The media are in a continuing struggle to defend their leading position against competing code-specific interpretations of social reality. However, for the foreseeable future we can envision no other function-specific area in society – neither politics nor science nor even religion – which could compete in its world-descriptions with mass media's constructions of reality in terms of thematic diversity, social reach, relevance, topicality and timeliness.
- *Autonomy*: Functional differentiation causes the media to execute its core function – producing and distributing self-descriptions of society – solely according to system-inherent structures and programs. The way it portrays reality is thus neither universally true nor entirely objective, nor does it necessarily correspond to the self-descriptions of those observed by the media. Rather, functional differentiation increases the likelihood that individual self-descriptions and their portrayal in the media will diverge, adding to the irritation potential often attributed to the mass media.

These three factors underscore the characteristics of ubiquity and social reach, and the binding character of mass media, and enhance the probability that media portrayals become a source of resonance and irritation in various places. These factors can therefore be seen as important *conditions for mediatization*. However, they are not the only necessary conditions. Otherwise, mediatization would have to be observable in somewhat similar form and intensity, and with similar consequences, in all social areas, which is clearly not the case. So, what *additional conditions* must be present?

To answer this question, we introduce a further theoretical distinction which is established in systems theory, one that allows us to describe primary systems of society with regard to their *function* and their *performance*. These two terms refer to two different ways of observing subsystems that must be kept strictly apart. When we speak of *function*, we are concerned with the role of the part within the whole (distinction between function-system and society). In contrast, the term *performance* is reserved for its relation to other parts (distinction between different function-systems). In the case of mass media, this corresponds to the distinction between the capacity to provide self-observation of society (function) and the creation of public attention and acceptance for selected social issues (performance). Therefore, function and performance do not refer to different "products" but merely to different forms of "recourse" to the media system, by society at large or individual subsystems.

A social system – such as media or politics – is not considered autonomous if or because it is entirely independent from its environment; rather it is autonomous if it is able to select certain elements in its environment from which it gets certain stimulations (although these external stimuli cannot determine the operations of and within the system). Systems have grown more autonomous and independent but at the same time more inter-dependent because they rely on tasks performed by other systems. The performance relations between systems are variable in the sense that, for example, science requires sometimes more and sometimes less public atten-tion; and they are potentially asymmetrical in the sense that not every performance is necessarily compensated by a counter-performance. Sys-tems also do not take advantage of performances merely because they are available, but only if and insofar as they require them. In their own com-munication they may frame this dependence as "prudently compensating a shortcoming" or as "undue (and potentially threatening) interference" by a foreign logic. However it is framed, the use of outside performances remains motivated and permitted by the receiving system which implements the input according to its own operating program.

Following these observations, we propose to use the terms "juridification", "scientification", "politicization", "economization" and also "mediatiza-tion" to denote specific forms of *performance relation* – i.e., the recourse to performances of certain social subsystems by systems in their environment. From this it follows that, first, it makes little sense to speak of the "mediatiza-tion of society". Mediatization takes place *within* society and does not affect it as a whole. Furthermore, mediatization takes place in a context of many systems cross-consuming services of other systems all the time, and these relationships can hardly be seen as a zero-sum game. Systems accessing each other's services may interfere with each other, but often they reinforce each other. An example of reinforcement is that if the economization of science were to lead to a preference for utility value in university research, this in turn would encourage the mediatization of science (by favoring high-profile research topics and research personalities).

Another consequence of this conceptualization is that it takes away the suspicion that mediatization is something extraordinary and allows us to understand the phenomenon in a more analytical frame of reference. Per-formance relations are in general based on the fact that a system, to some extent, absorbs foreign "raw materials" – for example, scientific knowledge, collective obligation, legitimate law – so as to keep its own communication going, which it does for that reason only. In addition, we can observe in many areas of society that such accesses are structurally guarded. This should always be mentioned when it is not only the actual "resource" but also criteria and norms of their production, i.e., programs that are incorporated into the program supply of the "requiring" system (cf. Schimank, 2006). The advantage of such a structural solution lies in the system's ability to observe and encourage continually its own performance needs and the performance capacity of other systems, and to provide long-term performance access or dispense it in a targeted way. We assume that such structural changes in a plurality of function-specific areas of society form the core of what is expressed in the social sciences by the already mentioned process terms: the increased involvement of hetero-referential selection considerations and programs within function-systems of society, especially at the organizational level. The anchoring of economic considerations in the field of science, the healthcare system, the media and elsewhere – i.e., commodification – is therefore only the most prominent example of "built-in hetero-reference" in modern societies.

With regard to mediatization, we can conclude that mass media's performance consists of providing public attention for issues of social communication. Other function-systems or organizations will absorb this performance according to their need for attention. It is typical for this access to occur when issues covered by mass media are taken up and become the basis of the system's own (system-internal) communication. But, it can also be achieved through prior communication of the mediatized system. In this case, issues are made available to mass media, which then take up the issues, provide them with public attention and acceptance, and play them back to society for further access.

By "simple" mediatization, we wish to denote the resonance impact of mass media's performances within systems in their environment. It indicates the degree to which other (now mediatized) social systems recognize mediated reality as a premise of further communication within mediatized social systems. The fact that other social systems' operations are geared towards the selection and presentation criteria of the mass media can be understood as "reflexive" mediatization. By taking performances of the media into account and making them objectives of strategic communication efforts, these other (now mediatized) systems aim to interlink their own interests and issues with those of the mass media. Finally, "consequences of mediatization" denote the various structural and procedural implications of this interrelation among the respective systems – for both the mass media and systems in its environment.

All major social systems of modern society require the scarce resource of "public attention", albeit at different levels of intensity, reach and frequency. In response to these and other parameters, the hetero-referential orientation towards mass media's selection criteria will lead to structure-formations which we can denote as the consequences of mediatization. We see examples of a structural integration of criteria for generating and directing public attention outside the system of mass media in many places of society. In competitive sports, we have seen them as changes to rules, sports facilities or competition schedules; in the political system in the form of organizational and content-related transformation of political election campaigns, changes to organizational and decision-making structures of political parties and the reorganization of parliamentary procedures; and in the academic system as a competitive relationship between academic reputation and public visibility. All of the above examples, to which we could add many more, have been variously examined by communication scholars. But only comparative-empirical research into mediatization can demonstrate systematically under which conditions the need for attention of which social systems leads to which forms of mediatization and to which structural formations, and what the implications are for the functionality and performance of mediatized systems.

The line of argumentation developed thus far reveals the dynamics of the development of the media sector as being "solely" a necessary condition of those phenomena which are denoted by the term "mediatization". Analyses that stop at this point obviously fall short. The process can only be causally explained when the analysis includes the contingent performance-need of social subsystems. Mediatization must therefore always be analyzed with regard to the structural conditions of each observed environmental system in society – instead of simply "externalizing" the reasons for the occurrence of the above phenomena and putting the blame on the media. For this reason, mediatization can also only be understood in a very limited sense as "media effect", because it is neither intended this way by media, nor does it occur without the "cooperation" of the mediatized systems themselves. Strictly speaking, the media can only bring about effects when it is enabled to cause them. In this sense, we have to investigate the conditions that trigger a need for (public) attention and acceptance in social systems.

We assume here that the degree of inclusivity of social systems represents one, if not the decisive, condition for the needs of a system. Inclusion refers here to the (active and passive) participation of people and organizations in the communications of a system. With inclusion, the dependence of the system in its function and performance capacities on the attention and acceptance of the included parties increases. We will return to this point in connection with the mediatization of politics. We can condense the previous observations into an initial theorem of mediatization:

T 1: The greater the inclusivity of a social system is, the greater is the need for attention and acceptance for its issues of communication (its "mediatization needs"). Conversely, the more exclusive a system is, the lower is its "receptivity" to mediatization.

From this general assumption, we can derive testable hypotheses. Thus, for example, the consequences of mediatization would be more observable in democratic politics where decision-making capacity relies heavily on public acceptance. It would also be more observable in (competitive) sports, which depend on the largest public audiences possible to generate financial and motivational incentives for winning, than in for example the legal or academic spheres. It is true that the public is granted access to various steps of the legal process, and the academic world also relies on its professional public. Nonetheless, judicial decisions and academic results require less (media-generated) public attention and approval. The procedural and professional public spheres that directly monitor the legality of decisions or the accuracy of results are much more exclusive – although for these areas, social-legitimacy deficits are also occasionally recognized which make the transition to the wider public appear promising (Weingart, 1998). In addition, we can presume that systemic interdependence relations are subject to economic cycles that are significantly influenced by social and extra-social events. For example, terrorist attacks lead to an increased politicization of media coverage, economic crises promote the economization of political decisions, increased competition for scarce research funds indirectly benefits the mediatization of the selection of academic issues, and so forth. We should therefore expect that peaks in mediatization are not only structurally determined but also triggered by certain key events.

The mediatization of politics

We can now also understand more precisely the "mediatization of politics". The formulation implies not only the autonomy of the system of mass media but also the autonomy of politics as an independent, function-specific area. By this we mean the overall process of making and implementing collectively binding decisions (cf. Luhmann, 2000). The capacity for making decisions collectively binding requires the legitimization of these decisions on the part of those affected; i.e., the (diffuse and specific) acceptance of political decisions as being collectively binding. This particular need for legitimization of political decisions is substantially produced or reproduced in the process of political communication. Politics must therefore secure acceptance from those (potentially) affected, which in turn essentially requires the generation of public attention for and acceptance of certain issues. This makes clear why politics is particularly dependent on media performances regarding the production and provision of issue-specific attention and acceptance. Our thesis is that this functional requirement under conditions of modern democracy and a differentiated media system produces precisely the effects that we denote as mediatization of the political sphere: the political system relies on mass-media performances and is orientated towards their selection and presentation criteria (in the sense of a reflexive mediatization) to be able to provide the kinds of issues to which the mass media can easily relate.

In this sense, the causes of mediatization lie in the fact that the political need for attention and acceptance has greatly increased during the transition to modern politics, and people can be expected less and less to give their "unmotivated" consent without further debate. At the same time, with the differentiation of a media system pursuing an autonomous operating logic, politics finds a unique addressee to meet this relevant need. The logic of the mediatization process becomes apparent only when we take account of the combination of both conditions. Nevertheless, we wish to deal here primarily with the first point, since it appears to us to be more important in terms of a differentiated description and explanation of the mediatization of politics, and because we have already outlined the main features regarding the second point.

The transition to modern politics can be described as a process of gradual differentiation and autonomization of a democratic political system. Two aspects of the differentiation of democratic politics are of particular importance in connection with mediatization:

- *Functional internal differentiation*: this is the conversion of political internal differentiation of stratification (state up/people down) into the political subsections of legislators, administration and public (cf. Luhmann, 2000). This functional internal differentiation of politics causes an immense increase in the internal complexity of the political system and thereby brings evolutionary advantages with it. It is also constitutive of the framework of democracy, the separation of the executive administration from the elected representatives, and the empowerment and inclusion of the public. The three subsections can no longer be placed in a hierarchical order of priority. Rather, they assume different functions in the political process: the public mandates governing elites, political elites create suitable framework conditions, and this in turn binds the public in its decision-making activity. The democratic circulation of power relies on the heterogeneity and essential equality of the subsections of the public, lawmakers and administration. This internal structure allows democracy to process highly complex interests and demands of the public, and to reduce this complexity through processes (elections, legislation, bureaucratic procedures) that facilitate the production and implementation of collectively binding decisions at the center of the system (cf. Luhmann, 2000).
- *Political inclusion*: this refers to the ever more complete inclusion of the public in the political system (cf. Luhmann, 2000), which is, in a sense, a corollary of the transition to the functional internal differentiation described above. Inclusion means passive and active involvement of the whole population in the political system. People are involved in

the political decision-making process and receive the formal power to select or deselect political personnel or to participate directly in the legislative process. People become active citizens who have interests which they can and should articulate and contribute. In addition to this active inclusion, there is also a transformation of passive inclusion, meaning access for more and more stakeholders to ever broader services of the political system. This increases the dependence on and claims to such performances. The crucial link between passive and active inclusion is that, due to the active-participation rights of the public, politicians must obtain the consent of the population and are therefore programmed to appeal to the population in their interests, to generate claims and to predict improvements (cf. Luhmann, 2000).

Both structural features have far-reaching implications for modern politics and its need for mass-media performances. Functional internal differentiation causes an increase in the diversity and heterogeneity of political claims and interests, especially of the periphery of the political system, leading to a general increase in the need for orientation and selection in the political system. This adds value to public opinion as orientation and selection structure, and thereby also to the mass media as central representatives of public opinion. Public opinion provides an indication as to which issues can be expected to find open ears and which cannot (Luhmann, 1970). In the light of public opinion politicians, citizens and the administration observe each other, and it becomes increasingly relevant how one is perceived by the wider public. In addition, increased political complexity also leads to a growing uncertainty with regard to political claims and interests. It is not enough to assume that the same interest groups will always make the same demands. When a virtually unlimited number of interests are at play and decisions could be made one way or another, then the need for approval and legitimization of each and every political decision increases. Unquestioned loyalty and acceptance can be assumed to a lesser degree than ever; they must instead be produced communicatively, from case to case. In each case, generating attention is the first step. These observations lead us to a second theorem in the research area of mediatization:

T 2: The higher the internal complexity of a social system and the greater the diversity of the resulting demands, the greater is its need for attention and acceptance, and the more important its ability to observe and effectively stimulate the issue-structure of mass-media communication.

In turn, the increasing inclusion causes a significant increase in the appreciation of the public as a source of legitimization for political concerns and decisions, and as a target for political communication. The inclusion of the public causes politics to be dependent on the public's consent and forces politics to monitor and address the specific interests and claims of certain public groups. This applies not only to the core area of party politics but also increasingly to the administration, which is faced with increased demands of its clientele. The more it relies on the cooperation of the public and organized groups, the less it can ignore these demands. Public opinion and mass-media reporting serve here as indispensable means to monitor the public.

Democratic political systems can therefore be regarded as particularly illustrative examples for what we stated in our first theorem. With regard to the internal differentiation of politics, it is fair to assume that, in those cases where potentially all citizens are involved (e.g., in an election or referendum), the consequences of mediatization can be observed particularly well, while actual decision-making in exclusive negotiation networks as well as the administrative implementation of decisions in the bureaucratic apparatus would lean much less towards the generating of public attention through mass media. With regard to the political subsystems mentioned above, this means that mediatization will have a greater significance in the areas of mediation between the public and other political subsystems (legislators or administration) than in the mediation between politics and administration. Nevertheless, the public also plays a direct or indirect role in the context of parliamentary legislation and bureaucratic processes. With regard to parliamentary initiatives, one must always bear in mind that they will be taken to the wider public, not only because of the public nature of the formal process but also because of the dependence of the parliamentarians on the consent of the electorate. The implementation of legal acts is dependent on the acceptance and cooperation of those concerned and must take into account their willingness to follow. The so-called "reflexive-preventive" public communication plays a significant role here too, as is obvious when we look at the increasing expenses for official information campaigns and public relations.

These examples show clearly how misleading it is to see the mediatization of election campaigns as *pars pro toto* (a part taken for the whole). Obviously, the need of politics for publicity and attention is not unlimited, even during election time. Outside campaign periods, it is not equally pronounced in all areas of politics. Rather, political access to media-generated "public awareness" will always be selective and vary according to the internal differentiation of the political system and the degree of inclusivity of the respective organization or process. When it comes to forms of inclusion (cf. Stichweh, 2005), it stands to reason that, wherever people are included in Hirschman's options of exit and voice, mass-media performances are in particular demand, because expression (voice) requires public attention (in order to have results). We can condense these observations into a third theorem:

T 3: If the ways of inclusion of political organizations and processes are based on exit and voice, they will regularly absorb mass-media performances and will therefore show more consequences of mediatization than social systems that involve people in their communication through education, professional care, secondary performance roles and so forth.

Up to this point, we can state that both aspects of political change – functional internal differentiation and political inclusion – must be seen as evolutionary preconditions for the increased need for public approval and attention in the political system and therefore for the mediatization of politics. These developments can be shown for different Western-style democracies, but they will differ greatly in their concrete formation and timescale. This is something that we cannot retrace here. Rather, we are interested in the structural and evolutionary preconditions for a mediatization of the political sphere, which can be opened up through an investigation of the functional conditions of modern political systems. So far, they have shown us that mediatization serves first and foremost to carry out modern politics.

To view mediatization as a developmental process that is, as it were, "imposed" onto the political system from the outside is to get it wrong. Mass media cannot (and do not want to) force anything on politics, not even media-savvy self-presentation. It is politics itself that realizes its dependence on media more than ever and is therefore reprogramming itself to appear more attractive. This does not exclude the possibility that the media's system-specific programs for the creation of their performance tasks (public attention and acceptance) at times prove fundamentally incompatible with political rationales, for instance when these political rationales demand exclusivity of small decision-making circles, discreteness of negotiations or confidentiality of administrative processes. Nonetheless, the media may successfully assert their claims. In such clashes, mediatization can be perceived in political circles (somewhat naively) as an intrusion of an alien logic, with potentially dysfunctional consequences.

However, the crucial difference between such cases and the assumption of a general "colonization" of political rationales by the media lies, in our view, in the fact that mass media can indeed impose unwanted public attention on political affairs, but they are hardly able to force politics to implement entirely new programs that are extrinsic to the system. Rather, it is to be expected that politics will react with system-specific adaptations. Such adjustments (as a result of transgressions by the media) may include enhancing the levels of confidentiality, shifting trouble spots into other institutional arenas, or creating "organizational buffers" between political processes and media – for instance in the form of personal agents who attract the majority of media attention to themselves and thereby distract attention from the actual processes.

Such responses may still be interpreted as "consequences of mediatization". But they are different from "colonization" because what is involved in these examples is the use of political structures to shield operations from media-induced publicity. This, however, may imply serious political dysfunctions or even legitimacy deficits if it concerns core areas of the interface between politics and public. Adapting political rationales to media logic, on the other hand, as may happen in selected political subsections such as government or administration, may have inflationary and deflationary consequences that ultimately block political decision-making processes (cf. Münch, 1991). From these observations we can draw our fourth and final theorem concerning mediatization:

> **T 4**: The consequences of mediatization may include both the structural "adaptation" of the political system to mass-media criteria in the generation of attention and structural measures to "shield" against public attention. The direction that the effect of mediatization takes will depend on the combinability and compatibility of media-specific and politics-specific operation programs.

Conclusion

In this paper, we have proposed to the discipline of communication science a series of revisions, additions and extensions to the concept of "mediatization". First, mediatization should not be characterized as the dominant meta-process of social change, which inevitably results in a "media society". The term "mediatization" refers to a specific perspective on social interdependency relations – namely, between media and their social environment. Other interdependency relations (e.g., to economization or judicialization) should not be disregarded – especially in view of a more differentiated understanding of mediatization. If interdependencies between functional areas should increase in the course of progressive functional differentiation, then mediatization will also gain in importance as a specific phenomenon of interdependency – as the recourse to media performances by other social systems. Mediatization does not stand alone and should thus not be understood as an all-encompassing primary phenomenon.

On the other hand, the phenomenon of mediatization cannot be attributed unilaterally to mass media as its cause. With the concept of "media causality" we are criticizing an idea of mediatization which sees organizational and social changes as being caused by media, an idea which cannot indicate persuasively what gives media this power to influence over and above their mere availability as well as what propels this power. Instead of this concept, we are here proposing a "push-and-pull model" of mediatization, one which locates the specific conditions of the process not within media but within the "mediatized" systems in the environment of media. An autonomous media system operating according to its own logic is a necessary but still not a sufficient condition for mediatization. Mass media themselves are treated in this model without normative bias as a highly specialized function-complex which equips issues of social communication with public attention and acceptance, and which has a virtually unrivaled performance capacity in this regard.

We then speak of "mediatization" when systems from the media's environment absorb these performances because and insofar as they need them for their own function and performance. This is to be expected to an even greater degree under conditions of high inclusivity and complexity (lack of transparency) of these systems, i.e., not in all (sub)systems with the same intensity and in the same way. If a system requires these performance tasks permanently, it will make appropriate adjustments to secure its access to them, and these structural changes can be observed and described empirically as "consequences of mediatization". Consequences are thereby to be understood as self-creations, since they are permitted or initiated by the "mediatized" systems and *not* imposed by media – even if some in politics may perceive (and describe) this differently.

Therefore, the mediatization of the political sphere is not to be interpreted as a sign of a declining political culture nor of the pathological colonization of politics by media; rather, it serves first and foremost to make politics possible under conditions of increased interdependencies, high political complexity and inclusivity. That media thereby become "summoned ghosts" that cannot be banished again, with unintended side-effects for the system, is by no means excluded. But even in this case they remain merely "summoned" ghosts and not diabolical visitations.

References

Hjarvard, S. (2008). The Mediatization of Society: A Theory of the Media as Agents of Social and Cultural Change. *Nordicom Review*, 29, 105–134.
Luhmann, N. (1970). Öffentliche Meinung [Public Opinion]. *Politische Vierteljahresschrift*, 11, 2–28.
Luhmann, N. (1982). *The Differentiation of Society.* New York, NY: Columbia University Press.
Luhmann, N. (1995). *Social Systems.* Stanford, CA: Stanford University Press.
Luhmann, N. (1996). *Die Realität der Massenmedien* [The Reality of Mass Media]. Opladen, Germany: Westdeutscher Verlag.
Luhmann, N. (1997). *Die Gesellschaft der Gesellschaft* [The Society of Society]. Frankfurt, Germany: Suhrkamp.
Luhmann, N. (2000). *Die Politik der Gesellschaft* [The Politics of Society]. Frankfurt, Germany: Suhrkamp.
Marcinkowski, F. (1993). *Publizistik als autopoietisches System* [Public Communication as an Autopoietic System]. Opladen: Westdeutscher Verlag.
Münch, R. (1991). *Dialektik der Kommunikationsgesellschaft* [Dialectic of Communication Society]. Frankfurt, Germany: Suhrkamp.
Nassehi, A. (2000). Das Politische der politischen Gesellschaft [The Politics of the Political Society]. *Soziologische Revue*, 23, 132–140.
Schimank, U. (2006). "Feindliche Übernahmen": Typen intersystemischer Autonomiebedrohung in der modernen Gesellschaft ["Unfriendly Mergers": Types

of Intersystemic Threats to Autonomy within Modern Societies]. In U. Schimank (Ed.), *Teilsystemische Autonomie und politische Gesellschaftssteuerung, Band 2* [Subsystemic Autonomy and the Political Regulation of Society] (Vol. 2, pp. 71–83). Wiesbaden, Germany: Verlag Sozialwissenschaft.

Schulz, W. (2004). Reconstructing Mediatization as an Analytical Concept. *European Journal of Communication*, 19, 87–101.

Stichweh, R. (2005). *Inklusion und Exklusion: Studien zur Gesellschaftstheorie* [Inclusion and Exclusion: Studies in Social Theory]. Bielefeld, Germany: Transcript Verlag.

Thompson, J. B. (1995). *The Media and Modernity: A Social Theory of the Media.* Cambridge: Polity Press.

Weingart, P. (1998). Science and the Media. *Research Policy*, 27, 869–879.

Part III
Dimensions of Mediatization

6
Mediation of Political Realities: Media as Crucial Sources of Information

Adam Shehata and Jesper Strömbäck

When we want to learn about the world around us, there are basically three perceptual sources of information: personal experiences, interpersonal communication and the media (Asp, 1986). We can learn things firsthand, by communicating with other people, or by taking part of different media.

For the most part, however, the media are the most important source of information. The reach of our own experiences is very limited, and the same holds true for most people we talk to. Particularly when it comes to politics and society, most of what we know – or think we know – we have learned from the media. Even in cases when we have some experiences on our own to base our knowledge on, without information from the media we do not know whether our experiences are representative of how things are or whether they are atypical (Mutz, 1998). For example, while we might have experiences of the local hospital, that does not tell us much about the quality of health care in general, and even less about factors influencing the health care system or what proposals there are to improve healthcare.

Consequently, it has become a truism that modern politics is largely mediated politics (Bennett & Entman, 2000; Kaid et al., 1991; Nimmo & Combs, 1983). The extent to which the media constitute the most important source of information about politics and society has also been labeled the first dimension of mediatization and singled out as a necessary prerequisite for further processes of mediatization (Strömbäck, 2008, 2011).

There might, however, be several reasons to revisit the notion that politics has become mediated and the evidence that the media are the most important source of information about politics and society. First and conceptually speaking, there is a need to distinguish between mediated and mediatized politics. Second, the media is a broad and heterogeneous category – including everything from books to newspapers, radio, television and increasingly digital media – and the relative importance of different media might vary across time as well as countries. Hence, there is a need

93

to take a closer look at our current knowledge about what kind of media people rely on for information about politics and society. Third, new media technologies and social media have caused old boundaries to become blurred and opened up for virtual interpersonal communication, raising new questions about what "the media" refers to and the extent to which it is valid to use "the media" as a shorthand for traditional mass media such as television, newspapers and radio.

Against this backdrop, the purpose of this chapter is to briefly discuss the conceptual relationship between mediated and mediatized politics, to analyze research on the importance of different kinds of media as sources of information about politics and society, and to analyze the implications of the findings for the notion that "the media" is the most important source of information about politics and society and for mediatization theory.

Mediation and mediatization: Conceptual similarities and differences

While scholarly interest in processes of mediation and mediatization has increased during the last decade, oftentimes these concepts are used without clear conceptualizations, and it is also common that mediation and mediatization are used to denote the same phenomena. Although there are exceptions, particularly British and US scholars often appear to prefer the term "mediation" when analyzing how the media influence various spheres in society (Altheide & Snow, 1988; Couldry, 2008; Davis, 2007; Livingstone, 2009; Nimmo & Combs, 1983; Silverstone, 2007), while scholars from continental Europe and Scandinavia appear to favor the term "mediatization" (Asp, 1986; Kepplinger, 2002; Lundby, 2009; Mazzoleni & Schulz, 1999; Hjarvard, 2013; Schillemans, 2012; Strömbäck, 2008). There might however be some development towards a convergence and an increasing consensus that "mediation" and "mediatization" refer to different processes (Hjarvard, 2013, p. 19).

From such a perspective and following Mazzoleni (2008a, 2008b), mediatization broadly refers to "the extension of the influence of the media (considered both as a cultural technology and as an organization)" in different spheres in society, whereas mediation refers to the rather neutral act of transmitting messages through different media (Strömbäck & Esser, 2009; Strömbäck, 2011). In the context of politics, politics is thus mediated whenever political messages are transmitted or whenever people learn about politics through any kind of media, regardless of whether this process yields any influence or transforms the style or content of political communication. To say that something is mediated is simply to say that it is communicated through some kind of media – and it matters less conceptually whether the media in question are television, newspapers, radio, the Internet or smartphones. Thus, mediated politics stands in contrast to interpersonal communication or personal experiences.

Beyond this distinction between mediation and mediatization, there are however reasons to distinguish between mediation at different levels of analysis. At the *micro level*, politics is mediated whenever a political message is communicated or someone learns about politics through some kind of media. At this level of analysis, politics has to some extent been mediated as long as there has been some kind of media. Politics can also be more or less mediated. At the one extreme would be those who never learn about politics from any kind of media, whereas at the other extreme would be those who learn about politics only through different media.

The extent to which people learn about politics through different media has an effect on mediation at the macro level. At the *macro level*, politics is mediated when the media has become the most important source of information about politics and society and the primary channel of communication between political actors and citizens (Bennett & Entman, 2001; Strömbäck, 2011). Mediated politics at the macro level can thus be understood as the aggregation of mediation of politics at the micro level.

The development of new media technologies has at the same time caused the concept of "the media" to become more heterogeneous and blurred. Most scholars analyzing the mediation and mediatization of politics usually apply "the media" as shorthand for traditional news media that function as *institutions*, i.e., television, newspapers and radio (Cook, 2005; Hjarvard, 2013; Strömbäck & Esser, 2009). The rise of the Internet and other digital media, which mix content produced by institutional mass media and different political and advocacy organizations, as well as by ordinary citizens, has however made this practice less valid, while also blurring the line between mass communication and interpersonal communication and de-institutionalizing the concept of "the media". Thus, not only is there a need to distinguish between mediated politics at the micro and the macro level, but also to separate mass-mediated politics from other kinds of mediation of political information and communication.

From the perspective of mediatization theory, the degree to which politics has become mediated constitutes an important part and necessary prerequisite for further processes of mediatization (Strömbäck, 2008, 2011; Mazzoleni, 2008a). What matters from that perspective is primarily the extent to which individuals rely on content produced and shaped by different news media *as institutions* (Esser, 2013; Hjarvard, 2013; Strömbäck, 2011), not whether they access the information through these media's traditional formats or their digital versions. It is thus less important whether people rely on the *New York Times* or nytimes.com for information about politics than if they rely on traditional news media institutions or on information coming directly, albeit through some kind of media, from, for example, political parties, governmental authorities or friends.

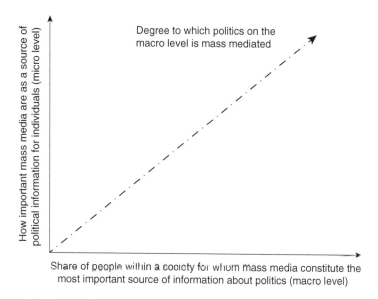

Figure 6.1   Mass-mediated politics at the micro and the macro level

The key question, then, is how important different mass media are as sources of political information for individuals *and* the share of people for whom the mass media constitute the most important source of information about politics and society. The more individuals rely on mass media for information about politics and society, and the larger the share of people for whom the mass media – in traditional or digital formats – constitute the most important source of information about politics and society, the more mass-mediated politics is (see Figure 6.1).

As the degree to which politics is mass-mediated theoretically influences further processes of mediatization, changes or differences across time or space in the degree to which politics is mass-mediated may have important implications for the mediatization of politics. Considering this and the changing media environments and patterns of media consumption, there is a need to take a closer look at the importance of media as sources of political information.

Media as sources of information

Because the notion that politics is mediated has become almost a truism, the claim that the media constitute the most important source of information is seldom critically examined. One additional reason may be that most media studies build on the idea that media is crucial for democracy, and research thus focuses not on *whether* but *how* and *in what ways* the media matter.

Thus, the mediation of political information serves as a taken-for-granted assumption from which to push the research agenda forward. Another reason may be that there is no straightforward way of empirically assessing the importance of the media as an information source in societies where citizens are more or less embedded in a media environment from the day they are born. Furthermore, there are no agreed-upon benchmarks for distinguishing between information sources and evaluating their relative "importance" – an issue that becomes even more pressing as various forms of media use, interpersonal communication and political behavior mix and mingle as a result of media convergence.

Hence, investigating the importance of the media as a source of information about politics and society is not a simple task. In the research review that follows we will thus discuss three ways of analyzing the importance of traditional mass media compared to other sources of information about politics and current affairs: (1) asking people about their reliance on mediated communications for information about politics and current affairs; (2) analyzing the relationship between media coverage and awareness of political and current events; and (3) analyzing different sources of citizens' sociotropic perceptions of reality.

Asking about citizens' reliance on mediated communications

The most straightforward approach to investigating the importance of traditional mass media as a source of information about politics and society – i.e., the mediation of politics – is to ask people explicitly about their main sources of political information (Althaus, 2007; Eurobarometer, 2012; Gidengil, 2008; Norris & Curtice, 2007; Pew, 2011). The literature contains various survey-based assessments of citizens' reliance on the media for information about politics and current affairs. Using respondents' self-reports of media reliance and use typically suggests a prominent role for mediated communication compared to personal experience and interpersonal communication as primary information sources.

For example, the Pew Research Center in the United States has for many years asked the following open-ended survey question: "How have you been getting most of your news about national and international issues? From television, from newspapers, from radio, from magazines, or from the Internet?" (Pew, 2008, 2011, 2013). Respondents are allowed to name two sources. As noted by Althaus and Tewksbury (2007), this approach has at least two advantages. First, it provides an estimate of respondents' self-reported relative importance of various media sources. Second, the question allows respondents to name other information sources than traditional news media, such as interpersonal discussions.

Evidence from both the United States and the 27 European member states, presented in Figure 6.2, suggests that television remains the dominant source

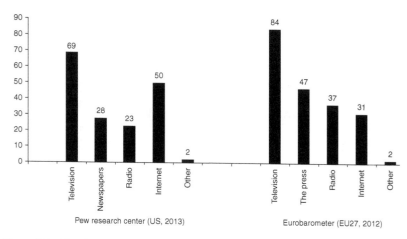

Pew research center (US, 2013)   Eurobarometer (EU27, 2012)

Figure 6.2   Most important source of news (%)

Note: Data from the United States come from Pew Research Center (2013), who asked respondents' the following question in 2013: "How do you get most of your news about national and international issues?" Data from the European Union countries come from Eurobarometer (2012), who asked respondents' the following question in 2012: "Where do you get most of your news on national political matters?"

of political information – at least as assessed by citizens themselves. The European data is based on a Eurobarometer survey conducted in the 27 member states in 2012, where respondents were asked a question similar to the Pew question: "Where do you get most of your news on national political matters?" Apart from the fact that television comes out on top of the list in both surveys, some other observations from these studies are worth pointing out.

First, while the 2013 US data shows that television is the most important source of news about national and international issues, it is increasingly challenged by the Internet. While 69% named television as the most important source of information, the Internet was placed second (50%), followed by newspapers (28%), radio (23%) and magazines (4%). Television tends to dominate as a source of information for most Europeans (84%) as well – it is perceived as the main source of information in all countries except for Luxemburg – but newspapers (47%) and radio (37%) are considered more important than the Internet (31%).

Second, the relative importance of different sources of information varies between European Union member states. Newspapers are, for instance, more prominent in some countries than others, which may reflect historical, political and media system differences (Elvestad & Blekesaune, 2008; Hallin & Mancini, 2004; Shehata & Strömbäck, 2011). Simply put, some countries are more television-centric while other countries are more newspaper-centric.

Third, the number of respondents who named a source other than these media was extremely low in both surveys (2%), which would indicate a negligible role for non-mediated forms of communication. It remains unclear from these data whether this is the case, though. Responses to open-ended questions like these may be highly sensitive to probing, i.e., whether interviewers explicitly mention specific news sources as examples when posing the questions (Schuman & Presser, 1996). Furthermore, respondents may be cued to think about media more than other types of information sources when asked about their ways of getting "news". Therefore, it is not clear to what extent these measures provide valid estimates of the relative importance of media sources on the one hand, and personal experience and interpersonal communication on the other.

A slightly modified question was therefore posed to a representative sample of Swedish citizens during the 2006 national parliamentary election campaign (Strömbäck, 2009). Asked about their main source of information about the election campaign, respondents were provided with a list of not only traditional and new media, but interpersonal communication and personal contacts with politicians and parties as well. Still, very few respondents considered these unmediated sources as the most important. Television was placed as the number one source by 54% of the sample, followed by newspapers (25%), Internet (8%) and radio (6%), while personal contacts with parties and politicians (4%) and interpersonal communication with friends and family members (3%) were the least important sources of campaign-related information.

Similar findings – based on similar survey items – indicating a prominent function of traditional media as sources of information during election campaigns have been documented in other countries as well, such as Britain and Canada (Gidengil, 2008; Norris & Curtice, 2007; Scammell & Semetko, 2008). Data from the 2005 British general election showed, for example, that traditional media such as television, newspapers and radio were by far the most commonly used sources of information (Norris & Curtice, 2007). Approximately 50% of the respondents reported that they got information about the election campaign from these media. Almost the same share, 46%, said they had discussed the election with friends or family members. By comparison, only 15% reported being contacted by a party or candidate, and even fewer (2%) attended a public meeting about the election.

It is important to note, however, that getting political information primarily from television does not necessarily equal exposure to regular newscasts or special elections programs moderated by journalists, but also to more infotainment-oriented talk shows as well as political ads or party election broadcasts. Similarly, getting information primarily from the "Internet" says little about what websites citizens use, whether political party websites and blogs, social media or the online version of traditional news media. In essence, this suggests that it is misleading to think of getting information from the Internet as opposed to getting information from traditional news media. We will return to this question below.

While asking people about their primary source of political information is straightforward, this strategy comes with methodological problems. Most importantly, this approach rests on the assumption that respondents are able to reliably estimate their dependence on different types of media and inter-personal communication, and weigh their importance in relation to one another. An alternative way of assessing the role of the media as an information source is to analyze the relationship between media coverage and respondents' awareness of political and current events information.

The relationship between media coverage and awareness of political and current events

As an alternative approach to asking citizens about their sources of information about politics, several studies analyze the importance of the media by analyzing the influence of media coverage on citizens' awareness of current events and issues. Theoretically and following the OMA framework, variations in political knowledge among citizens are typically considered a function of learning *opportunities*, *motivations* and *abilities* (Delli Carpini & Keeter, 1996; Luskin, 1990; Prior, 2007; Strömbäck et al., 2012). While motivations and abilities are individual-level factors expressing differences in personal interest and cognitive resources, the opportunities to learn are determined by the availability of political information in any given context (Aalberg et al., 2010; Esser et al., 2012). By using variations in the supply of media coverage of various topics, and thereby the opportunities for citizens to acquire this information, several studies have analyzed the influence of information provided by the media on citizens' awareness of current political issues and events (Curran et al., 2009; Delli Carpini et al., 1994; Jerit et al., 2006). The major lesson from this research is that citizens acquire a good deal of information about national and international political issues when this information is widely available in those media they have access to.

Several of the studies within this research area are particularly relevant in light of our interest in the media as a source of political information. While substantial scholarly attention has been devoted to the relationship between media use and political knowledge in general, the specific focus on aware-ness of current affairs news – what Delli Carpini and Keeter (1996) refer to as "surveillance facts" – is better suited for assessing the news media's role as an information source than more common measures of political knowledge. Compared to measures tapping knowledge of historical facts, institutions, rules of the game, party ideology and issue positions, acquiring surveillance knowledge "depends upon recent exposure to information in the media rather than learning that occurred years ago" (Jerit et al., 2006, p. 269).

In a study of "passive learning", Zukin and Snyder (1984) compared citizens' awareness of candidates running for office in New Jersey and New York elections, based on geographical variations in the amount of media coverage devoted to the election campaigns. Despite equal interest in the election, residents living in media-rich markets with extensive coverage were 40% more likely to know about the candidates than citizens residing in media markets with substantially less election coverage (see also Delli Carpini et al., 1994).

While these results ascribe to the media a prominent role as information sources in election campaigns, the media markets of the late 1970s and early 1980s were very different from today's unconstrained high-choice media environments (Prior, 2007). Despite this, a number of recent studies have supported the idea that variations in information opportunities provided by major news media explain differences in awareness of current events and issues, beyond what is accounted for by individual-level characteristics. A number of cross-national comparative studies, using extensive media content analyses and survey data, have linked differences in the supply of hard and soft news to variations in citizens' awareness of domestic and international issues (Aalberg & Curran, 2011; Curran et al., 2009; Iyengar et al., 2010; Iyengar et al., 2009). People living in media systems providing extensive hard news, and thereby greater opportunities for the average citizens to encounter political and current affairs information, were also more knowledgeable about those issues that were covered by the media. The availability of such information in the media was also related to smaller gaps in knowledge based on personal motivation and resources.

Evidence of the important role of media as disseminators of current events information in today's high-choice media environments does not only come from cross-national comparative research. A growing number of both cross-sectional and longitudinal studies conducted in the United States as well as Europe show that the supply of political information in major news media increases knowledge and awareness of these issues among the electorate (Barabas & Jerit, 2009; Elenbaas et al., 2012, 2013; Jerit et al., 2006; Nadeau et al., 2008). For instance, Barabas and Jerit (2009) used a large number of surveys conducted in the United States to analyze how policy-specific knowledge on a range of issues – such as gun control, health care and social security – was influenced by media coverage of these topics. Among other things, they found not only that increases in the amount of coverage devoted to an issue were related to higher levels of policy-specific knowledge, but also that the breadth and prominence of these news stories increased the opportunities to acquire this information. Using a very similar research design but in a European context, Elenbaas et al. (2012, 2013) showed "that a wider distribution of political information in the media strongly increases the odds that citizens acquire that information" (Elenbaas et al., 2012, p. 15).

These studies clearly suggest that media matter and that politics is mediated: awareness and knowledge of political current affairs varies according to the availability and prominence of this information in major news media outlets. What is less clear, however, is whether this information mainly spreads to citizens directly from media exposure, or through various indirect communication flows. To be sure, there are studies indicating that some of the variation in current events knowledge can be attributed to citizens' personal media exposure diets, and that both passive and motivated learning occur from the media (Elenbaas et al., 2013; Shehata, 2013; Soroka et al., 2012), but several obstacles inhibit firm conclusions regarding the relative importance of various sources of information at the individual level. To begin with, despite the fact that many studies have investigated the relationship between news media use and political knowledge, there are – apart from the research discussed above – few that focus on awareness of current news events or surveillance knowledge. In addition, survey measures of individual-level news consumption are plagued with methodological problems such as overreporting, which limits their use as reliable indicators of actual news exposure (Price & Zaller, 1993; Prior, 2009). Finally, analyzing the relationship between individual-level news exposure and knowledge of current events becomes problematic in situations of information saturation, i.e., when the information is widely available across media outlets and in public deliberation – which tends to be the case with major breaking news that dominate the agenda (Druckman, 2005; Elenbaas et al., 2012; Zukin & Snyder, 1984). In those cases it becomes almost impossible to distinguish the influence of media coverage from other sources of information such as interpersonal communication. This can be perceived as an example of amalgamation, which Schulz (2004) suggested is one effect of mediatization.

While the research discussed above undoubtedly suggests that the media play a significant role as providers of political and current affairs information, these studies say little about the relative importance of mediated communication compared to interpersonal discussions and personal experience. This question has, however, been at the heart of research on the formation of sociotropic perceptions.

Mediated communication in the formation of sociotropic perceptions

The relative influence of media coverage, interpersonal communication and personal experience on citizens' sociotropic perceptions has been a key issue in research on voting and agenda-setting. The sources of citizens' perceptions of collective experience became a critical question as research on economic voting consistently showed that judgments of national economic (sociotropic) trends were more important than personal pocketbook issues for explaining electoral behavior (Kinder, 1981; Lewis-Beck & Stegmaier,

2007). Similarly, the sources of sociotropic perceptions have been at the center of research on agenda-setting theory, according to which the traditional news media are hypothesized to exert a strong influence on what issues the public consider important national problems (McCombs, 2004).

Both these research traditions ascribe to the media a central role in forming citizens' sociotropic perceptions, i.e., perceptions of societal or national-level conditions. Media influence is not considered unconditional, however. Rather, most of this research builds on some version of media system dependency (MSD) theory (Ball-Rokeach, 1985). MSD is founded on the idea that power relations originate from control over resources that other actors need in order to fulfill their goals. The more exclusive these resources are, and the more other actors require these resources, the more asymmetric the power relation. According to MSD, media power is based on controlling access to information that media consumers require in order to achieve their particular goals, whatever these goals are:

> The process of media effects is initiated by media control over scarce and prized information sources – gathering, processing, and dissemination – that must be accessed in order for the larger social system, as well as members of the media audiences, to achieve a range of goals [...] The more exclusive the media system's control over these resources, and the more essential it is to have access to these resources to achieve goals, the more likely it is that there will be media effects.
>
> (Ball-Rokeach & Jung, 2009, p. 533)

Exclusivity is crucial in this regard. Citizens who have access to other sources of information on a given topic are consequently less dependent on the media when forming perceptions and opinions. Research on the formation of sociotropic perceptions has primarily addressed the competing or complementary influences of personal experience and interpersonal communication as alternative sources of information. While some of this research has treated personal experience and interpersonal communication as *competing* factors, others emphasize the interactive and reciprocal relations between different sources of information as citizens form perceptions of collective experience. The basic question, though, concerns the conditions under which citizens use information from the mass media, personal experience and interpersonal communication when making inferences about collective experience.

Agenda-setting research focusing on the contingencies of media influence on sociotropic perceptions has – based on MSD – analyzed the role of issue obtrusiveness, i.e., citizens' direct personal experience of various topics, as a moderating factor (Demers et al., 1989; Watt et al., 1993). Several of these studies support the basic premise of MSD theory: the agenda-setting influence of the mass media is stronger for issues that people have little direct experience with. Limited personal experience means less information from non-mediated sources, and media dependency becomes stronger. Soroka (2002) found, for instance, that agenda-setting effects on public opinion were stronger for unobtrusive issues such as environmental problems and government debt and deficits than for the obtrusive inflation issue. While unobtrusiveness seems to enhance the role of mediated communication, the findings are somewhat mixed for obtrusive issues. Some studies suggest that personal experiences constrain the agenda-setting impact of the media, while others find that media coverage influences citizens' sociotropic perceptions of obtrusive issues as well (Demers et al., 1989; Goss & Aday, 2003; Hügel et al., 1989; Iyengar & Kinder, 1987; Watt et al., 1993).

Even though there is mixed evidence regarding whether issue obtrusiveness reduces the media's agenda-setting influence, there is less disagreement that both personal experience and interpersonal communication exert independent effects on perceived issue importance at the societal level (Iyengar & Kinder, 1987; Wanta & Hu, 1990) People experiencing unemployment are, for example, more likely to consider this an important issue, just as talking to friends and family about crime influences sociotropic perceptions.

The most convincing account of how media coverage, personal experience and discussions influence sociotropic perceptions emphasizes the mutual and interactive – rather than competing – effects of these factors. Such a perspective may explain (1) some of the inconsistent findings regarding the role of personal experience as a moderator of agenda-setting effects, as well as (2) the relatively weak findings for agenda-setting effects at the individual level (Erbring et al., 1980; Roessler, 2008). Whenever citizens can rely on personal experience or interpersonal discussion networks, mediated communication may be an integral factor in the formation of sociotropic perceptions, but rarely in an unfiltered way. Alternative information sources can both reduce or enhance media influence on perceptions of collective experience. Conversely, the impact of personal experience on perceptions of collective experience may be dependent on mediated communications.

In one of the most extensive analyses of the influence of personal experiences and mediated communication on sociotropic perceptions, Mutz (1998) found that the mass media have a dual role in politicizing personal experience. Focusing on unemployment, she found that the mass media were the primary influence on perceptions of national trends while personal experience was the main source of personal-level judgments (see also Goss & Aday, 2003). In the absence of mediated information, however, sociotropic perceptions depended more on personal experiences:

> [i]ndividual-level variations in perceptions of unemployment conditions are, in fact, meaningful; they primarily demonstrate differences in the amount and type of information available to people. Those with much

information from mass media sources will have perceptions of unemployment consistent with media presentations, while those relying on more parochial sources will have perceptions that reflect their immediate environments.

(Mutz, 1992, p. 502)

With respect to the interaction between mediated communication and personal experience, Mutz (1994) also found that heavy media coverage of unemployment increasingly colored national-level unemployment perceptions. Thus, extensive media coverage helps citizens to connect the personal with the political by "exposing people to the similar experiences of others" (Mutz, 1994, p. 692).

The importance of the media as a source of information about politics and society (sociotropic perceptions) at the individual level depends, therefore, on other factors. Research on the contingent conditions of media influence suggests that mediated information flows are more likely to be adopted if these messages are consonant with citizens' perceptions of their personal experiences as well as the content of their interpersonal discussions (Chong & Druckman, 2007; Demers et al., 1989; Mutz, 1998). Several agenda-setting studies have also supported the "issue sensitivity" hypothesis, indicating that sociotropic perceptions are shaped by an interactive influence of media coverage and audience characteristics (Erbring et al., 1980; Iyengar & Kinder, 1987; Roessler, 1999). Based on their experimental studies of media effects, Iyengar and Kinder concluded, for instance, that "when problems flare up and capture the attention of the media, agenda-setting effects show up most immediately among those directly affected by the problem" (1987, pp. 52–53). Similarly, another individual-level agenda-setting analysis found weak direct effects of media coverage on perceived issue importance, concluding that "[p]ieces of information are retrieved from many other sources and permanently modified by discussions with other people or individual processing of the respondent" (Roessler, 1999, p. 691). In a similar vein, several agenda-setting studies suggest that individual variations in citizens' need for orientation with respect to certain issues influence the tendency to seek out information from the media (McCombs, 2004).

In sum, while it remains difficult to assess the relative importance of various sources of information on sociotropic perceptions, research suggests that mediated communication, personal experience and interpersonal discussions are best conceived of as interactive factors in the formation of sociotropic perceptions. Based on the discussion above, it thus seems reasonable to conclude that (1) personal experiences and interpersonal discussions do shape perceptions of collective experience, and even more so in the absence of media coverage; (2) mediated information flows can both weaken and strengthen the relationship between personal experiences and sociotropic perceptions; (3) media coverage has the strongest influence on sociotropic perceptions of unobtrusive issues; and (4) the impact of mediated communication on sociotropic perceptions is dependent on whether media messages are in line or at odds with personal experiences and interpersonal discussions.

The mediation of politics in high-choice media environments

Learning about politics and society is obviously a function of various contextual and individual-level factors. As noted previously, the OMA framework provides a general overview of how information opportunities as well as personal motivations and abilities influence learning about politics and society (Delli Carpini & Keeter, 1996; Luskin, 1990). While mediated communication is likely to be crucial as a source of political information, the specific importance of various media is thus dependent not only on differences in interests, preferences and resources among citizens, but also on the larger social, technological and cultural transformations that have occurred during the last few decades (Bennett & Iyengar, 2008; Prior, 2007; Stroud, 2011).

In particular, the profound media environmental changes – with a multiplication of output across platforms, channels and outlets – have substantially altered the opportunities for citizens to encounter political information as part of their everyday lives. Not only has the number of media sources from which people can learn grown, but so has the complexity and variation in how citizens can acquire such information through a combination of mediated offline and online sources. As argued by Bennett and Manheim (2006, p. 22), information consumption has shifted away from mass to individualized experience, which becomes evident as one compares "the appointment-based society that gathered around network broadcast news with the emergence of the podcast society increasingly driven by personalized, on-demand news aggregators" (see also Chaffee & Metzger, 2001). While the societal and individual-level consequences of these media environmental changes in terms of media use, political involvement and opinion formation have yet to be thoroughly analyzed as the process unfolds, the implications for the mediation of politics may become substantial.

Using MSD theory (Ball-Rokeach & Jung, 2009) as a point of departure, the transformation from low-choice to high-choice media environments most obviously seems to liberate individuals from their dependency on traditional news media for information about politics and society. If dependency is based on controlling others' access to scarce resources, the proliferation of alternative sources of political information undermines the unique role of traditional mass media as possessors and disseminators of exclusive information. What is theoretically possible, however, may not necessarily equal actual changes and practices.

To be sure, the trend of shrinking audiences for news media on traditional platforms seems to be consistent across Western democracies (Blekesaune et al., 2012; Prior, 2007; Strömbäck et al., 2012). However, this does not mean that citizens are necessarily becoming less dependent on media per se, or that they actively seek information about politics from the full range of alternative sources now available to them. While a recent study found that citizens who rely on multiple online news sources were less inclined to base their sociotropic perceptions on cues from the traditional news media (Shehata & Strömbäck, 2013), evidence strongly suggests that citizens who get their news about politics from the Internet mainly turn to the websites of the traditional media. Among Europeans who use the Internet as a source of information about national politics, almost 70% said they got their news from information websites such as newspapers and news magazines, followed by social network sites (27%), government websites (24%), blogs (11%) and video hosting websites (8%) (Eurobarometer, 2012). Based on a similar pattern in the United States, Mutz and Young (2011, pp. 1027–1029) concluded that "even in the realm of new media, traditional media sources dominate. And, while an increasing number of people get their news online, few online newspaper sites look much different from their paper-and-ink predecessors and most present the same news to their online and offline readers."

Thus, it would be a mistake to equate the rising importance of the Internet as a source of information about politics and society with a declining importance of traditional news media. As long as people when using the Internet as a source of information mainly turn to the digital versions of traditional mass media, the Internet does not substitute traditional mass media, and politics does not become less mediated.

The most important consequence of digital media in the realm of information flows and mediation is thus probably not the substitution of traditional mass media. What is likely to become more important is rather (1) the increasing mixing and mingling of information coming from traditional mass media and advocacy organizations, businesses and other non-media organizations, as well as through traditional or virtual interpersonal communication; (2) the increasing fragmentation and individualization of media and information consumption patterns; and (3) the continuous formation of multiple-step flows of information, where information originating with traditional mass media flow – and in the process mix and mingle with other information – through social networks of communication online and offline before reaching the individual consumers of information. There will be less inadvertent exposure to traditional news media in their traditional formats and more to different types of mediated multiple-step flows of information in the future than in the past, but this does not in itself make traditional news media as an institution less important or politics less mediated.

Discussion and conclusions

It has long been a truism that modern politics largely is mediated politics, i.e., politics mainly communicated through different mass media with the mass media being the most important source of information about politics and society. The (mass) mediation of politics is also an important prerequisite for the mediatization of politics, so changes in this respect would potentially have significant implications for the mediatization of politics. The mediation of politics is however not a question of either/or. It is rather a matter of degree, and to fully understand the extent to which politics is mediated, there is reason to distinguish between mediation at the micro and the macro level. At the micro level, the key question is how important mass media are as a source of information about politics and society for individuals, while at the macro level the key question is the share of people within a society for whom the mass media are the most important source of information about politics and society. The more individuals rely on mass media for information about politics and society, and the larger the share of people for whom mass media – in traditional or digital formats – constitute the most important source of information about politics and society, the more mediated politics is (see Figure 6.1).

Despite the taken-for-granted assumption that modern politics is largely mediated politics, our review shows that it is not easy to determine the extent to which individuals rely on mass media for information about politics and society, and hence the degree to which politics at the micro and the macro levels is mediated. While all evidence suggests that mass media are extremely important as a source of information about politics and society, and that politics is indeed mediated, there is no obvious approach in examining exactly *how important* the media are as a source of political information. Different approaches yield somewhat different, albeit not contradictory results, and the degree of media dependency might vary across not only individuals within or between countries, but also depending on the nature of different issues and the availability of alternative sources of information.

Thus, if one conclusion is that politics is still highly mediated, another conclusion is that it is difficult to determine the degree to which politics at the micro or the macro level is mediated. One implication is hence that there is a need for further research on the relative importance of different sources of information about politics and society, and that the mediation of politics should not just be treated as a truism.

Still, if it is difficult to assess the extent to which people rely on mass media for information about politics and society today, it will become even more difficult in the future as media environments continue to change, different media continue to converge, different sources of information continue to mix and mingle, and different multiple-step flows of information through various social networks continue to develop and blur the distinction between types of information as well as the origins of information.

Considering the focus in contemporary research and public discourse on the increasing importance of the Internet, it is however important not to focus too much on the technical platforms through which information flows. What matters most from the perspective of the mediation and mediatization of politics is not primarily the technical platforms through which people get information about and experience politics and society. What matters most is how important the mass media *as an institution* is as a source of information about politics and society. More important than how many use the Internet to learn about politics and society is thus *how* people use the Internet and the extent to which they turn to mass media in their traditional or digital versions to find information about politics and society.

Thus, the rising importance of the Internet does not necessarily herald the demise of mediated politics, nor of the mediatization of politics. It might rather herald the re-mediation of politics. This might have implications for the mediatization of politics in the future, but as long as the mass media – in their traditional or digital formats – continue to be the most important source of information about politics and society, while being largely autonomous from political institutions, politics will continue to be both mediated and mediatized.

References

Aalberg, T., & Curran, J. (Eds.) (2011). *How Media Inform Democracy: A Comparative Approach.* London: Routledge.

Aalberg, T., van Aelst, P., & Curran, J. (2010). Media Systems and the Political Information Environment: A Cross-National Comparison. *International Journal of Politics*, 15(3), 255–271.

Althaus, S. (2007). Free Falls, High Dives, and the Future of Democratic Accountability. In D. Graber, D. McQuail & P. Norris (Eds.), *The Politics of News – The News of Politics*. Washington, DC: CQ Press.

Althaus, S., & Tewksbury, D. (2007). *Toward a New Generation of Media Use Measures.* Pilot study report presented to the Board of Overseers of the American National Election Studies.

Altheide, D. L., & Snow, R. P. (1988). Toward a Theory of Mediation. In J. A. Anderson (Ed.), *Communication Yearbook 11* (pp. 194–223). Newbury Park: Sage.

Asp, K. (1986). *Mäktiga massmedier: Studier i politisk opinionsbildning.* Stockholm: Akademilitteratur.

Ball-Rokeach, S. (1985). The Origins of Individual Media-system Dependency Theory: A Sociological Framework. *Communication Research*, 12(4), 485–510.

Ball-Rokeach, S., & Jung, J. (2009). The Evolution of Media System Dependency Theory. In R. Nabi & M. B. Oliver (Eds.), *The Sage Handbook of Media Processes and Effects*. Thousand Oaks: Sage.

Barabas, J., & Jerit, J. (2009). Estimating the Causal Effects of Media Coverage on Policy-Specific Knowledge. *American Journal of Political Science*, 53(1), 73–89.

Bennett, W. L., & Entman, R. M. (Eds.) (2001). *Mediated Politics: Communication and the Future of Democracy*. New York, NY: Cambridge University Press.

Bennett, L., & Iyengar, S. (2008). A New Era of Minimal Effects? The Changing Foundations of Political Communication. *Journal of Communication*, 58(4), 707–731.

Bennett, L., & Manheim, J. (2006). The One-Step Flow of Communication. *The ANNALS of the American Academy of Political and Social Science*, 608(1), 213–232.

Bennett, W. L., & Entman, R. M. (Eds.) (2001). *Mediated Politics: Communication in the Future of Democracy*. New York, NY: Cambridge University Press.

Blekesaune, A., Elvestad, E., & Aalberg, T. (2011). Tuning Out the World of News and Current Affairs. An Empirical Study of Europe's Disconnected Citizens. *European Sociological Review*, 27(6), 110–126.

Chaffee, S., & Metzger, M. (2001). The End of Mass Communication? *Mass Communication & Society*, 4(4), 365–379.

Chong, D., & Druckman, J. (2007). A Theory of Framing and Opinion Formation in Competitive Elite Environments. *Journal of Communication*, 57(1), 99–118.

Cook, T. E. (2005). *Governing with the News: The News Media as a Political Institution*. 2nd Edition. Chicago, IL: University of Chicago Press.

Couldry, N. (2008). Mediatization or Mediation? Alternative Understandings of the Emergent Space of Digital Storytelling. *New Media & Society*, 10(3), 373–391.

Curran, J., Iyengar, S., Lund, A. B., & Salovaara-Moring, I. (2009). Media System, Public Knowledge & Democracy: A Comparative Study. *European Journal of Communication*, 24(1), 5–26.

Davis, A. (2007). *The Mediation of Power: A Critical Introduction*. London: Routledge.

Delli Carpini, M., Keeter, S., & Kennamer, D. (1994). Effects of the News Media Environment on Citizen Knowledge of State Politics and Government. *Journalism Quarterly*, 71(2), 443–456.

Delli Carpini, M. X., & Keeter, S. (1996). *What Americans Know about Politics and Why It Matters*. New Haven, CT: Yale University Press.

Demers, D., Craff, D., Choi, Y., & Pessin, B. (1989). Issue Obtrusiveness and the Agenda-Setting Effects of National Network News. *Communication Research*, 16(6), 793–812.

Druckman, J. (2005). Media Matter: How Newspapers and Television News Cover Campaigns and Influence Voters. *Political Communication*, 22(4), 463–481.

Elenbaas, M., Boomgaarden, H., Schuck, A., & De Vreese, C. (2013). The Impact of Media Coverage and Motivation on Performance-Relevant Information. *Political Communication*, 30(1), 1–16.

Elenbaas, M., De Vreese, C., Schuck, A., & Boomgaarden, H. (2012, 2013). Reconciling Passive and Motivated Learning: The Saturation-Conditional Impact of Media Coverage and Motivation on Political Information. *Communication Research*, first online 20 November 2012, DOI 0093650212467032.

Elvestad, E., & Blekesaune, A. (2008). Newspaper Readers in Europe: A Multilevel Study of Individual and National Differences. *European Journal of Communication*, 23(4), 425–447.

Erbring, L., Goldenberg, E., & Miller, A. (1980). Front-Page News and Real-World Cues: A New Look at Agenda-Setting by the Media. *American Journal of Political Science*, 24(1), 16–49.

Esser, F. (2013). Mediatization as a Challenge: Media Logic Versus Political Logic. In H. Kriesi, S. Lavenex, F. Esser, J. Matthes, M. Bühlmann & D. Bochsler (Eds.), *Democracy in the Age of Globalization and Mediatization* (pp. 155–176). Basingstoke: Palgrave Macmillan.

Esser, F., de Vreese, C. H., Strömbäck, J., van Aelst, P., Aalberg, T., Stanyer, J., Lengauer, G., Berganza, R., Legnante, G., Papathanassopoulos, S., Salgado, S., Sheafer, T., & Reinemann, C. (2012). Political Information Opportunities in Europé: A Longitudinal and Comparative Study of Thirteen Television Systems. *International Journal of Press/Politics*, 17(3), 247–274.

Eurobarometer (2012). Media Use in the European Union, Standard Eurobarometer 78. Survey carried out by TNS Opinion & Social at the request of the European Commission, Directorate-General Communication. Available at http://ec.europa.eu/public_opinion/archives/eb/eb78/eb78_media_en.pdf

Gidengil, E. (2008). Media Matter: Election News in Canada. In J. Strömbäck & L. Lee Kaid (Eds.), *The Handbook of Election News Coverage around the World*. New York, NY: Routledge.

Goss, K., & Aday, S. (2003). The Scary World in your Living Room and Neighborhood: Using Local Broadcast News, Neighborhood Crime Rates, and Personal Experience to Test Agenda Setting and Cultivation. *Journal of Communication*, 53(3), 411–426.

Hallin, D. C., & Mancini, P. (2004). *Comparing Media Systems: Three Models of Media and Politics*. New York, NY: Cambridge University Press.

Hjarvard, S. (2013). *The Mediatization of Culture and Society*. London: Routledge.

Hügel, R., Degenhardt, W., & Weiss, H. (1989). Structural Equation Models for the Analysis of the Agenda-setting Process. *European Journal of Communicaiton*, 4(2), 191–210.

Iyengar, S., Curran, J., Brink Lund, A., Salovaara-Moring, I., Hahn, K. S., & Coen, S. (2010). Cross-National Versus Individual-Level Differences in Political Information: A Media Systems Perspective. *Journal of Elections, Public Opinion & Parties*, 20(3), 291–309.

Iyengar, S., Hahn, K., Bonfadelli, H., & Marr, M. (2009). "Dark Areas of Ignorance" Revisited. *Communication Research*, 36(3), 341–358.

Iyengar, S., & Kinder, D. R. (1987). *News That Matters*. Chicago, IL: University of Chicago Press.

Jerit, J., Barabas, J., & Bolsen, T. (2006). Citizens, Knowledge and the Information Environment. *American Journal of Political Science*, 50(2), 266–282.

Kaid, L. L., Gerstlé, J., & Sanders, K. R. (Eds.) (1991). *Mediated Politics in Two Cultures: Presidential Campaigning in the United States and France*. Westport: Praeger.

Kepplinger, H. M. (2002). Mediatization of Politics: Theory and Data. *Journal of Communication*, 52(4), 972–986.

Kinder, D. (1981). Presidents, Prosperity, and Public Opinion. *Public Opinion Quarterly*, 45(1), 1–21.

Lewis-Beck, M. S., & Stegmaier, M. (2007). "Economic models of voting." In R. Dalton & H.-D. Klingemann (Eds.), *The Oxford Handbook of Political Behavior*. Oxford: Oxford University Press.

Livingstone, S. (2009). On the Mediation of Everything. *Journal of Communication*, 59(1), 1–18.

Lundby, K. (2009). Introduction: 'Mediatization' as Key. In K. Lundby (Ed.), *Mediatization. Concept, Changes, Consequences* (pp. 1–18). New York, NY: Peter Lang.

Luskin, R. (1990). Explaining Political Sophistication. *Political Behavior*, 12(4), 331–361.

Mazzoleni, G. (2008a). Mediatization of Politics. In W. Donsbach (Ed.), *The International Encyclopedia of Communication* (Vol. VII, pp. 3047–3051). Malden, MA: Blackwell.

Mazzoleni, G. (2008b). Mediatization of Society. In W. Donsbach (Ed.), *The International Encyclopedia of Communication* (Vol. VII, pp. 3052–3055). Malden, MA: Blackwell.

Mazzoleni, G., & Schulz, W. (1999). Mediatization of Politics: A Challenge for Democracy? *Political Communication*, 16(3), 247–261.

McCombs, M. (2004). *Setting the Agenda: The Mass Media and Public Opinion.* Cambridge, MA: Polity Press.

Mutz, D. (1992). Mass Media and the Depoliticization of Personal Experience. *American Political Science Review*, 36(2), 483–508.

Mutz, D. (1994). Contextualizing Personal Experience: The Role of the Mass Media. *The Journal of Politics*, 56(3), 689–714.

Mutz, D. (1998). *Impersonal Influence: How Perceptions of Mass Collectives Affect Political Attitudes.* Cambridge, MA: Cambridge University Press.

Mutz, D., & Young, L. (2011). Communication and Public Opinion: Plus Ça Change? *Public Opinion Quarterly*, 75(5), 1018–1044.

Nadeau, R., Nevitte, N., Gidengil, E., & Blais, A. (2008). Election Campaigns as Information Campaigns: Who Learns What and Does It Matter? *Political Communication*, 25(3), 229–248.

Nimmo, D., & Combs, J. E. (1983). *Mediated Political Realities.* New York, NY: Longman.

Norris, P., & Curtice, J. (2007). Getting the Message Out: A Two-Step Model of the Role of the Internet in Campaign Communication Flows during the 2005 British General Election. *Journal of Information Technology & Politics*, 4(4), 3–13.

Pew Research Center. (2008). *Internet Overtakes Newspapers as News Outlet.* Washington, DC: Pew Research Center.

Pew Research Center. (2011). *Internet Gains on Television as Public's Main News Source. More Young People Cite Internet than TV.* Washington, DC: Pew Research Center.

Pew Research Center. (2013). *Amid Criticism, Support for Media's "Watchdog" Role Stands Out.* Washington, DC: Pew Research Center.

Price, V., & Zaller, J. (1993). Who Gets the News? Alternative Measures of News Reception and Their Implications for Research. *Public Opinion Quarterly*, 57, 133–164.

Prior, M. (2007). *Post-Broadcast Democracy: How Media Choice Increases Inequality in Political Involvement and Polarizes Elections.* New York, NY: Cambridge University Press.

Prior, M. (2009). The Immensely Inflated News Audience: Assessing Bias in Self-reported News Exposure. *Public Opinion Quarterly*, 73(1), 130–143.

Roessler, P. (1999). The Individual Agenda-Designing Process: How Interpersonal Communication, Egocentric Networks, and Mass Media Shape the Perception of Political Issues by Individuals. *Communication Research*, 26(6), 666–700.

Roessler, P. (2008). Agenda-Setting, Framing and Priming. In W. Donsbach & M. Traugott (Eds.), *The Sage Handbook of Public Opinion Research.* London: Sage.

Scammell, M., & Semetko, H. (2008). Election News Coverage in the U.K. In J. Strömbäck & L. Lee Kaid (Eds.), *The Handbook of Election News Coverage around the World.* New York, NY: Routledge.

Schillemans, T. (2012). *Mediatization of Public Services: How Organizations Adapt to News Media.* Frankfurt am Main: Peter Lang.

Schulz, W. (2004). Reconstructing Mediatization as an Analytical Concept. *European Journal of Communication*, 19(1), 87–101.

Schuman, H., & Presser, S. (1996). *Questions and Answers in Attitude Surveys: Experiments on Question Form, Wording, and Context.* Thousand Oaks: Sage.

Shehata, A. (2013). Active or Passive Learning from Television? Political Information Opportunities and Knowledge Gaps during Election Campaigns. *Journal of Elections, Public Opinion & Parties*, 23(2), 200–222.

Shehata, A., & Strömbäck, J. (2011). A Matter of Context: A Comparative Study of Media Environments and News Consumption Gaps in Europe. *Political Communication*, 28(1), 110–134.

Shehata, A., & Strömbäck, J. (2013). Not (Yet) a New Era of Minimal Effects: A Study of Agenda Setting at the Aggregate and Individual Levels. *International Journal of Press/Politics*, 18(2), 234–255.

Silverstone, R. (2007). *Media and Morality: On the Rise of the Mediapolis*. Cambridge, MA: Polity.

Soroka, S. (2002). Issue Attributes and Agenda-Setting by the Media, the Public, and Policymakers in Canada. *International Journal of Public Opinion Research*, 14(3), 264–285.

Soroka, S., Andrew, B., Aalberg, T., Iyengar, S., Curran, J., Coen, S., Hayashi, K., Jones, P., Mazzoleni, G., Rhee, J., Rowe, D., & Tiffen, R. (2012). Auntie knows Best? Public Broadcasters and Current Affairs Knowledge. *British Journal of Political Science*, 43(4), 719–739.

Strömbäck, J. (2008). Four Phases of Mediatization: An Analysis of the Mediatization of Politics. *The International Journal of Press/Politics*, 13(3), 228–246.

Strömbäck, J. (2009). Att studera valrörelser. In L. Nord & J. Strömbäck (Eds.), *Väljarna, partierna och medierna: En studie av politisk kommunikation i valrörelsen 2006* (pp. 9–28). Stockholm: SNS Förlag.

Strömbäck, J. (2011). Mediatization of Politics: Toward a Conceptual Framework for Comparative Research. In E. P. Bucy & R. L. Holber (Eds.), *Sourcebook for Political Communication Research. Methods, Measures, and Analytical Techniques*. New York, NY: Routledge.

Strömbäck, J., Djerf-Pierre, M., & Shehata, A. (2012). The Dynamics of Political Interest and News Media Consumption: A Longitudinal Perspective. *International Journal of Public Opinion Research*, 25(4), 414–435.

Strömbäck, J., & Esser, F. (2009). Shaping Politics: Mediatization and Media Interventionism. In K. Lundby (Ed.), *Mediatization. Concept, Changes, Consequences* (pp. 205–224). New York, NY: Peter Lang.

Stroud, N. J. (2011). *Niche News: The Politics of News Choice*. New York, NY: Oxford University Press.

Wanta, W., & Hu, Y. (1990). Interpersonal Communication and the Agenda-Setting Process. *Journalism & Mass Communication Quarterly*, 69(4), 847–855.

Watt, J., Mazza, M., & Snyder, L. (1993). Agenda-Setting Effects of Television News Coverage and the Effects Decay Curve. *Communication Research*, 20(3), 408–435.

Zukin, C., & Snyder, R. (1984). Passive Learning: When the Media Environment Is the Message. *Public Opinion Quarterly*, 48(3), 629–638.

7
Mediatization at the Structural Level: Independence from Politics, Dependence on the Market

Linards Udris and Jens Lucht

Whenever we examine the mediatization of politics, we address inherently normative and fundamental issues concerning the quality of democracy (Kriesi, 2013). So far, it seems that media system analyses at the macro level with links to democracy theory have tended to be conceptual and only rarely include empirical tests, such as analyses of media structures and content. At the same time, the empirically rich mediatization research that focuses on the media logic reflected in the media content (the third dimension of mediatization, according to Strömbäck, 2008) relies on sophisticated analyses to explain how structural features, such as the degree of media autonomy (the second dimension of mediatization), shape news coverage. However, this research tends to concentrate on finding mechanisms for specific types of news outlets and devotes less attention to the media system as a whole and the (normative) social implications of these mechanisms. For instance, although it may be possible to explain why a certain media type shows more signs of media logic over the course of time, it would also be useful to know whether this media type becomes more or less representative in the context of a specific media system over time and what this may mean for the quality of democratic debate.

In this chapter, we attempt to work towards this direction and to contribute empirical analyses of two dimensions of mediatization, namely, the second (the degree to which the media have become independent of other political and social institutions) and the third (the degree to which media content and the coverage of politics and current affairs are governed by media logic; Strömbäck, 2008). By building on the theoretical conceptualizations set out in the introductory chapter (see Strömbäck & Esser, in this volume), we will concentrate on concrete empirical and comparative observations and not treat theoretical issues in any detail.[1]

The (de)differentiation of the press at the structural level

According to the mediatization thesis, the media must become a system or an institution in their own right and with their own logic in order to have an independent impact on politics and other social systems. At the level of media structures, this means that the media had to break their organizational ties to the political sphere (and further possible dependencies on other social systems). At the same time, this new autonomy is only fully realized if the media also remain independent of the economic system and follows a logic that exclusively follow market considerations (Habermas, 2006, p. 419). There is, of course, a long tradition of research applying different approaches (field theory, systems theory, sociology of news, etc.) which examines how the media in general and various media outlets in particular position themselves in relation to both the political *and* economic fields (cf. Benson & Hallin, 2007). As regards the structural independence of the media from political actors such as parties, the concept of "press-party parallelism", introduced by Seymour-Ure (1974), has been increasingly referenced in comparative political communication research (e.g., Berkel, 2006), most notably by Hallin and Mancini (2004). In the matter of the structural independence of the media from the market, the research stresses the importance of commercial pressures on media organizations, which have implications for the structure of ownership and the degree of profit-orientation (e.g., Picard, 2004; Wadbring, 2013). One frequently used main indicator captures the difference between public and private broadcasting (e.g., Strömbäck & van Aelst, 2010; Esser, 2008). However, where this difference does not exist (such as in the press sector) or where company data are unavailable, the research has come to rely on another indicator that is measurable and meaningful for cross-national comparative analyses over time, namely, whether a media organization is publicly traded on the stock exchange. This is because market-listed media organizations experience higher shareholder pressures and are more highly profit-driven than other types of media organizations (McMenamin et al., 2012; Benson & Hallin, 2007, p. 28; Benson, 2004, p. 282; Picard, 2004, pp. 7–8).

Along these lines, academics in the field of comparative political communication have argued that media (de)differentiation varies substantially, even within similar Western democracies. Hallin and Mancini (2004) chose political parallelism, a variant of press–party parallelism, as a main indicator to distinguish their three "models of media and politics", namely, the extent to which the media are associated with political parties or follow general political tendencies. In their analysis, the liberal model shows the lowest degree and the polarized-pluralist model the highest degree of political parallelism, with the democratic-corporatist model falling in between. In the polarized-pluralist and democratic-corporatist models, however, political parallelism declines over time. The concept has so far remained on a theoretical level, and few attempts have been made to actually measure the degree of press–party parallelism, especially with regard to comparisons between countries (but see van Kempen, 2007) and particularly across time. Similarly, there is a lack of empirical data that systematically trace the degree of (de)differentiation of the media from the economic system across countries and over time.

Against this theoretical background, we have conducted a cross-spatial and cross-temporal analysis of what Strömbäck (2008) calls the second dimension (the degree to which the media have become independent of other political and social institutions) and the third dimension (the degree to which the media content and coverage of politics and current affairs are governed by media logic) of the mediatization of politics. To cover the three main models of media and politics (as defined by Hallin & Mancini, 2004) at least to a certain extent, we included Great Britain as representative of the liberal model, France as representative of the polarized-pluralist model, and three countries – one large and two small as representatives of the democratic-corporatist model: Germany, Austria and Switzerland. We assume that "size matters" (such as small production and sales markets; Puppis, 2009) and we also wish to demonstrate that Hallin and Mancini's ideal typical models can show considerable internal heterogeneity. We begin our analysis of media structures in the year 1960, representing a time in which, according to Hallin and Mancini (2004, pp. 300–301), the differences between the models were most pronounced and in which the party-oriented press still played an important role in democratic-corporatist countries (cf. Brants & van Praag, 2006). We also include data for 1970, 1980, 1990, 2005 and 2010. This allows us to check whether the three models are converging at the level of media structures, as well as to determine the timing and speed of any possible transformations.

We will initially focus our analysis on the newspapers for theoretical and pragmatic reasons. Taking into account the historical perspective applied by Hallin and Mancini (2004), the "development of the mass circulation press" has played a principal role in shaping the respective media systems to this day (p. 22). On the pragmatic side of the argument, there is a serious lack of comparable data for radio and television across five decades and these five countries, especially considering that we are interested in audience numbers of specific information programs (e.g., *Tagesschau* on ARD) and not of channels in general (e.g., ARD).

By way of structural analysis, we consequently examined the 30 largest-circulation print titles (dailies or weeklies) for their links to political parties, churches, associations and other intermediary institutions. Figure 7.1 shows the number of general news providers with "social and political ties" (marked as black columns) in the five countries over time. General news providers without social and political ties are organized primarily as private businesses. Figure 7.1 subdivides the private press outlets further into

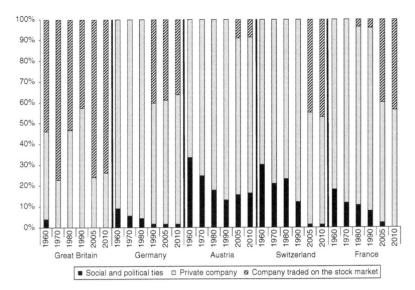

Figure 7.1   Print news providers in Great Britain, Germany, Austria, Switzerland and France, 1960–2010

Note: The graph shows the 30 largest-circulation print news outlets per country and year that are published at least once a week and provide public affairs coverage. The basis for classifying their structural links are (self-) declarations (e.g., "official organ of XY"), personal or organizational relations at a high level (e.g., an editor who also has political functions), and the legal form (e.g., company listed on the stock exchange).

those that are publicly listed ("company traded on the stock market", shown hatched) and those that are not ("private company", shown grey).[2] The percentages given for the three types represent their circulation shares out of the total circulation of all 30 newspapers.[3]

The basic finding is that the emancipation of the press has progressed first and foremost in the liberal system (Great Britain), followed by the largest democratic-corporatist system (Germany) and the polarized-pluralist system (France). By 2010, the share of press outlets with clear ties to social and political actors had dropped to 0% in Britain and France, and 1% or 2% in Germany and Switzerland. In Austria, the process is still underway and the political parallelism of the press is still fairly noticeable.

We can identify at least three reasons for the overall decline in press outlets with social and political ties. First, media providers have been transforming themselves primarily into economic actors, if not into stock exchange-listed companies. In Switzerland, for instance, the *Zürichsee-Zeitung* newspaper had clear links to the Liberal Democrats (a center-right government party) in the 1980s. Its publisher had served as a representative of this party in regional and national parliaments. These connections have now largely disappeared, and the paper was acquired by what is (currently) the largest stock-listed media organization in Switzerland, namely, the Tamedia corporation. We consequently assigned the same newspaper to different categories over the course of time. Second, the circulation of outlets with social and political ties has been falling more rapidly than the circulation of those with no (or significantly fewer) social and political ties. In Austria, for instance, the social-democratic party paper *Arbeiterzeitung* lost a quarter of its circulation from 1960 to 1980, whereas the popular *Kronenzeitung*, published by a private company, gained massively in circulation in the same period, from around 100,000 to almost 900,000. Third, formerly important newspapers linked to "intermediary" actors such as the social-democratic *Arbeiterzeitung* in Austria, *Reynolds News* (associated with the Labour Party in Great Britain), or the Catholic-conservative *Vaterland* in Switzerland, went out of business.

At the same time, there are clear indications that this growing independence from politics coincides with a growing dependence on the market. In all countries examined, listed companies now play a larger role than in the 1960s. Thus, expectations of high shareholder value are on the rise, and more capital is flowing into the press market from companies with no traditional links to journalism.

Comparing these cases, our analysis supports the three models and the argument for a growing convergence towards the liberal model while adding "size" as a factor that explains the heterogeneity within the democratic-corporatist model. As expected, in the liberal model, the differentiation of the press from politics and its commercialization starts much earlier than in the other models. According to our data, Great Britain had only a weak intermediary press in 1960, and private (commercial) providers – often publicly listed – have dominated the press market ever since. This is not to deny certain remaining forms of political parallelism at the level of the audience (van Kempen, 2007) and of content; on the structural side, however, stable links to social and political actors have disappeared. This phenomenon is also reflected by the fact that newspapers do not consistently follow party lines but instead tend to switch sides when this appears to be beneficial for "commercial reasons" (Kuhn, 2007, pp. 217–218), as demonstrated by the famous example of *The Sun* in the 1990s. Typical of a press market that was commercialized early on, we also saw fluctuations in ownership across the decades, with rather frequent selling, reselling and launching of press titles in Great Britain.

Taking a closer look at the democratic-corporatist model, we can observe a degree of heterogeneity because the processes of differentiation and commercialization had begun much later in the small states, whereas Germany exhibits greater similarities to the liberal model. One reason for this is market size, which facilitates economies of scale. Another is the sudden transformation imposed upon Germany by the Western Allies immediately after the Second World War ("zero hour"), which allowed a diversified and somewhat more party-independent press system to develop more quickly than in the small states. For a time, the structures of a small state constrained the rapid transformation of intermediary media providers into purely commercial enterprises. Furthermore, in Switzerland, and even more so in Austria, "pillarization" prevailed longer than in Germany, contributing to the important role of the party press (and vice versa). More recently, the Swiss press has experienced a strong push towards commercialization, with stock corporations becoming more common (from 0% in 1990 to 47% in 2010). Only in Austria's press system do we still observe a significant number of large press outlets with social and political ties (see, for instance, the role of Styria Medien, financed by the *Katholischer Medienverein* of the Diocese of Graz; see Seethaler & Melischek, 2006) and a comparatively minor role for media companies traded on the stock market.

The polarized-pluralist model, represented by France in our sample, offers a more ambivalent picture. As in the other two models, France has seen an emancipation of its press during the period under study, largely because "intermediary" titles such as *L'Humanité* (the organ of the Communist Party) or *La Croix* (Christian-conservative) suffered declining circulation rates and decreasing significance in comparison to (new) titles published by commercial enterprises. Furthermore, outlets forming part of publicly listed conglomerates have become more important, especially in the last two decades. At the same time, to a higher degree than in the other two models, newspapers operating on the polarized-pluralist model often have political ties *and* experience strong shareholder pressures because they are traded on the stock exchange. This situation is best illustrated by Serge Dassault, who integrated *SOC Presse* (which publishes titles such as *Le Figaro*) in his Dassault Group (which includes publicly traded companies from non-media fields) and served as a senate member for the conservative government party UMP. However, we would like to argue that this political involvement differs from a stable "embedding" of the media in a party milieu because it was limited to the principal owner, who was more a business-oriented media tycoon than a political figure. Similar (historical) cases are known from the United States (Udris, 2012).[4]

An often overlooked form of differentiation: Growing stratification of the press

Although the mediatization of politics clearly affects the functional dimension of social differentiation, reviewing the "giants" of social theory reminds us that social processes typically show effects in two additional forms of social differentiation, namely, the stratificatory and segmentary dimensions (Imhof, 2006). Researchers who study mediatization should consequently also address phenomena such as new allocations of power in the context of media concentration and growing inequality, involving an increasing division between "up-market" and "down-market" media (stratificatory) and increasing disentanglement between the political and media domains, so that political systems, especially at regional and supra-national levels, lack a corresponding public sphere (segmentary). Empirically, the literature on media systems and mediatization tends to focus on the functional dimension and, to a lesser degree, on the segmentary dimension, only rarely touching upon questions of power and social (in)equality. This situation may be illustrated by looking at the short length of the chapters on "critiques of differentiation theory" and "the question of power" compared to the overall argument in Hallin and Mancini's (2004, pp. 80–84) book, and at the main criticism by Curran (2011, pp. 36–40), who, in "questioning a new orthodoxy", challenges these models on the grounds that they do not take social inequality into account.

Regardless of which side of the argument one takes, it becomes empirically clear that the process of disentanglement (functional) is accompanied by a process of growing press stratification. This becomes evident when newspapers are systematically classified into "quality press", "mid-market press" and "tabloids/free papers" and we track their importance over time. This classification is based on the assumptions that these three press types exhibit different degrees of media logic and that social divisions are also reflected in these press sectors – typically observed in Great Britain in the distinction of "up-market", "mid-market" and "down-market" media (see Ward, 2007, p. 75; Sparks, 2000, p. 29). Although the tabloid press covers public (as opposed to private) issues less frequently than the other two types (Sparks, 2000), it is subject to greater commercial pressures due to its dependence on street sales, and preferentially addresses the lower social strata as readers or buyers. At the other end of the spectrum, the up-market papers usually offer the highest quality of news reporting and rely more on (loyal) subscribers from the social elites. The mid-market papers usually fall between these two types. Lastly, free or "commuter" papers might not necessarily address the lower social strata, but their high dependence on advertising usually leads to their news content being similar to that of the tabloids, as studies from Switzerland and Austria suggest (fög, 2012; Stark & Magin, 2011). In the following, therefore, we subsume the free papers under the tabloid press.

Our categorization of tabloid, mid-market and quality media is based on an etic approach designed to ensure that press types are comparable across countries and over time. Drawing on a random sample of one week per issue and year, we classified the papers as follows:

Quality papers report more often than the mid-market and tabloid papers on domestic and foreign politics, economics and culture, devote less attention to lifestyle issues and more frequently address "structural changes in the world" (Sparks, 2000), which is also typically seen in an extensive "feuilleton" section. Examples of quality papers are *Le Monde* in France, *Die*

Zeit in Germany, *Neue Zürcher Zeitung* in Switzerland, *The Observer* in Great Britain and *Die Presse* in Austria.

Mid-market papers more often include press titles with a regional focus, such as *Ouest France* (France), *Westdeutsche Allgemeine Zeitung* (Germany), *Kurier* (Austria), *Tages-Anzeiger* (Switzerland) and *Wolverhampton Express & Star* (Great Britain), as well as some national papers like the British *Daily Mail*.

Lastly, the tabloid and free papers often mingle politics with private and human interest issues and often lack differentiated sections. Examples include *Bild* and *Express* in Germany, *Blick* or *20 Minuten* in Switzerland, *Kronenzeitung* in Austria, the *Daily Mirror* in Great Britain, and *Le Parisien* in France.

This classification brings the stratification of the press to light (see Figure 7.2). Furthermore, we can see similar patterns in the degree, timing and speed of these transformations to those we found in the emancipation of the press. The data for Great Britain reflects a commercialized press system, whose dependence on street sales rather than subscriptions puts media organizations under additional pressure to capture the attention of their audience daily. The development of the popular press has been far from linear (cf. also Kuhn, 2007; McNair, 2003), but we see tendencies towards a growing "polarization between prestige and mass newspapers"

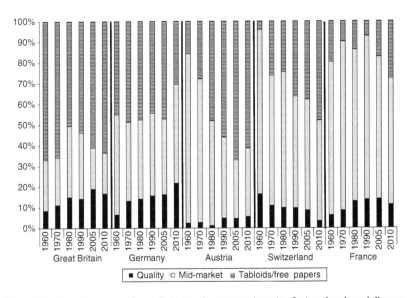

Figure 7.2 Press types in Great Britain, Germany, Austria, Switzerland and France, 1960–2010

Note: Assignment to the three formats (quality, mid-market, tabloid/free paper) was made after examining, for each country, random samples of the 30 largest print news outlets for each year under study. As in Figure 7.1, the percentages represent shares in the total circulation of all 30 papers.

(Curran, 2000, p. 128), with the mid-market press taking up 20% in 2010. In this respect, Germany again shows more similarities to Great Britain and the liberal model than to the other two members of the democratic-corporatist model; it had several important tabloids in 1960 (making up 45% of the cumulative circulation). But it is the only country we examined in which popular papers lost market share (2010: 30%, down from 49% in 1970). In addition to the quality papers, the national and regional "mid-market" newspapers (e.g., *Westdeutsche Allgemeine Zeitung*) still play an important role (2010: 48%) here, reflecting a press market in which publishing houses still do comparably good business (Brüggemann et al., 2012).

Switzerland and Austria again fall into the same category. In both countries, the rise of the tabloid press started late and then developed quickly (Magin, 2013), primarily at the expense of the mid-market papers. In Switzerland, tabloid and free papers now have circulation shares that are practically as high as those of the mid-market papers (2010: 48%, up from 4% in 1960), and in Austria these papers now constitute the majority of the cumulative circulation (2010: 56%, up from 16% in 1960). In the last decade, the "classic" tabloids have suffered from substantial readership losses, but this situation has been more than compensated for by the rise of free papers. Again, France is a case in which this process points in the same direction but starts at a lower level. In view of generally lower newspaper use and a rather "elite" orientation of newspapers (Hallin & Mancini, 2004), it is not surprising to see the tabloids playing a smaller role (2010: 17%) than in the other countries, where the quality and especially the "mid-market" papers with a regional focus have dominated the scene (Adam & Berkel, 2006).

In summary, these findings have clear social and theoretical implications. At a social level, the growing division between quality papers on the one hand, and tabloid and free papers on the other hand, makes it increasingly relevant for researchers to more intensively address questions of readership fragmentation and social cohesion. In terms of comparative research based on the three models of media and politics, our findings on degrees of press autonomy (Figure 7.1) and press sectors pursuing different types of news logic (Figure 7.2) both support the three models and modify them insofar as "size matters", with the small states of Austria and Switzerland experiencing changes later but more rapidly than Germany. Significantly, the growing importance of the tabloid media seems to go hand-in-hand with the disentanglement and commercialization of the press already described. At the level of media structures, both the functional (differentiation from politics) and stratificatory (elite vs. tabloid) dimensions point to an increasing mediatization of politics. The growing importance of the tabloids on the press market means that political actors are increasingly challenged to craft their messages to fit the popular news logic of these papers (the fourth dimension of mediatization). However, with regard to structural implications, the rise of the tabloids puts pressure on the mid-market papers, which may react to this challenge by incorporating more elements based on the logic of the commercial media (the third dimension of mediatization). In the next section, we will examine whether we can find any support for these assumptions and whether mediatization at a structural level affects the actual media content of the mid-market papers.

Only slightly increasing mediatization of media content in mid-market papers ...

A basic argument of the mediatization thesis, which assumes that the four dimensions of mediatization are interrelated, is that media content is increasingly characterized by media logic (Altheide & Snow, 1979; Mazzoleni, 2008). In light of our analysis of media structures presented above, there are good reasons to assume that this is in fact happening, especially in the mid-market papers.

Of course, not all features of media logic are a result of commercial pressures; professionalization and technological change also affect the logic of the media (Esser, 2013, p. 167). One indicator that comes closer to the commercial aspect of media logic is the proportion of "soft news" (Patterson, 2000; Curran et al., 2010, pp. 7–9; fög, 2012). Commercialized or market-driven media organizations devote substantial attention to "soft news" (rather than "hard news" such as political, economic, or cultural issues) because they consider this a viable and promising strategy to capture the attention of an increasingly volatile readership (cf. also Beam, 2003). Soft news can be operationalized on at least four dimensions, as Reinemann et al. (2012) have recently proposed: first, in the *topic* dimension, soft news excludes all topics that are relevant to politics. Second, in the *focus* dimension, a soft news item stresses "individual relevance" rather than "societal relevance", meaning "the personal, private meaning or consequences of the incidents" rather than the "overall meaning [...] for society at large" (Reinemann et al., 2012, p. 237). This can also be described as the *personalization frame*, because this type of news reporting suggests that it is mainly the actions of (a few) individuals, and not the structures in which they are embedded, that actually matter (fög, 2012, p. 466). Although political structures (e.g., Kriesi, 2012) or an "institutionalized personalization" conducted by political actors (Rahat & Sheafer, 2007) influence the degree or level of personalization, there are good reasons for explaining personalization by the process of the commercialization of the media (Esser & Hemmer, 2008, pp. 294–296; Imhof, 2011, pp. 126–127). By blaming politicians personally for grievances and for moral and political failures, and by downplaying the structural bases and the complexity of political problems, the media hope to better connect to their readership (Blumler & Kavanagh, 1999, pp. 219–221).

This *overall personalization frame*, in which actors can still be described in conjunction with their roles, should be differentiated from a *personalization frame without a role focus*, in which the private aspects of an actor come to dominate (fög, 2012, p. 466). Fourth, in the *style* dimension, soft news shows increasing levels of moralization and emotionalization at the expense of cognitive-normative reporting, which could be captured with the *sensationalism frame* (Strömbäck & Dimitrova, 2006; fög, 2012, p. 464). So far, empirical studies on the development of soft news over time provide inconclusive results. In their extensive literature review, Reinemann et al. (2012) show that some studies find an increase in soft news and some do not, whereas others distinguish between different dimensions of soft news and note an increase in some dimensions and a decrease in others.

If we take the mid-market papers as a yardstick and use three of the core indicators just discussed – depoliticization, personalization and sensationalism – our findings suggest a very modest transformation of media content over time. Specifically, we content-analyzed the news coverage of one mid-market paper in each of the five countries in 1960, 1980, and 2005 using constructed week sampling. We selected mid-market papers with comparatively high circulations that were in business for the entire 45-year period. The results displayed in Table 7.1 show that this very modest transformation does not affect all mid-market papers to the same degree, and it does not appear in all indicators. The proportion of *political news coverage* remains more or less stable, at least in relative terms. In the German *Westdeutsche Allgemeine Zeitung*, for instance, political news coverage constitutes close to one-half of all longer articles in our sample, and this amount is almost identical for *Ouest France* and the *Kurier* of Austria. The Swiss *Tages-Anzeiger* peaked in 1980, reaching the levels of the quality papers (Udris & Lucht, 2011, p. 169), but remained closer to the level of other mid-market papers in 1960 and 2005. The British *Wolverhampton Express & Star* remained at a rather low level of political reporting, with no significant changes over time. In the mid-market papers examined here, we found no indication of a depoliticization of media content in the sense that human interest issues were increasingly covered in the "hard news" and mixed news sections. As for country differences, in line with our expectations we see the greatest focus on politics in the polarized-pluralist model, where newspapers, with their generally more "elite" orientation, follow a political logic, and the lowest focus on politics in the liberal model.

As with depoliticization, we find only very moderate evidence for increasing *sensationalism* in the political news coverage. In fact, there is no clear trend over time. Whereas the *Westdeutsche Allgemeine Zeitung* of Germany made less use of the sensationalism frame in 2005 than in 1960, and *Ouest France* generally almost never uses this frame, the *Kurier* in Austria, the Swiss *Tages-Anzeiger,* and, especially, the *Express & Star* in Great Britain, all show a tendency towards sensationalism. The increase in these three papers may

Table 7.1 News coverage in mid-market papers, 1960–2005

	1960	1980	2005
Share of political news coverage (in %)			
Ouest France (*n* = 317)	52%	52%	57%
Westdeutsche Allgemeine (*n* = 458)	47%	45%	48%
Tages-Anzeiger (*n* = 580)	48%	64%	48%
Kurier (*n* = 270)	*	57%	51%
Wolverhampton Express & Star (*n* = 450)	35%	30%	32%
Sensationalism in political news coverage (in %)			
Ouest France (*n* = 169)	0%	1%	0%
Westdeutsche Allgemeine (*n* = 215)	9%	3%	0%
Tages-Anzeiger (*n* = 302)	4%	0%	6%
Kurier (*n* = 143)	*	4%	13%
Wolverhampton Express & Star (*n* = 145)	2%	0%	24%
Personalization in political news coverage (in %) (in brackets: without role focus)			
Ouest France (*n* = 169)	13% (11%)	21% (6%)	13% (13%)
Westdeutsche Allgemeine (*n* = 215)	25% (0%)	24% (1%)	24% (20%)
Tages-Anzeiger (*n* = 302)	20% (0%)	13% (11%)	25% (8%)
Kurier (*n* = 143)	*	19% (4%)	8% (6%)
Wolverhampton Express & Star (*n* = 145)	12% (5%)	10% (0%)	24% (20%)

* no data available for 1960.
Note: The content analysis of six editions per year from five newspapers each yielded 2,075 articles. Out of these articles, 974 dealt with political affairs and were coded for sensationalism and personalization frame.

not be surprising if we bear in mind our earlier finding that the decreasing importance of the mid-market press is most notable in the liberal model as well as in the small states in the democratic-corporatist model. However, the low level of sensationalism and the moderate changes lead us to be skeptical about any substantial increases in sensationalism in the political news coverage.

Our findings regarding the possible *personalization* of politics also yield an ambivalent picture. Overall, there is little increase in the focus on persons rather than collectives, structures, or issues. Some researchers have shown that personalization as such is not a new phenomenon, and media content is not shaped more by the personalization frame today than it used to be (e.g., Wilke & Reinemann, 2001; Vliegenthart et al., 2011). However, personalization rises substantially in the British mid-market paper, in line with our expectations. Additionally, we can observe increasing personalization without a role focus in three of the five papers, which means that actors are increasingly portrayed with no connection to their (functional) roles, and private aspects come to dominate instead. However, in contrast to the sensationalism frame, the British paper is the only one that confirms our expectations regarding the direction of the personalization frame over time. Neither the Austrian nor the Swiss papers show increasing levels (despite radically transformed media structures), while the German paper begins to use the personalization frame more often over time.

In sum, our indicators suggest that most of the mid-market papers we analyzed have proved somewhat resistant to profound changes in content despite major structural transformations in their environment, at least with regard to the three indicators we used. Of course, our analysis was meant to be a "hard test": we measured sensationalism and personalization on the basis of whether they were "dominant" in an article or not. Therefore, the proportion of sensationalism and personalization in the news coverage could be slightly higher if we had measured whether these frames were merely "present" in an article. Despite these limitations, and in line with our expectations and the theoretical models, slight "spill-over" effects resulting from the commercialization of the media structures (i.e. a higher propensity to display media logic) occur most often in the relatively commercialized liberal model (*Wolverhampton Express & Star*). In this paper, the proportion of political reporting was low to begin with, and the share of sensationalism and personalization, especially without a role focus, is increasing. However, neither the proportion nor the direction of the other indicators of soft news corresponded to our findings on the changing media structure in the two other models. This leads us to conclude that the presence of media logic has not necessarily increased significantly *within* certain media types, but has increased at the level of media systems as a whole due to shifts in the *proportions of* the three media types (tabloid, mid-market and quality).

... But growing mediatization of politics at the media system level

To address shifts in the sectoral shares of media types and to provide a more nuanced and more representative picture of the mediatization of politics at the systemic level, we ought to account for other important media types from television, radio and the online sector. We will do so by focusing on Switzerland: this is an interesting case because the structures of the press changed here later but more rapidly than in the other countries analyzed. The findings suggest that media markets in small countries such as Switzerland are typically strongly affected by the processes of commercialization and globalization (see Puppis, 2009, pp. 10–11). However, these transformations must be considered against possible changes in broadcasting, as small states typically tend to adopt a regulatory approach to counter these pressures (by means of strong public service broadcasting), as well as changes in the online sector, which is largely out of regulators' control. First, it is important to determine the degree of media logic demonstrated by different media in comparison to others (at meso and micro levels). Second, it is important to determine what role these different media play in a given media system (at macro level). In the following analysis, we examine news content (i.e. political news coverage in Switzerland) from 37 different news outlets that can be subsumed under several parent categories as shown in Table 7.2. Typically, outlets within the same media type share certain characteristics, such as similar business models (e.g., reliance on advertising rather than subscription), ownership structures (e.g., party papers, stock corporation), political or legal frameworks (e.g., public broadcaster with official mandate vs. lightly regulated commercial provider) and production schedules (weekly, daily, 24/7). Thus, we follow Strömbäck's and van Aelst's (2010) appeal to systematically use "media types" as "structural antecedents" of news coverage to explain why the media are shaped differently by media logic. Turning to the systems level, we show the actual media use of these media types and how this has changed in the last decade, for which data are available.

The findings presented in Table 7.2 come from a large-scale content analysis (fög, 2012), a project similar to the "State of the News Media" annual report by the Project for Excellence in Journalism (PEJ 2013). The results suggest both a clear stratification of the degree of soft news among the media types and a clear stratification with regard to changes in media use in the last decade. Again, we used the dimensions of soft news as indicators of the commercial aspects of media logic. This analysis reveals that different media types are shaped by commercial media logic to substantially different degrees. Additionally, with very few exceptions, the four indicators point in the same direction: a higher focus on politics tends to go hand-in-hand with fewer elements of media logic within the political news coverage, especially lower use of the overall personalization frame and the sensationalism frame and, partially, the type of personalization that does not focus on a role.[5] Overall, this large-scale content analysis shows remarkable differences not only (and not mainly) between media channels but also between media types. In the press sector, the share of attention to politics is lowest in the tabloid dailies (19%) and free commuter papers (25%) and highest in paid-for dailies. This is more apparent in the quality paper (73%) published by a non-listed media company than in the more regionally focused

Table 7.2 Soft news in media types in Switzerland (2011) and change in media use

	News coverage in general		Political news coverage				Media use	
	Topic dimension (focus on politics)	n	Personalization (overall)	Personalization (without role focus)	Sensationalism	n	2011 (online: 2010)	Change since 2001 (online: since 2005)
PRESS								
Quality daily (1)	73%	484	26%	1%	1%	355	122,803	−28%
Regional/mid-market dailies (3)	57%	1,252	34%	4%	3%	711	324,317	−25%
Tabloid dailies (2)	19%	1,033	43%	8%	20%	220	265,467	−29%
Free commuter papers (2)	25%	502	40%	2%	6%	126	699,612	133%
Sunday and weekly papers (5)*	56%	1,053	33%	3%	15%	593	582,032	66%
NEWSPAPER INTERNET SITES								
Quality daily (1)	64%	402	35%	1%	0%	258	9,042,914	105%
Regional/mid-market dailies (3)	44%	1,013	37%	2%	3%	462	16,363,351	267%
Tabloid dailies (2)	20%	685	51%	4%	12%	128	22,664,235	221%
Free commuter papers (2)	35%	774	45%	2%	6%	270	16,842,125	246%

RADIO NEWSCASTS								
Public broadcasting (4)	64%	1,837	24%	1%	0%	1,190	1,070,600	−23%
Private broadcasting (4)	46%	1,318	25%	2%	1%	599	97,900	13%
TV NEWSCASTS								
Public broadcasting (4)	55%	1,847	30%	2%	2%	1,021	1,780,100	−27%
Private broadcasting (4)	37%	1,279	30%	3%	9%	472	111,400	1%
All media types (% average, *n* total)	**46%**	**13,479**	**35%**	**3%**	**6%**	**6,405**		

* These Sunday and weekly papers do not offer newspaper Internet sites.

Note: Content analysis of randomly sampled front-page and lead stories published between January and December 2011 by 37 Swiss news outlets (fög, 2012). Data on audience use of these outlets based on newspaper circulation rates (WEMF), online site visits (Netmetrix), and viewers or listeners (Mediapulse).

Reading example: Two of the newspaper Internet sites are from tabloid dailies. They devote an average of 20% of their stories to politics (*n* = 685). Of these, 51% use a personalization frame, 4% a personalization frame without a role focus, and 12% a sensationalism frame. The audience of these two news sites grew by 221% between 2005 and 2011.

"mid-market" dailies (57%), all of which are published by the stock corporation Tamedia (see also fög, 2012, p. 74). Similar disparities can be observed in the websites of the different newspaper types, and in television and radio stations with different ownership structures. Interestingly, online news sites tend to perform worse than their printed parent papers – mostly due to a lack of resources and a faster news cycle. Thus, one main result is that what matters are not the actual channels (print, broadcast, online) but rather the outlet types and their structural conditions. Specific structures, such as the overall revenue and the level of dependence on advertising (e.g., paid dailies vs. free commuter papers), the targeting of specific social strata (e.g., tabloid papers) and the type of (statutory) public service obligations to produce hard news (public vs. private broadcasting), are closely related to varying levels of soft news.

This stratification of the Swiss media system is apparent not only in terms of its media content but also of actual media use and changes in this use. Taking the developments in the last decade as a yardstick, we can clearly see that the media types that offer more soft news are on the rise, whereas those that offer less soft news suffer audience losses. Public broadcasting programs, which continue to play a dominant role in the radio and television sector, and the quality paper *Neue Zürcher Zeitung* lost approximately a quarter of their audience in ten years. In contrast, the free commuter papers, the Sunday and weekly papers as well as all examined online news sites (especially those offering less political news coverage) have been enjoying audience gains in this period. Thus, at the macro level, an increasingly commercialized media system, intensified by the new media, tends to lead to further stratification and, with regard to the quality of the news coverage offered to citizens, to less favorable "political news environments" (Shehata & Strömbäck, 2011; fög, 2012, pp. 22–23).

Conclusion

We conclude our discussion by reiterating that press systems in Western Europe have experienced an emancipation from their former social and political ties and a growing dependence on the market, a process reflected in the growing number of media organizations traded on the stock market. In addition to this transformation of media structures in the functional dimension in the last five decades, they have experienced substantial transformations in the stratificatory dimension, which is usually overlooked by mediatization research. Hence, we see not only a growing dependence of the press on the market but also an increase in tabloid and free papers offering lower-quality journalism and a growing division between down-market and up-market papers at the systems level, primarily at the expense of the mid-market papers. This wider theoretical perspective allows the ramifications of mediatization to be studied more comprehensively, thus countering the trends in research on media performance that have shifted "from broad issues of public purpose" to a narrow focus on "particular features of content or use that can provide quantifiable measures and indicators" (McQuail, 2013, p. 62). In the field of comparative political communications, the stratificatory dimension adds further proof of the level of "fitness" of the three models of media and politics proposed by Hallin and Mancini (2004). A comparison of these processes of commercialization and stratification between the varying cases based on our results primarily confirms the three models as well as their authors' argument for a convergence towards the liberal model. However, we also showed that specific path dependencies resulting from former levels of pillarization and market size have an impact on the degree and timing of this commercialization and stratification of the press, which leads to heterogeneity within the democratic-corporatist model. Hence, these transformations of media structures fit the three models, but only with certain qualifications.

Apart from this clearly visible mediatization of politics in the second dimension, our findings on the mediatization of politics in terms of media content, the third dimension, are ambivalent. Our content analysis, which captured several dimensions of soft news and compared mid-market papers across countries and over time, suggests a slight increase in media logic in the liberal model, but only very modest trends in the other countries. Further research, including a wider media sample, is naturally needed to substantiate these findings. Furthermore, qualitative case studies may be better suited than constructed week sampling to capture the alleged increase in sensationalist news waves or "media hypes" (cf. Vasterman, 2005), for instance. Nevertheless, although the results for the British case fit the expectation that factors at the media system level are especially influential for journalism (cf. Hanitzsch, 2008), the somewhat surprising findings regarding the other four cases challenge the notion of more or less direct causal links between structural change at the macro (market composition) and meso (media organizations) levels, and the micro level (news content features). These findings indicate the resilience of certain media types, which position themselves quite clearly towards other types of journalism. Thus, the mediatization of politics is intensified not so much by the relatively stable content of the mid-market papers as by the decreasing importance of these papers in the media system in favor of the tabloid media.

Ideally, of course, further research would map the degree of mediatization on this third dimension beyond the press sector, however important that may still be. The case of Switzerland shows us that the processes of commercialization and stratification are apparent in other media types, including radio, television and newspaper websites. A large-scale content analysis of 37 media outlets and programs and of media use shows that, first, media content is heavily stratified along different media types. Thus, media types and the structural conditions they share clearly matter with regard to the degree of media logic. Second, the media types that show fewer elements of media logic and soft news, most notably the regional "mid-market" press, the quality press and public broadcasting, have been losing substantial parts of their audience (and advertising revenue). Conversely, the media types that offer more soft news have gained in importance. Strikingly, the "new media" (i.e. newspaper websites) all show a higher degree of soft news than their counterparts in the press, further contributing to the commercialization and stratification of the media system. One major implication of our studies is that future research on the mediatization of politics should pay even more attention to the representativeness of media outlets and media types and their shifting importance in a media system. Audience numbers are one possible proxy, but to obtain a more nuanced picture, the research should add survey data on political actors (to examine, for instance, which media types are claimed to have an impact on citizens and politics) as well as content data on inter-media agenda-setting (Vliegenthart & Walgrave, 2008). Despite the limitations of our studies, the cases of Austria and, especially, of Switzerland, show that small media markets tend to be particularly vulnerable to commercialization and stratification processes, so that media systems move substantially towards a "market model" within a relatively short period of time. This is an important finding because media systems that do not rely on the "market model" tend to promote political learning, knowledge and participation and to reduce social inequality (cf. Curran et al., 2009, p. 22; Imhof, 2011, pp. 132–135). From a comparative perspective, to better understand the transformation of Western democracies through the process of mediatization we believe it is necessary to consider not only the overall degree of media autonomy, commercialization and stratification but also the timing and speed of this process. Thus, Germany and Great Britain might show higher levels of politically independent, commercialized media and a generally high importance of tabloid media, but journalists and political actors (and citizens) in these countries have had time to adapt to these transformations. In France, Austria and, especially, Switzerland, this late but somewhat rapid process might be perceived by these groups as particularly pervasive, shifting formerly stable role expectations (perhaps only temporarily). In summary, examining the timing and speed of the transformation of media structures and comparing them with adaptation processes by political actors and audiences may prove a fruitful avenue for further research.

Notes

1. This chapter draws on findings from two large-scale projects. The first one, "Democracy in a Media Society", part of the National Center of Competence in Research on Challenges to Democracy in the 21st Century (NCCR Democracy), was funded by the Swiss National Science Foundation. The second project, an ongoing

media monitoring initiative on "The Quality of the News Media in Switzerland", is funded by various foundations and donors (for a list, see fög, 2012, p. 19). The authors are grateful for this support.

2. We assume that being traded on the stock market is more influential for a news organization than having a proprietor with political ties. Thus, a press outlet controlled by a "media tycoon" with political ties that, at the same time, is part of a conglomerate with publicly traded companies (e.g., newspapers belonging to French businessman and politician Serge Dassault) is coded "company traded on the stock market" and not "social and political ties".

3. List of consulted sources for circulation rates, 1960–2010: Österreichische Auflagenkontrolle, Pressehandbuch, Handbuch Österreichs Presse, Werbung, Grafik, Melischek and Seethaler (1999) (Austria), Stamm Leitfaden für Presse und Werbung, Presse- und Medienhandbuch Stamm, IVW Quartalsauflage (Germany), Répértoire de la presse française, Association pour le côntrole de la diffusion des médias (OJD) (France), The newspaper press directory and advertisers' guide (and subsequent publications by Benn's Brothers, based on circulation data from ABC), Seymour-Ure (1996), www.abc.org.uk, www.newspapersoc.org.uk (Great Britain), Schweizerischer Zeitungstarif, WEMF Auflagenbulletin, Impressum (Switzerland).

4. See, for instance, the case of newspaper publisher W. R. Hearst, who was elected a Congressman for the Democratic Party twice and tried to get his party to nominate him as a candidate for the US presidency in 1924. Interestingly, nowhere in the literature are Hearst's newspapers described as belonging to the "party press", and no one claims that the American press market in the interwar years showed high levels of press-party parallelism, despite the dominance of the Hearst papers (cf. Udris, 2012).

5. The only exceptions are private broadcasts. In radio, low resources in terms of news staff translate into a high reliance on factual, macro-level news agency reports, which are more or less "read out loud". Private television broadcasters use the sensationalism frame fairly often, but, as argued above, the personalization of politics cannot be observed more frequently in this media sector.

References

Adam, S., & Berkel, B. (2006). Media Structures as an Obstacle to the Europeanization of Public Spheres? Development of a Cross-National Typology. In M. Maier & J. Tenscher (Eds.), *Campaigning in Europe – Campaigning for Europe: Political Parties, Campaigns, Mass Media and the European Parliament Elections 2004* (pp. 45–66). Berlin: Lit.

Altheide, D. L., & Snow, R. P. (1979). *Media Logic.* Beverly Hills, London: Sage.

Beam, R. A. (2003). Content Differences between Daily Newspapers with Strong and Weak Market Orientations. *Journalism and Mass Communication Quarterly*, 80(2), 368–390.

Benson, B. (2004). Bringing the Sociology of Media Back In. *Political Communication*, 21(3), 275–292.

Benson, R., & Hallin, D. C. (2007). How States, Markets and Globalization Shape the News: The French and US National Press, 1965–1997. *European Journal of Communication*, 22(27), 27–48.

Berkel, B. (2006). Political Parallelism in News and Commentaries on the Haider Conflict: A Comparative Analysis of Austrian, British, German, and French Quality Newspapers. *Communications*, 31(1), 85–104.

Blumler, J. G. & Kavanagh, D. (1999). The Third Age of Political Communication: Influences and Features. *Political Communication*, 16(3), 209–230.

Brants, K., & van Praag, P. (2006). Signs of Media Logic: Half a Century of Political Communication in the Netherlands. *Javnost/The Public*, 13(1), 24–40.

Brüggemann, M., Esser, F., & Humprecht, E. (2012). The Strategic Repertoire of Publishers in the Media Crisis: The "Five C" Scheme in Germany. *Journalism Studies*, 13(5–6), 742–752.

Curran, J. (2000). Rethinking Media and Democracy. In J. Curran & M. Gurevitch (Eds.), *Mass Media and Society* (pp. 120–154). London: Arnold.

Curran, J. (2011). *Media and Democracy*. London: Routledge.

Curran, J., Iyengar, S., Brink Lund, A., & Salovaara-Moring, I. (2009). Media System, Public Knowledge and Democracy: A Comparative Study. *European Journal of Communication*, 24(1), 5–26.

Curran, J., Salovaara-Moring, I., Coen, S., & Iyengar, S. (2010). Crime, Foreigners and Hard News: A Cross-national Comparison of Reporting and Public Perception. *Journalism*, 11(1), 3–19.

Esser, F. (2008). Dimensions of Political News Cultures: Sound Bite and Image Bite News in France, Germany, Great Britain, and the United States. *The International Journal of Press/Politics*, 13(4), 401–428.

Esser, F. (2013). Mediatization as a Challenge: Media Logic versus Political Logic. In H. Kriesi, S. Lavenex, F. Esser, J. Matthes, M. Bühlmann & D. Bochsler (Eds.), *Democracy in the Age of Globalization and Mediatization* (pp. 155–176). Basingstoke: Palgrave Macmillan.

Esser, F., & Hemmer, K. (2008). Characteristics and Dynamics of Election News Coverage in Germany. In J. Strömbäck & L. Lee Kaid (Eds.), *The Handbook of Election News Coverage around the World* (pp. 289–307). New York: Routledge.

fög – Forschungsbereich Öffentlichkeit und Gesellschaft/Universität Zürich (Ed.) (2012). *Jahrbuch 2012 Qualität der Medien. Schweiz – Suisse – Svizzera*. Basel: Schwabe.

Habermas, J. (2006). Political Communication in Media Society: Does Democracy Still Enjoy an Epistemic Dimension? The Impact of Normative Theory on Empirical Research. *Communication Theory*, 16(4), 411–426.

Hallin, D. C., & Mancini, P. (2004). *Comparing Media Systems: Three Models of Media and Politics*. Cambridge: Cambridge University Press.

Hanitzsch, T. (2008). Comparing Media Systems Reconsidered: Recent Development and Directions for Future Research. *Journal of Global Mass Communication*, 1(3/4), 111–117.

Imhof, K. (2006). Mediengesellschaft und Medialisierung. *Medien & Kommunikationswissenschaft, M & K*, 54(2), 191–215.

Imhof, K. (2011). *Die Krise der Öffentlichkeit: Kommunikation und Medien als Faktoren des sozialen Wandels*. Frankfurt am Main: Campus.

Kriesi, H. (2012). Personalization of National Election Campaigns. *Party Politics*, 18(6), 825–844.

Kriesi, H. (2013). Conclusion: An Assessment of the State of Democracy Given the Challenges of Globalization and Mediatization. In H. Kriesi, S. Lavenex, F. Esser, J. Matthes, M. Bühlmann & D. Bochsler (Eds.), *Democracy in the Age of Globalization and Mediatization* (pp. 202–215). Basingstoke: Palgrave Macmillan.

Kuhn, R. (2007). *Politics and the Media in Britain*. Basingstoke: Palgrave Macmillan.

Magin, M., & Stark, B. (2011). Österreich – Land ohne Leuchttürme? Qualitätszeitungen im Spannungsfeld zwischen publizistischer Leistung und strukturellen Zwängen. In R. Blum, K. Imhof, H. Bonfadelli & O. Jarren (Eds.),

Krise der Leuchttürme öffentlicher Kommunikation – Vergangenheit und Zukunft der Qualitätsmedien (pp. 97–114). Wiesbaden: VS Verlag.

Magin, M. (2013). Die "Abflachungsspirale" – Fakt oder Fiktion? Boulevardisierungstendenzen in der Wahlkampfberichterstattung deutscher und österreichischer Tageszeitungen (1949–2006). In T. Roessing & N. Podschuweit (Eds.), Politische Kommunikation in Zeiten des Medienwandels (pp. 257–287). Berlin: de Gruyter.

Mazzoleni, G. (2008). Media Logic. In W. Donsbach (Ed.), *The International Encyclopedia of Communication* (pp. 3052–3055). Oxford: Blackwell.

McMenamin, I., Flynn, R., O'Malley, E., & Rafter, K. (2012). Commercialism and Election Framing: A Content Analysis of Twelve Newspapers in the 2011 Irish General Election. *The International Journal of Press/Politics*, 18(2), 167–187.

McNair, B. (2003). *News and Journalism in the UK*. London: Routledge.

McQuail, D. (2013). Media Structure and Performance: Reflections on a Changed Environment. In M. Puppis, M. Künzler & O. Jarren (Eds.), *Media Structures and Media Performance. Medienstrukturen und Medienperformanz* (pp. 45–66). Vienna: Verlag der Österreichischen Akademie der Wissenschaften.

Melischek, G., & Seethaler, J. (Eds.) (1999). *Die Wiener Tageszeitungen: Eine Dokumentation. Bd. 5: 1945–1955. Mit einem Überblick über die österreichische Tagespresse der Zweiten Republik bis 1998*. Frankfurt am Main: Lang.

Patterson, T. E. (2000). *Doing Well and Doing Good: How Soft News and Critical Journalism are Shrinking the News Audience and Weakening Democracy – and What News Outlets Can Do about It*. Cambridge: Harvard University, Joan Shorenstein Center on the Press, Politics, and Public Policy.

Pew Research Center. (2013). *The Pew Research Center's Project for Excellence in Journalism. The State of the News Media 2013: An Annual Report on American Journalism*. http://stateofthemedia.org/, date accessed 15 May 2013.

Picard, R. G. (2004). Commercialism and Newspaper Quality. *Newspaper Research Journal*, 25(1), 54–65.

Puppis, M. (2009). Media Regulation in Small States. *International Communication Gazette*, 71(1–2), 7–17.

Rahat, G., & T. Sheafer (2007). The Personalization(s) of Politics: Israel, 1949–2003. *Political Communication*, 24(1), 65–80.

Reinemann, C., Stanyer, J., Scherr, S., & Legnante, G. (2012). Hard and Soft News: A Review of Concepts, Operationalizations and Key Findings. *Journalism*, 13(2), 221–239.

Seethaler, J., & Melischek, G. (2006). Die Pressekonzentration in Österreich im europäischen Vergleich [Press concentration in European comparison]. *Österreichische Zeitschrift für Politikwissenschaft* [Austrian Journal for Political Science], 35(4), 337–360.

Seymour-Ure, C. (1974). *The Political Impact of Mass Media*. London: Constable.

Seymour-Ure, C. (1996). *The British Press and Broadcasting since 1945*. Oxford: Blackwell.

Shehata, A., & Strömbäck, J. (2011). A Matter of Context: A Comparative Study of Media Environments and News Consumption Gaps in Europe. *Political Communication*, 28(1), 110–134.

Sparks, C. (2000). Introduction: The Panic over Tabloid News. In C. Sparks & J. Tulloch (Eds.), *Tabloid Tales. Global Debates over Media Standards* (pp. 1–40). Oxford: Rowman & Littlefield.

Strömbäck, J. (2008). Four Phases of Mediatization: An Analysis of the Mediatization of Politics. *The International Journal of Press/Politics*, 13(3), 228–246.

Strömbäck, J., & Dimitrova, D. V. (2006). Political and Media Systems Matter: A Comparison of Election News Coverage in Sweden and the United States. *The Harvard International Journal of Press/Politics*, 11(4), 131–147.

Strömbäck, J., & van Aelst, P. (2010). Exploring Some Antecedents of the Media's Framing of Election News: A Comparison of Swedish and Belgian Election News. *The International Journal of Press/Politics*, 15(1), 41–59.

Udris, L. (2012). The Press and the Repeal of National Prohibition. In T. Welskopp & A. Lessoff (Eds.), *Fractured Modernity – America Confronts Modern Times, 1890s to 1940s* (pp. 97–127). München: Oldenbourg.

Udris, L., & Lucht, J. (2011). Qualitätsmedien in Pressesystemen: Wandel der Medienstrukturen gleich Wandel der Medieninhalte? In R. Blum, H. Bonfadelli, K. Imhof & O. Jarren (Eds.), *Krise der Leuchttürme öffentlicher Kommunikation – Vergangenheit und Zukunft der Qualitätsmedien* (pp. 151–176). Wiesbaden: VS Verlag für Sozialwissenschaften.

van Kempen, H. (2007). Media-Party Parallelism and Its Effects: A Cross-National Comparative Study. *Political Communication*, 24(3), 303–320.

Vasterman, P. L. M. (2005). Media-Hype: Self-Reinforcing News Waves, Journalistic Standards and the Construction of Social Problems. *European Journal of Communication*, 20(4), 508–530.

Vliegenthart, R., Boomgaarden, H. G., & Boumans, J. W. (2011). Changes in Political News Coverage: Personalization, Conflict and Negativity in British and Dutch Newspapers. In K. Brants & K. Voltmer (Eds.), *Political Communication in Postmodern Democracy: Challenging the Primacy of Politics* (pp. 92–110). Basingstoke: Palgrave Macmillan.

Vliegenthart, R., & Walgrave, S. (2008). The Contingency of Intermedia Agenda Setting: A Longitudinal Study in Belgium. *J&MC Quarterly*, 85(4), 860–877.

Wadbring, I. (2013). Levels of Commercialisation. In M. Puppis, M. Künzler & O. Jarren (Eds.), *Media Structures and Media Performance. Medienstrukturen und Medienperformanz* (pp. 119–134). Vienna: Verlag der Österreichischen Akademie der Wissenschaften.

Ward, G. (2007). UK National Newspapers. In P. J. Anderson & G. Ward (Eds.), *The Future of Journalism in the Advanced Democracies* (pp. 73–88). Aldershot: Ashgate.

Wilke, J., & Reinemann, C. (2001). Do the Candidates Matter? Long-Term Trends of Campaign Coverage – A Study of the German Press since 1949. *European Journal of Communication*, 16(3), 291–314.

8
Mediatization of News: The Role of Journalistic Framing

Claes H. de Vreese

Framing has become one of the most popular concepts in the field of communication science. Recent overviews all document the popularity and tremendous increase in the use of the concept (Borah, 2011; Chong & Druckman, 2007b; d'Angelo & Kuypers, 2009; de Vreese & Lecheler, 2012; Matthes, 2009, 2012; Scheufele & Tewksbury, 2007; Vliegenthart & van Zoonen, 2011). Despite this proliferation, the framing concept has virtually gone unnoticed in the also burgeoning literature on mediatization (Mazzoleni, 1987; Mazzoleni & Schulz, 1999; Esser, 2013; Strömbäck, 2008). This is surprising since the notions of framing and mediatization would benefit from more simultaneous consideration. In this chapter, I develop an argument for the linkages between framing and mediatization, show how in particular journalistic news framing is a key indicator of mediatization, and reflect on the consequences of different types of news framing. The chapter first defines and identifies *journalistic news frames*. This then becomes an articulation of a media and journalism perspective at the intersection between framing and mediatization research.

Journalistic news frames are frames that play a transformative role vis-à-vis frames sponsored by (political) elites. They take as their starting point journalistic discretion and the autonomy of journalists, they focus on what journalists and news media organizations actively do to the topics they select and they stress the adaptation and modification of frames from elites. For example, in a policy discussion on a welfare issue where two political actors offer different framings of the topic, a journalist or news organization may transform this into a story focusing on a human example of the implementation of a new policy. Or the policy discussion can become subsidiary to a story focusing on the political conflict and disagreement between the political actors while also juxtaposing their two frames. Both cases are examples of journalistic news frames through which a template is offered for how to understand an issue or event. The journalistic news frame stresses some aspects of the case and pushes others to the background and the frame highlights the *active* role of journalists in constructing news stories, a process which is at the core of mediatization.

Mediatization

As the current volume acknowledges, mediatization is a term that has been used by many with different meanings. According to Mazzoleni and Schulz (1999), it is a process by which politics has "lost its autonomy, has become dependent in its central functions on mass media, and is continuously shaped by interactions with mass media" (p. 250). Strömbäck and Esser (2014b) look at the concept more comprehensively and define the mediatization of politics as "a long-term process through which the importance and influence of media in political processes and over political institutions, organizations and actors has increased". Specifically they introduce four dimensions of mediatization, based on Strömbäck (2008, 2011; Strömbäck & Esser, 2009). In their conceptualization, the third dimension refers to "the degree to which media content and the coverage of politics and society is governed by media logic as opposed to political logic" (Esser & Strömbäck, 2014a). As they argue, the second dimension, referring to the degree to which media have become independent from other political and social institutions, is a prerequisite for the third dimension. In the third dimension, the crucial question at stake is whether "news media coverage reflect news media's professional, commercial or technological needs and interests, rather than the needs and interests of political institutions and actors" (Esser & Strömbäck, 2014b). If the latter is the case, this would be seen as news coverage governed by media logic. They highlight *"media interventionism"* (Esser, 2008) and the *"media's discretionary power"* (Semetko et al., 1991) as additional indicators that the news is actively shaped by media logic. Referring to the former, Esser (2008) investigated news in four countries across time. He found that journalistic voices are more heard than politicians' voices. Moreover, he found that the more controlled and tightly managed political campaigns are, the less journalists rely on soundbites and the more they provide input in the news. Blumler and Gurevitch (see Semetko et al., 1991) distinguished between sacerdotal and pragmatic approaches to news reporting. The former is indicative of a respectful approach to politics, where the agenda and framing are largely determined by politics and the latter is indicative of a selective approach, where politics is packaged according to the mechanisms of news selection.

In research on the third dimension of mediatization, the framing concept is, however, virtually absent (but see Strömbäck & Dimitrova, 2011). Strömbäck and Esser (2014b) mention in passing that the mediatization of politics includes traditional media effects – such as, for example, framing. As will become clear below, some frames are highly relevant for the mediatization literature as well as relevant and consequential for public understanding of politics.

News framing: A process

The research on journalistic news frames is contextualized by long research traditions in neighboring disciplines. Research in political science has been particularly occupied with the effects of elite framing of political issues (Zaller, 1992). Research in economics and psychology has been concerned with the behavioral consequences of framing and the underlying mechanisms (Kahneman & Tversky, 1984). Studies in sociology have paid attention to power relations and how frames interact with the social and cultural surroundings (Gamson, 1992). For communication science, the potential of the framing concept is its integrative nature (Reese, 2007). To realize this potential, it is important to stress that framing is a *process* (de Vreese, 2005a; Matthes, 2012; Scheufele, 1999). However, most studies tend to focus *either* on the analysis and presence of frames *or* on the effects of framing. In the exploding literature on how different issues are framed, there seems to be no limit to the number of operationalizations of frames (Hertog & McLeod, 2001) or to the issues that are analyzed. News framing helps to understand dynamic processes that involve frame-building (how frames emerge), the presence and development of frames in the media and frame-setting (the interplay between frames and citizens). Entman (1993) noted that frames have several locations, including the communicator, the text, the receiver and in the surrounding culture. These locations emphasize framing as a process that consists of distinct stages: frame-building, frame-setting and individual and societal level consequences of framing (d'Angelo, 2002; Hänggli, 2012; Matthes, 2012; de Vreese, 2005a; Scheufele, 1999).

Frame-building concerns the interaction between different actors over how to frame an issue and how this, at the end of the day, is framed in the news. Most issues are open for multiple interpretations and framing strategies. Journalists are in a position to choose or modify frames that are offered by actors and bring in their own angles and frames (which is at the core of the notion of journalistic news frames). Journalists are thus active actors that define the coverage, with a considerable amount of autonomy and discretion. Frame-building thus refers to *the process of competition, selection, and modification of frames from elites or strategic communicators by the media*. This process is influenced by forces internal to the news room and news organizations as well as by external forces such as political elites, social movements or interest groups. The influence of these external forces is apparent, for example, when journalists use parts of political speeches, or "sound-bites", to illustrate an issue whereas the influence of internal forces is visible in the structure and emphasis of a news story. The forces endogenous to the news organization corroborate Shoemaker and Reese's (1996) general observations regarding the multiple influences on news production. More specifically, de Vreese (2005a) names internal factors such as editorial policies and news values, which shape the day-to-day work of journalists, as particularly relevant for understanding the frame-building process. Others have emphasized factors such as the type or political orientation of a medium that a journalist is working for (Donsbach, 2004) or how more general role concepts can affect news content (van Dalen et al., 2012). Elites, political parties and their staff are engaged in attempts that involve unprecedented resources to manage campaigns, streamline communication and marketing, manage public relations and affect the news coverage. Even after an election, strategic communication is an integral part of governing (Sanders, 2011). The media, meanwhile, appear to have become more commercialized (Hamilton, 2004), more interpretive (Salgado & Strömbäck, 2012), more critical towards political institutions and actors (Lengauer et al., 2012), more focused on covering politics as a strategic game (Aalberg et al., 2012) and more inclined to deconstruct strategies of elites.

Currently we know little about the conditions under which journalists or elite sources are more or less likely to dominate the news framing. Arguably, in line with the mediatization literature, the more elites control the news framing, the less mediatization dominates and vice versa. Scheufele (1999) voiced the idea that journalists are most likely to adapt elite framing, when the issue at stake is "relatively new" (p. 116) on the media agenda. Extrapolating from indexing theory (Bennett et al., 2006), we would also expect a strong dominance of elite framing. These propositions, however, are still open for empirical testing. At the individual level, Druckman (2001a, 2001b, 2004) proposes an alternative perspective and offers evidence of the conditions under which elite framing does *not* take place (see also Baden, 2010). He focuses mostly on the limits of framing vis-à-vis citizens' attitudes, i.e., when framing effects are limited by, for example, the credibility of sources. However, there is good reason to assume that if citizens are sufficiently competent (in his terminology) to at times resist elite framing, then journalists under certain conditions can do so too.

Analyses of frames in the news have focused on either *equivalency* or *emphasis* frames (Chong & Druckman, 2007b). Equivalency frames refer to alike content, which is presented or phrased differently (Kahneman & Tversky, 1984; O'Keefe & Jensen, 2006). Emphasis frames present "qualitatively different yet potentially relevant considerations" (Chong & Druckman, 2007b, p. 114). The concept of equivalency stems from the series of "Asian disease" studies by Kahneman and Tversky (1984). Though their framing manipulation – altering the wording of a scenario outlining the consequences of a fatal illness – was appropriate to explore the psychological process, this definition of framing is rather narrow.

Theoretical arguments have been made in favor of using a narrow conceptualization in framing research (Scheufele, 2000; Scheufele & Iyengar, forthcoming) – also to limit the broadening horizons of the concepts – but few empirical studies of news framing or framing effects have investigated the equivalence phenomenon. The vast majority of framing studies, more or less explicitly, apply an *emphasis* definition of frames. One strong argument for the use of emphasis frames is that most issues – political and social – cannot be meaningfully reduced to two identical scenarios. Simple question wording differences that reverse information are not easily compatible with more complex communicative situations and politics (Sniderman & Theriault, 2004). Political, economic and social events and issues are more often presented to citizens as alternative characterizations of a course of action. In the case of oil drilling, for example, citizens may be presented with frames such as economic costs of gas prices, unemployment, environment or the US dependency on foreign energy sources (Zaller, 1992).

There is a large variety of definitions of what a news frame is in both theoretical and empirical contributions. *Conceptually*, news frames can be defined as "a central organizing idea or story line that provides meaning to an unfolding strip of events, weaving a connection among them. The frame suggests what the controversy is about, the essence of the issue" (Gamson & Modigliani, 1989, p. 143). In short, a news frame can affect an individual by stressing certain aspects of reality and pushing others into the background – it has a selective function. In this way, certain issue attributes, judgments and decisions are suggested (Scheufele, 2000; Berinsky & Kinder, 2006). Again, corroborating the mediatization literature, the more journalistic news frames dominate the news, the higher is the degree of mediatization.

Frame-setting refers to the interaction between media frames and individuals' prior knowledge and predispositions. Frames in the news may affect learning, interpretation and evaluation of issues and events. This part of the framing process has been investigated most elaborately, often with the goal of exploring the extent to which and under what circumstances audiences reflect and mirror frames made available to them in, for example, the news. The *consequences* of framing can be conceived on the individual and the societal level. An individual-level consequence may be altered attitudes about an issue based on exposure to certain frames. At the societal level, frames may contribute to shaping social level processes such as political socialization, decision-making and collective actions. News frames have been shown to affect citizens' sense-making on a variety of political issues (e.g., Berinsky & Kinder, 2006; Iyengar, 1991; Nelson et al., 1997). Studies have tested effects on a number of dependent variables, such as issue interpretation (Valkenburg et al., 1999), cognitive complexity (Shah et al., 2004), public opinion and issue support (Druckman & Nelson, 2003; Sniderman & Theriault, 2004), voter mobilization (Valentino et al., 2001) and vote choice (Elenbaas & de Vreese, 2008).

Framing effects research has gone through a number of stages. Early studies focused mostly on direct, across the board, main effects. The oft-cited piece by Nelson et al. (1997) focused on how participants who viewed a free speech frame expressed more tolerance for the Ku Klux Klan than participants who viewed a public order frame. In later framing effects research, the attention shifted (as in media effects research more generally; Nabi & Oliver, 2009) to a greater interest in the process of framing effects and the conditional nature of the effects. In terms of the process, research has focused on three different processes that can mediate framing effects: accessibility change, belief importance change and belief content change (de Vreese & Lecheler, 2012). Collectively, these studies suggest that frames may have effects through different routes (Slothuus, 2008; de Vreese et al., 2011). In terms of conditioning factors, framing effects research has focused on individual and contextual moderating factors. At the individual level, the roles of political knowledge and need to evaluate have been assessed while the role of frame strength, source credibility and issue salience have been investigated at the contextual level (Druckman, 2001b; Lecheler et al., 2009).

The most recent generation of framing effects research takes the notion of framing as a *process* more seriously in the designs and investigates effects as a dynamic and diachronic process. Earlier studies in this area found conflicting evidence as to how enduring framing effects were, with de Vreese (2004) finding effects vanished quickly in the absence of new information while Tewksbury et al. (2000) and Lecheler and de Vreese (2011) found some effects over time. Lecheler and de Vreese (2013) investigated exposure to repetitive and competitive framing over time and Chong and Druckman (2012) and Baden and Lecheler (2012) provide a series of theoretical propositions about framing effects over time, depending on the information-processing mode.

In terms of mediatization, the more important news frames are for citizens' understanding and evaluations of political issues, the higher is the degree of mediatization. This is particularly true if journalistic news frames, which indeed can be quite consequential, dominate the coverage.

Mediatization and the use of journalistic news frames

The key goal of this chapter is relate the notion of journalistic news frames to the broader concept of mediatization. To do so, we need to distinguish between sponsored frames, often proposed by political elites and strategic communicators, and journalistic frames. Journalistic news frames are examples of generic news frames. Generic frames are frames that can transcend issues and sometimes even time or context. For example, a morality frame (Semetko & Valkenburg, 2000) or risk and opportunity frames (Schuck & de Vreese, 2006) can be applied to different issues and are as such not issue specific but generic in nature. Journalistic news frames form a special type of generic frame. While journalistic production processes involve the selection of topics that become the subjects of news coverage, these processes, very importantly, also play a transformative role. As Gamson and Modigliani (1989) pointed out, what journalists *do* to topics that their sources focus upon, or that are generated by other means (e.g., acts of nature), become a story's "organizing principle", or frame. Tuchman (1978) described journalistic frames as useful tools that journalists apply when dealing with the ongoing flow of information. Matthes (2012) also emphasizes that journalistic frames result in different news outlets framing issues in different ways.

In a seminal study, Neuman et al. (1992) identified *human impact, economics* and *conflict* as common frames used by the news media (and by audience members as well; see also Price et al., 1997). Similarly, Cappella and Jamieson (1997) and Patterson (1993) identified the strategy and games frames as frequently used by the media. Reviewing the work of the past couple of decades on how the media frame political issues, we can distill a number of distinct, frequently used, journalistic news frames. These frames have been identified as some of the most common in the framing literature (Matthes, 2009) and have been found in media content analyses spanning from the United States to Europe and Asia (Luther & Zhou, 2005; Semetko & Valkenburg, 2000). Below, each of these key journalistic news frames are discussed, the overlap between neighboring notions of news coverage addressed, and the effects summarized. Journalistic news frames are consequential. They are the explicit and manifest presence of journalistic selection and work routines in the news – and thus indicative of media logic as part of mediatization – and they matter for public opinion. The four types of framing are

(1) Episodic and human interest framing
(2) Conflict and competitive framing
(3) Economic consequences framing
(4) Strategy and game framing

Episodic and human interest framing. In communication science, there is an abundance of literature that pays tribute to the journalistic emphasis on human examples, specific instances and exemplars. Human interest framing "brings a human face or an emotional angle to the presentation of an event, issue, or problem" (Semetko & Valkenburg, 2000). Likewise, episodic framing shows specific instances and human examples of larger political issues, such as for example a news story about an elderly disabled woman unable to get public home care (Iyengar, 1991). In the same vein, journalists often use exemplars, i.e., "personal descriptions by people who are concerned with or interested in an issue" (Brosius, 2003, p. 179).

Human interest framing, episodic framing and the use of exemplars are all part of the underlying journalistic approach to political topics that favors the example, the illustration, the human face above the more general, abstract and thematic approach to covering politics. A thematic approach to political issues and events puts them in a broader context and presents collective, abstract and general evidence (Iyengar, 1991). A news story about cuts in government welfare expenditures substantiated by statistical figures is an empirical example of thematic framing and can be contrasted with the example of the elderly woman. This type of news framing is among the most common in media reports (Neuman et al., 1992). It dovetails with news selection criteria and the use of popular examples in the news is increasing (Lefevere et al., 2012).

Looking at the *effects* of human interest and episodic framing, ground-breaking work was conducted by Iyengar (1991). His demonstration of how episodic news frames influence the attribution of causal and treatment responsibility and thereby individuals' policy evaluations – across a number of issues – was an important vehicle for research in this area. Research on learning from human interest and personalization in the news shows a positive effect of such news features on learning (Jebril, 2010; Price & Czilli, 1996). Graber (1990), Robinson and Levy (1986) and Gunter (1987) also showed that personalized and close-to-home news stories are better recalled. Valkenburg et al. (1999) showed that for the issue of crime, human interest framing dampened learning, while for the issue of euro, human interest framing did not affect learning in comparison with other news frames. Finally, research has shown that exemplars are more effective than general, often statistical information (Lefevere et al., 2011), and that a focus on individuals yields more intense aversive and empathic emotional reactions (Gross, 2008).

Conflict and competitive framing. The conflict frame reflects conflict and disagreement among individuals, groups, organizations or countries. In both the United States (Neuman et al., 1992) and in Europe (Semetko & Valkenburg, 2000), this frame has been readily identified in the news. The latter study found that the conflict frame was the second most common news frame and that the more serious the newspaper, the more the conflict frame was present. Previous research has pointed to the high news value of stories that focus on conflict between political actors (Price, 1989). News media indeed tend to focus on stories where there is conflict – where two sides can be juxtaposed (Neuman et al., 1992). Thus, the presence of conflict is an essential criterion for a story to make it into the news, not only because it "sells", but also to meet professional standards of balanced reporting (Galtung & Ruge, 1965). Conflict is also inherent to politics. It is embodied in political reasoning (Lupia et al., 2000) and in democratic theory conflict is seen as an essential part of democratic decision-making (Sartori, 1987). Schattschneider (1960) defined democracy as "a competitive political system" with elites defining policy options so that citizens can make a choice: "conflict, competition, organization, leadership and responsibility are the ingredients of a working definition of democracy" (p. 135).

While scholars have long recognized the importance of elite competition in affecting opinion formation (Entman, 1993; Schattschneider, 1960), conflict framing is also a manifest expression in news of some of the most important journalistic hallmarks: balance, hearing the other side, and offering actors a chance to react and provide "their side of the story". In framing research, the presence of multiple and often conflicting perspectives has been considered both within and between news reports. In political discourse, citizens are likely to be exposed to repetitive or competitive news messages over time, and the outcome of these two is likely to vary (Zaller, 1992, 1996). In turn, *competitive news framing* has received considerable attention (Sniderman & Theriault, 2004; Chong & Druckman, 2007a). This makes sense, both when considering the dynamics of politics and of journalism.

The *effects* of exposure to conflict and competitive frames have shown that such frames invite individuals to incorporate elements from both sides or both frames in their thoughts on an issue (de Vreese, 2004). Competing messages may also annul the effects of messages on opinions (de Vreese & Boomgaarden, 2006; Zaller, 1992). Most studies focus on the effects of competitive framing when *two competing frames are presented at the same time*. For instance, Sniderman and Theriault (2004) found that competitive framing increases the influence of existing personal beliefs in the process, and decreases the effects of news framing (see also Chong & Druckman, 2007a). Conflicting information may also have a mobilizing function, especially during election time when conflict news cues an electorate that there is something to choose between (de Vreese & Tobiasen, 2007; Schuck et al., 2014).

Increasingly, studies also test how competitive news frames affect opinion formation over time (Lecheler & de Vreese, 2013). In the most comprehensive study so far, Chong and Druckman (2010) showed that competing messages received simultaneously might neutralize one another. When investigating the dynamics of this, they found that when messages are separated by days or weeks, most people give greater weight to the most recent communication because previous effects decay over time. This effect is conditioned by individual differences, with individuals who engage in deliberate processing of information displaying more attitude stability and giving more weight to previous messages. As Chong and Druckman (2010) conclude, "these results show that people typically form significantly different opinions when they receive competing messages over time than when they receive the same messages simultaneously" (p. 663).

Economic consequences. This frame reports an event, problem or issue in terms of the consequences it will have economically for entities such as groups, organizations or countries. Neuman et al. (1992) identified it as a common frame in the news and found that the wide impact of an event, often in terms economic ramifications, is an important news value (Graber,

1993). The extensive use of the economic consequence frame by journalists is apparent in studies of a wide range of issues such as the introduction of the European common currency, the euro (de Vreese et al., 2001), immigration (D'Haenens, 2001), Turkey (Koenig et al., 2006), the Olympic Games (Zaharopoulos, 2007) and SARS (Beaduoin, 2007; Luther & Zhou, 2005).

In terms of *effects* of exposure to the economic consequences frame, it has been demonstrated how the frame can guide individuals' train of thought about an issue (de Vreese, 2004) and affect participants' economic expectations and support for the enlargement of the European Union (contingent upon the frame's valence so that negative interpretations of economic consequences depressed economic expectations and support for the enlargement of the EU while positive interpretations led to more positive economic assessments and greater support for enlargement) (de Vreese, 2009). De Vreese et al. (2012) found that economic frames were persuasive across the board, whereas the effects of cultural (religious) frames were strongly conditioned by individual predispositions. Finally, Lecheler and de Vreese (2011) found that the effect of exposure to this frame depends on a person's level of political knowledge, with moderately knowledgeable individuals displaying the most persistent framing effects.

Strategy and game framing. The news media's focus on the electoral race and politicians' strategies is a major topic in research and popular discourse. This frame has previously been hailed as an indicator of mediatization in news (Strömbäck & Dimitrova, 2011). Patterson (1993) showed how American campaign news has shifted away from a descriptive and issue-oriented mode to a more interpretive and game-oriented approach. Cappella and Jamieson (1997) added to this the focus on motivations and political strategies, arguing that a strategy frame now dominates mainstream political news coverage (see also Farnsworth & Lichter, 2011). Lawrence (2000) confirmed this even for routine political coverage. Extant research has confounded different aspects involved in this coverage. As Aalberg et al. (2012) argue, the *game frame*

> refers to news stories that portray politics as a game and are centered around: who is winning or losing elections, in the battle for public opinion, in legislative debates, or in politics in general; expressions of public opinion (polls, vox pops); approval or disapproval from interest groups or particular constituencies or publics; or that speculate about electoral or policy outcomes or potential coalitions.

This is distinct from the *strategy frame*, which

> refers to news stories that are centered around interpretations of candidates' or parties' motives for actions and positions; their strategies and tactics for achieving political or policy goals; how they campaign;

and choices regarding leadership and integrity, including personal traits. It also involves different types of media strategies, including news coverage of press behavior.

They further note that at a meta-conceptual level it makes sense to consider both elements as part of a strategic game frame, which in its focus on process is distinct from more policy- and content-oriented political reporting.

The reasons for the use of the strategic game frame can be linked to changes in the political system, journalism and the news business. Political campaigns relying on highly managed strategies are met by journalists trying to expose and uncover these strategies. By focusing on strategic aspects of the political game, political reporters maintain an apparent stance of both independence and objectivity (Aalberg et al., 2012). Zaller (2001) phrases it in terms of "product substitution": "the harder presidential campaigns try to control what journalists report about their candidate, the harder journalists try to report something else instead" (p. 248).

The use of the strategy frame varies significantly. In an Israeli study, Sheafer et al. (2008) found that newspapers applied the game frame more often than the issue frame in all elections. For Germany, Esser and Hemmer (2008) similarly found that "strategic framing" was dominant on television news in all elections between 1994 and 2005. In international comparisons, Strömbäck and colleagues have found that the game metaframe was dominant in between 50% (Sweden) and 67% (the US) of the news, with Belgian, British, Norwegian and Spanish news stories falling between these two points (Strömbäck & Aalberg, 2008; Strömbäck & Luengo, 2008; Strömbäck & Shehata, 2007; Strömbäck & van Aelst, 2010). Taken together, these studies suggest that this frame is widely applied despite important differences across countries. It is therefore safe to conclude that this is one of the most important journalistic news frames.

The *effects* of the strategic game frame have been center stage in much research. The seminal studies by Cappella and Jamieson (1997) demonstrated some of the effects: if the focus is less on substantive issues and more on strategies and politicians' character traits, political cynicism is activated and political engagement undermined. Strategic news frames make politicians' self-interest more salient and depress knowledge on policy positions as well as dampening political efficacy (Pedersen, 2012). Acknowledging that in most cases strategic news stories also carry substantive and policy relevant information, Cappella and Jamieson (1997), however, argue that strategic news frames favor attention to and recalling of strategic rather than substantive information. Other research has provided a more nuanced picture of the effects of the strategic game frame. Valentino et al. (2001) for example demonstrated that it is *not* the presence of polls in the news that causes cynicism. Also when looking at the more strategy focused elements, recent research is more nuanced; de Vreese and Semetko (2002) showed that strategic news can indeed induce cynicism, but this may not per se lead to political disengagement. De Vreese (2005b) showed that a certain threshold of strategic news is required for cynicism to be activated at all and Adriaansen et al. (2010) showed strategy news may not cause cynicism in all instances and that substantive news can even reduce political cynicism.

A research agenda on mediatization and journalistic news frames

Journalistic news frames are important because they showcase how journalistic conventions and production processes translate political events into templates for news stories. They transform politics on the premise of media and journalism. They can therefore be considered indicative of mediatization where journalism has the upper hand in determining not only what is covered but also how it is covered in the news. The frames are also important because these templates make a real difference for the audience. As succinctly formulated by Nelson et al. (1997), frames are important because they "shape individual understanding and opinion concerning an issue by stressing specific elements or features of the broader controversy, reducing a usually complex issue down to one or two central aspects" (p. 568). While journalists and news organizations may follow or deviate from a political elite actor's agenda, it is obvious that there is considerable leeway and autonomy on the side of journalism when deciding how to frame issues. This is something that current and future journalists and editors should be aware of. Their "framing power" is not negligible and has implications both for our understanding of mediatization processes and for the dynamics of public opinion. And understanding this is one of the key contributions of communication science to the interdisciplinary body of framing research.

Based on extant research, I identified four journalistic news frames that are of importance for understanding the frame-building process, how news is framed and the frame-setting process. The four frames (human interest and episodic framing, conflict and competitive framing, economic consequences framing, and strategy and game framing) were defined and an overview of their presence in the news and their effects was provided. What's next for communication science's study of journalistic news framing as an indicator of mediatization? Two areas of research are in need of further understanding and empirical work: (1) the interaction between journalistic news framing and elite framing; and (2) the diversity of frames in the news and the normative implications.

Concerning the *interaction between journalistic news framing and elite framing*: frames in the news are the outcomes of how (elite) sources frame issues, how journalists and news organizations select, possibly adopt or contrast these frames, or renegotiate and reframe them into a frame following the logics of journalism, the news organization and the news genre. While frame-building is often singled out as an area in need of further attention (de Vreese, 2012), there is only modest research on this topic (for an exception see Hänggli, 2012). The process and the interactions between elite frames and sponsored and strategic frames on the one hand, and journalistic news frames on the other, need to be studied to better understand the framing in the news. This research should also extend to effects studies so as to assess whether elite frames in the news or journalistic news frames are most important and for whom. Such an approach would take full advantage of the framing concept as a process and as an empirical indicator of the mediatization concept. It would also allow for the bridging of research in journalism and communication on the one hand and political science and public opinion formation on the other with the backdrop of mediatization processes as an underlying concept.

With respect to the *diversity of frames in the news and the normative implications*, some frames are more present in the news than others. This goes both for sponsored frames and journalistic frames. Future research should engage with existing research on political balance in the news on the one hand (see Hopmann et al., 2012 for a recent overview) and normative implications of communication research on the other (see Althaus, 2012 for a recent overview) to make informed observations about the diversity in frames in the news. If mediatization is conducive to journalistic news frames taking the lead, what does this mean for the role of the media in democratic processes?

Framing research has a full agenda laid out for the future. A concept that gains in popularity as quickly as framing has, has the inherent danger of losing importance due to a watering down of its meaning and significance (see also Scheufele & Iyengar, forthcoming). Journalistic news frames offer a perspective to articulate the meaning and significance of framing in relation to the broader observations about mediatization. It sounds like a truism to say that "what journalists do matters", but in the intersection of framing and mediatization research, we should take this observation seriously.

References

Aalberg, T., Strömbäck, J., & de Vreese, C. H. (2012). The Framing of Politics as Strategy and Game: A Review of Concepts, Operationalizations and Key Findings. *Journalism*, 13(2), 162–178.

Adriaansen, M., van Praag, P., & de Vreese, C. H. (2010). Substance Matters: How News Content Can Reduce Political Cynicism. *International Journal of Public Opinion Research*, 22, 433–457.

Althaus, S. L. (2012). What's Good and Bad in Political Communication Research? Normative Standards for Evaluating Media and Citizen Performance. In H. A. Semetko & M. Scammell (Eds.), *Sage Handbook of Political Communication* (pp. 97–113). London, UK: Sage.

Beaduoin, C. E. (2007). SARS News Coverage and Its Determinants in China and the US. *Gazette*, 69(6), 509–524.

Baden, C. (2010). *Communication, Contextualization, & Cognition: Patterns & Processes of Frames' influence on People's interpretations of the EU Constitution*. Delft: Eburon Academic Publishers.

Baden, C. & Lecheler, S. (2012). Fleeting, Fading, or Far-Reaching? A Knowledge-Based Model of the Persistence of Framing Effects. *Communication Theory*, 22(4), 359–382.

Bennett, L., Lawrence, R., & Livingston, S. (2006). None Dare Call It Torture: Indexing and the Limits of Press Independence in the Abu Gharib Scandal. *Journal of Communication*, 56(3), 467–485.

Berinsky, A. J., & Kinder, D. R. (2006). Making Sense of Issues through Media Frames: Understanding the Kosovo Crisis. *The Journal of Politics*, 68(3), 640–656.

Borah, P. (2011). Conceptual Issues in Framing Theory: A Systematic Examination of a Decade's Literature. *Journal of Communication*, 61(2), 246–263.

Brosius, H. (2003). Exemplars in the News: A Theory of the Effects of Political Communication. In J. Bryant, D. Roskos-Ewoldsen & J. Cantor (Eds.), *Communication and Emotion: Essays in Honor of Dolf Zillmann* (pp. 179–194). Mahwah, NJ: Lawrence Erlbaum.

Cappella, J. N., & Jamieson, K. H. (1997). *Spiral of Cynicism: The Press and the Public Good*. New York: Oxford University Press.

Chong, D., & Druckman, J. N. (2007a). A Theory of Framing and Opinion Formation in Competitive Elite Environments. *Journal of Communication*, 57(1), 99–118.

Chong, D., & Druckman, J. N. (2007b). Framing Theory. *Annual Review of Political Science*, 10(1), 103–126.

Chong, D., & Druckman, J. N. (2010). Dynamic Public Opinion: Communication Effects over Time. *American Political Science Review*, 104(4), 663–680.

Chong, D., & Druckman, J. N. (2012). Dynamics in Mass Communication Effects. In H. A. Semetko & M. Scammell (Eds.), *The Sage Handbook of Political Communication* (pp. 307–323). London, UK: Sage.

d'Angelo, P. (2002). News Framing as a Multiparadigmatic Research Program: A Response to Entman. *Journal of Communication*, 52(4), 870–888.

d'Angelo, P., & Kuypers, J. A. (Eds.) (2009). *Doing News Framing Analysis: Empirical and Theoretical Perspectives*. New York: Routledge.

D'Haenens, L. (2001). Framing of Asylum Seekers in Dutch Regional Newspapers. *Media, Culture & Society*, 23(6), 847–860.

de Vreese, C. H. (2004). The Effects of Strategic News on Political Cynicism, Issue Evaluations, and Policy Support: A Two-Wave Experiment. *Mass Communication and Society*, 7(2), 191–214.

de Vreese, C. H. (2005a). News Framing: Theory and Typology. *Information Design Journal Document Design*, 13(1), 51–62.

de Vreese, C. H. (2005b). The Spiral of Cynicism Reconsidered: The Mobilizing Function of News. *European Journal of Communication*, 20, 283–301.

de Vreese, C. H. (2009). The Effects of Journalistic News Frames. In P. d'Angelo & J. Kuypers (Eds.), *Doing News Framing Analysis: Empirical and Theoretical Perspectives* (pp. 187–214). New York: Routledge.

de Vreese, C. H. (2012). New Avenues for Framing Research. *American Behavioral Scientist*, 56(3), 365–375.

de Vreese, C. H., & Boomgaarden, H. (2006). Media Message Flows and Interpersonal Communication: The Conditional Nature of Effects on Public Opinion. *Communication Research*, 33, 1–19.

de Vreese, C. H., Boomgaarden, H. G., & Semetko, H. A. (2011). (In)direct Framing Effects: The Effects of News Media Framing on Public Support for Turkish Membership in the European Union. *Communication Research*, 38(2), 179–205.

de Vreese, C. H., & Lecheler, S. (2012). News Framing Research: An Overview and New Developments. In H. Semetko & M. Scammell (Eds.), *SAGE Handbook of Political Communication* (pp. 292–306). London, UK: Sage.

de Vreese, C. H., Peter, J., & Semetko, H. A. (2001). Framing Politics at the Launch of the Euro: A Cross-national Comparative Study of Frames in the News. *Political Communication*, 18(2), 107–122.

de Vreese, C. H., & Semetko, H. A. (2002). Cynical and Engaged: Strategic Campaign Coverage, Public Opinion and Mobilization in a Referendum. *Communication Research*, 29(6), 615–641.

de Vreese, C. H., & Tobiasen, M. (2007). Conflict and Identity: Explaining Turnout and Anti-integrationist Voting in the Danish 2004 Elections for the European Parliament. *Scandinavian Political Studies*, 30, 87–114.

de Vreese, C. H., van der Brug, W., & Hobolt, S. (2012). Turkey in the EU: How Cultural and Economic Frames Affect Support for Turkish Membership. *Comparative European Politics*, 10, 218–235.

Donsbach, W. (2004). Psychology of News Decisions: Factors behind Journalists' Professional Behavior. *Journalism*, 5(2), 131–157.

Druckman, J. N. (2001a). On the Limits of Framing Effects: Who Can Frame? *Journal of Politics*, 63(4), 1041–1066.

Druckman, J. N. (2001b). The Implications of Framing Effects for Citizen Competence. *Political Behavior*, 23(3), 225–256.

Druckman, J. N. (2004). Political Preference Formation: Competition, Deliberation, and the (Ir)relevance of Framing Effects. *American Political Science Review*, 98(4), 671–686.

Druckman, J. N., & Nelson, K. R. (2003). Framing and Deliberation: How Citizens Conversations Limit Elite Influence. *American Journal of Political Science*, 47(4), 729–745.

Elenbaas, M., & De Vreese, C. H. (2008). The Effects of Strategic News on Political Cynicism and Vote Choice among Young Voters. *Journal of Communication*, 58(3), 550–567.

Entman, R. M. (1993). Framing: Toward Clarification of a Fractured Paradigm. *Journal of Communication*, 43(4), 51–58.

Esser, F. (2008). Dimensions of Political News Cultures: Sound Bite and Image Bite News in France, Germany, Great Britain, and the United States. *International Journal of Press/Politics*, 13(4), 401–428.

Esser, F. (2013). Mediatization as a Challenge: Media Logic versus Political Logic. In H. Kriesi, S. Lavenex, F. Esser, J. Matthes, M. Bühlmann & D. Bochsler (Eds.), *Democracy in the Age of Globalization and Mediatization* (pp. 155–176). Basingstoke: Palgrave Macmillan.

Esser, F., & Hemmer, K. (2008). Characteristics and Dynamics of Election News Coverage in Germany. In J. Strömbäck & L. L. Kaid (Eds.), *Handbook of Election News Coverage around the World* (pp. 289–307). London: Routledge.

Farnsworth, S., & Lichter, R. (2011). The Contemporary Presidency: The Return of the Honeymoon: Television News Coverage of New Presidents, 1981–2009. *Presidential Studies Quarterly*, 41(3), 590–603.

Galtung, J., & Ruge, M. H. (1965). The Structure of Foreign News: The Presentation of the Congo, Cuba, and Cyprus Crises in Four Norwegian Newspapers. *Journal of Peace Research*, 1, 64–91.

Gamson, W. A. (1992). *Talking Politics*. New York: Cambridge University Press.

Gamson, W. A., & Modigliani, A. (1989). Media Discourse and Public Opinion on Nuclear Power: A Constructionist Approach. *American Journal of Sociology*, 95(1), 1–37.

Graber, D. A. (1990). Seeing Is Remembering: How Visuals Contribute to Learning from Television News. *Journal of communication*, 40(3), 134–156.

Graber, D. A. (1993).*Processing the News*. Chicago: Chicago University Press.

Gross, K. (2008). Framing Persuasive Appeals: Episodic and Thematic Framing, Emotional Response, and Policy Opinion. *Political Psychology*, 29, 169–192.

Gunter, B. 1987. *Poor Reception: Misunderstanding and Forgetting Broadcast News*, Hillsdale, NJ: Lawrence Erlbaum Associates, Inc.

Hamilton, J. (2004). *All the News That's Fit to Shell: How the Market Transforms Information Into News*. Princeton, NJ: Princeton University Press.

Hänggli, R. (2012). Frame Construction and Frame Promotion (strategic frame choices). *American Behavioral Scientist*, 56(3), 260–278.

Hertog, J. K., & McLeod, D. M. (2001). Multiperspectival Approach to Framing Analysis: A Field Guide'. In S. D. Reese, O. H. Gandy & A. E. Grant (Eds.), *Framing Public Life* (pp. 139–162). Mahwah, NJ: Lawrence Erlbaum.

Hopmann, D., van Aelst, P., & Legnante, G. (2012). Political Balance in the News: A Review of Concepts, Operationalizations and Key Findings. *Journalism*, 13(2), 240–257.

Iyengar, S. (1991). *Is Anyone Responsible? How Television Frames Political Issues*. Chicago: University of Chicago Press.

Iyengar, S., & Kinder, D. R. (1987). *News That Matters: Television and American Opinion*. Chicago: University of Chicago Press.

Jebril, N. (2010). *Political Journalism in Comparative Perspective: Reconfiguring Malign News Media Effects on Political Perception and Cognition*. Doctoral dissertation, University of Southern Denmark.

Kahneman, D., & Tversky, A. (1984). Choices, Values and Frames. *American Psychologist*, 39(4), 341–350.

Koenig, T., Mihelk, S., Downey, J., & Bek, M. G. (2006). Media Framings of the Issue of Turkish Accession to the EU. *Innovation*, 19(2), 149–169.

Lawrence, R. (2000). Game-framing the Issues: Tracking the Strategy Frame in Public Policy News. *Political Communication*, 17(2), 93–114.

Lecheler, S., & de Vreese, C. H. (2011). Getting Real: The Duration of Framing Effects. *Journal of Communication*, 61, 959–983.

Lecheler, S., & de Vreese, C. H. (2013). What a Difference a Day Makes? Repetitive and Competitive Framing over Time. *Communication Research*, 40(2), 147–175.

Lecheler, S., de Vreese, C. H., & Slothuus, R. (2009). Issue Importance as a Moderator of Framing Effects. *Communication Research*, 36(3), 400–425.

Lefevere, J., de Swert, K., & Walgrave, S. (2012). Effects of Popular Exemplars in Television News. *Communication Research*, 39(1), 103–119.

Lengauer, G., Esser, F., & Berganza, R. (2012). Negativity in Political News: A Review of Concepts, Operationalizations and Key Findings. *Journalism*, 13(2), 179–202.

Lupia, A., McCubbins, M. D., & Popkin, S. L. (2000). *Elements of Reason: Cognition, Choice, and the Bounds of Rationality*. Cambridge: Cambridge University Press.

Luther, C. A., & Zhou, X. (2005). Within the Boundaries of Politics: News Framing of SARS in China and the United States. *Journalism & Mass Communication Quarterly*, 82(4), 857–872.

Matthes, J. (2009). What's in a Frame? A Content Analysis of Media-Framing Studies in the World's Leading Communication Journals 1990–2005. *Journalism and Mass Communication Quarterly*, 86(2), 349–367.

Matthes, J. (2012). Framing Politics: An Integrative Approach. *American Behavioral Scientist*, 56(3), 247–259.

Mazzoleni, G. (1987). Media Logic and Party Logic in Campaign Coverage: The Italian General Election of 1983. *European Journal of Communication*, 2(1), 81–103.

Mazzoleni, G., & Schulz, W. (1999). Mediatization of Politics: A Challenge for Democracy? *Political Communication*, 16(3), 247–261.

Nabi, R. L., & Oliver, M. B. (Eds.) (2009). *The Sage Handbook of Media Processes and Effects*. Thousand Oaks, CA: Sage.

Nelson, T. E., Oxley, Z. M., & Clawson, R. A. (1997). Toward a Psychology of Framing Effects. *Political Behavior*, 19(3), 221–246.

Neuman, W. R., Just, M. R., & Crigler, A. N. (1992). *Common Knowledge: News and the Construction of Political Meaning*. Chicago: University of Chicago Press.

O'Keefe, D. J., & Jensen, J. D. (2006). The Advantages of Compliance or the Disadvantages of Noncompliance? A Meta-Analytic Review of the Relative Persuasive Effectiveness of Gain-Framed and Loss-Framed Messages. *Communication Yearbook*, 30, 1–43.

Patterson, T. E. (1993). *Out of Order*. New York: Knopf.

Pedersen, R. (2012). The Game Frame and Political Efficacy: Beyond the Spiral of Cynicism. *European Journal of Communication*, 27(3), 225–240.

Price, V. (1989). Social Identification and Public Opinion: Effects of Communicating Group Conflict. *Public Opinion Quarterly*, 53, 197–224.

Price, V. & Czilli, E. J. (1996). Modeling Patterns of News Recognition and Recall. *Journal of Communication*, 46(2), 55–78.

Price, V., Tewksbury, D., & Powers, E. (1997). Switching Trains of Thought. *Communication Research*, 24(5), 481–506.

Reese, S. D. (2007). The Framing Project: A Bridging Model for Media Research Revisited. *Journal of Communication*, 57(1), 148–154.

Robinson, J. P. & Levy, M. R. (1986). Interpersonal Communication and News Comprehension. *Public Opinion Quarterly*, 50(2), 160–175.

Salgado, S. & Strömbäck, J. (2012). Interpretive Journalism: A Review of Concepts, Operationalizations and Key Findings. *Journalism*, 13(2), 144–161.

Sanders, K. (2011). Political Public Relations and Government Communication. In J. Strömbäck & S. Kiousis (Eds.), *Political Public Relations: Principles and Applications* (pp. 254–273). New York: Routledge.

Sartori, G. (1987). *The Theory of Democracy Revisited*. New Jersey: Chatham.

Schattschneider, E. E. (1960). *Semi-sovereign People: A Realist's View of Democracy in America*. New York: Harcourt Publishers.

Scheufele, D. A. (1999). Framing as a Theory of Media Effect. *Journal of Communication*, 49(1), 103–122.

Scheufele, D. A. (2000). Agenda-Setting, Priming, and Framing Revisited: Another Look at Cognitive Effects of Political Communication. *Mass Communication and Society*, 3(2), 297–316.

Scheufele, D. A., & Iyengar, S. (forthcoming). The State of Framing Research: A Call for New Directions. In K. Kenski & K. H. Jamieson (Eds.), *The Oxford handbook of political communication theories*. New York: Oxford University Press.

Scheufele, D. A., & Tewksbury, D. A. (2007). Framing, Agenda-Setting, and Priming: The Evolution of Three Media Effects Models. *Journal of Communication*, 57(1), 9–20.

Schuck, A., Vliegenthart, R., & de Vreese, C. H. (2014). Who's Afraid of Conflict? How Conflict Framing in Campaign News Coverage Mobilized Voters in the 2009 European Parliamentary Elections. *British Journal of Political Science*, doi:10.1017/S0007123413000525.

Schuck, A. R. T., & de Vreese, C. H. (2006). Between Risk and Opportunity: News Framing and Its Effects on Public Support for EU Enlargement. *European Journal of Communication*, 21(1), 5–23.

Semetko, H. A., Blumler, J. G., Gurevitch, M., Weaver, D. H., Barkin, S., & Wilhoit, G. C. (1991). *The Formation of Campaign Agenda*. Mahwah, NJ: Lawrence Erlbaum Associates.

Semetko, H. A., & Valkenburg, P. M. (2000). Framing European Politics: A Content Analysis of Press and Television News. *Journal of Communication*, 50(2), 93–109.

Shah, D. V., Kwak, N., Schmierbach, M., & Zubric, J. (2004). The Interplay of News Frames on Cognitive Complexity. *Human Communication Research*, 30(1), 102–120.

Sheafer, T., Weimann, G., & Tsfati, Y. (2008). Campaigns in the Holy Land: The Content and Effects of Election News Coverage in Israel. In J. Strömbäck & L. L. Kaid (Eds.), *Handbook of Election News Coverage around the World* (pp. 209–225). London: Routledge.

Shoemaker, P., & Reese, S. D. (1996). *Mediating the Message*. New York: Longman Publishers.

Slothuus, R. (2008). More Than Weighting Cognitive Importance: A Dual Process Model of Issue Framing Effects. *Political Psychology*, 29(1), 1–28.

Sniderman, P. M., & Theriault, S. M. (2004). The Structure of Political Argument and the Logic of Issue Framing. In W. E. Saris & P. M. Sniderman (Eds.), *Studies in Public Opinion* (pp. 133–165). Princeton, NJ: Princeton University Press.

Strömbäck, J. (2008). Four Phases of Mediatization: An Analysis of the Mediatization of Politics. *The International Journal of Press/Politics*, 13(3), 228–246.

Strömbäck, J. (2011). Mediatization of Politics: Toward a Conceptual Framework for Comparative Research. In E. P. Bucy & R. L. Holber (Eds.), *Sourcebook for Political Communication Research. Methods, Measures, and Analytical Techniques* (pp. 367–382). New York: Routledge.

Strömbäck, J., & Aalberg, T. (2008). Election News Coverage in Democratic Corporatist Countries: A Comparative Study of Sweden and Norway. *Scandinavian Political Studies*, 31(1), 91–106.

Strömbäck, J., & Dimitrova, D. V. (2011). Mediatization and Media Interventionism: A Comparative Analysis of Sweden and the United States. *International Journal of Press/Politics*, 16(1), 30–49.

Strömbäck, J., & Esser, F. (2009). Shaping Politics: Mediatization and Media Interventionism. In K. Lundby (Ed.), *Mediatization. Concept, Changes, Consequences* (pp. 205–224). New York: Peter Lang.

Strömbäck, J., & Esser, F. (2014a). Mediatization of Politics: Transforming Democracies and Reshaping Politics. In K. Lundby (Ed.), *Mediatization*. Berlin: de Gruyter.

Strömbäck, J., & Esser, F. (2014b). Mediatization of Politics: Towards a Theoretical Framework. In F. Esser & J. Strömbäck (Eds.), *Mediatization of Politics. Understanding the Transformation of Western Democracies* (pp. 3–28). Basingstoke: Palgrave Macmillan.

Strömbäck, J., & Luengo, Ó. G. (2008). Polarized Pluralist and Democratic Corporatist Models: A Comparison of Election News Coverage in Spain and Sweden. *The International Communication Gazette*, 70(6), 547–562.

Strömbäck, J., & Shehata, A. (2007). Structural Biases in British and Swedish Election News Coverage. *Journalism Studies*, 8(5), 798–812.

Strömbäck, J., & Van Aelst, P. (2010). Exploring Some Antecedents of the Media's Framing of Election News: A Comparison of Swedish and Belgian Election News. *International Journal of Press/Politics*, 15(1), 41–59.

Tewksbury, D., Jones, J., Peske, M. W., Raymond, A., & Vig, W. (2000). The Interaction of News and Advocate Frames: Manipulating Audience Perceptions of a Local Public Policy Issue. *Journalism and Mass Communication Quarterly*, 77(4), 804–829.

Tuchman, G. (1978). *Making News: A Study in the Construction of Reality*. New York: Free Press.

Valentino, N. A., Beckmann, M. N., & Buhr, T. A. (2001). A Spiral of Cynicism for Some: The Contingent Effects of Campaign News Frames on Participation and Confidence in Government. *Political Communication*, 18(4), 347–367.

Valkenburg, P. M., Semetko, H. A., & de Vreese, C. H. (1999). The Effects of News Frames on Readers' Thoughts and Recall. *Communication Research*, 26(5), 550–569.

van Dalen, A., Albaek, E., & de Vreese, C. H. (2012). Different Roles, Different Content? A Four Country Comparison of the Role Conceptions and Reporting Style of Political Journalists. *Journalism*, 13(7) 903–922.

Vliegenthart, R., & Van Zoonen, E. A. (2011). Power to the Frame: Bringing Sociology Back to Frame Analysis. *European Journal of Communication*, 26(2), 101–115.

Zaharopoulos, T. (2007). The News Framing of the 2004 Olympic Games. *Mass Communication and Society*, 10(2), 235–249.

Zaller, J. (1992). *The Nature and Origins of Mass Opinion*. Cambridge: Cambridge University Press.

Zaller, J. (2001). *A Theory of Media Politics: How the Interests of Politicians, Journalists and Citizens Shape the News*. Unpublished manuscript UCLA.

Zaller, J. (1996). The Myth of Massive Media Impact Revived: New Support for a Discredited Idea. In D. Mutz, R. Brody & P. Sniderman (Eds.), *Political Persuasion and Attitude Change* (pp. 17–79). Ann Arbor, MI: University of Michigan Press.

9
Mediatization of Campaign Coverage: Metacoverage of US Elections

Paul D'Angelo, Florin Büchel and Frank Esser

If mediatization, like globalization and modernization, is a meta-process of societal change (Krotz, 2008) whereby "the media have become integrated into the operations of other social institutions [and] acquired the status of social institutions in their own right" (Hjarvard, 2008, p. 113), then, arguably, this is nowhere more evident than in contemporary election campaigns. In most Western democracies, there are reciprocal dependencies – mutual need but different goals – between media organizations and the political parties and campaign organizations that vie for votes during elections (Gurevitch & Blumler, 1990). To be sure, the nature of these interdependencies is shaped by structural and cultural features of the media and political institutions within a country (Blumler & Gurevitch, 2001; see Strömbäck & Esser, 2009, pp. 217–218 for a useful summary). However, on the whole, mediatization theorists and researchers are interested in the processes and mechanisms through which these interdependencies typically tilt over time towards the media (Strömbäck, 2008). News organizations lie at the center of interest in work on the mediatization of politics (Esser, 2013). Accordingly, in election settings, the concern is with how the *media logic* of commercial imperatives, professional routines and message formats not only comes to dominate the content of campaign news, but also how it gets integrated into the *political logic* of political rules, organizational structures and routines, and self-presentational strategies that political parties and campaign organizations must follow in order to campaign effectively (Strömbäck, 2008; Strömbäck & Esser, 2009).

An omnipresent and, some would argue, intrusive media logic characterizes candidate-centered US elections at the presidential level (Arterton, 1984; Patterson, 1993), perhaps more so than in federal-level elections of any other country (e.g., Mazzoleni & Schulz, 1999; Strömbäck & Dimitrova, 2011). This chapter examines the role played by *metacoverage*, a type of news that foregrounds media organizations, formats and technologies, in the mediatization of US presidential elections. Our thesis is that metacoverage provides documentary evidence of the media logic operating in US campaign politics; thus, an empirical analysis of metacoverage allows researchers to infer ways that metacoverage influences the political campaign logic.[1] This chapter develops a theoretical framework and presents an empirical analysis that aim to show how metacoverage is a "molding force" (Hepp, 2012) in US presidential elections.

Mediation and mediatization in US presidential elections

The mediatization of US presidential campaigns can be understood in relation to "media politics", an institutional perspective that US scholars have been developing since the beginning of the so-called "modern" campaign. In US electoral politics, the modern campaign began when the Republican and Democratic parties put into effect procedural changes suggested by the 1970 McGovern–Fraser Commission. Thereafter, primary elections became more important in the nomination of each party's candidate for president (Wattenberg, 1994). Thus, from the 1972 presidential election on, parties have played an attenuated role in nominating a candidate for president and vice-president at their late-summer national conventions (Polsby, 1983). Although the Commission primarily aimed to democratize the candidate selection process, these changes also had ramifications for the news media (Arterton, 1984). "Major unintended by-products of reform have been an increased dependency on the mass media as an electoral intermediary and the emergence of the press as an independent force in the electoral process," noted Davis (1992, p. 254).

Absent the strong organizational role of political parties – contemporary candidate organizations are "temporary, built anew for each election", noted Arterton (1984, p. 7) – the modern US presidential election operates at the confluence of campaign organizations and mass media industries. To fit mediatization into this picture, we must distinguish the concept "mediation" from the institutionalization of media logic (Hjarvard, 2008; Strömbäck, 2008; Strömbäck & Esser, 2009).

As Strömbäck (2008) stated, mediatization can occur only after politics becomes infused with mediation. In the first phase of mediatization, therefore, media "constitute the dominant source of information and [the dominant] channel of communication between the governors and the governed" (p. 236). In the election campaign setting, mediation is evident in the communications technologies and devices candidates used to connect with voters and constituents. It is also evident in the variety of media organizations that campaign organizations interact with in order to carry out the political campaign logic.

Mediation permeates each stage of the US presidential election cycle. For example, candidates "surface" via announcement speeches that punctuate the campaign's pre-primary stage. Although each speech is always delivered to a live audience (thus its mode of delivery is non-mediated), candidates may stream the speech on the Internet, record it for use in campaign ads and court news coverage of the live speech. Political advertisements on television are perhaps the prototypical form of mediation in contemporary US presidential elections. Television ads are ubiquitous during the intra-party primaries and caucuses in each state, and during the general election period after Labor Day, when each party's nominee engages in a ten-week battle for the presidency itself. In fact, television ads began to change US electoral politics well before the McGovern–Fraser Commission. Going back to the 1952 presidential election, four years after the three major radio networks (ABC, NBC, and CBS) began regular television broadcasts, the Republican Party advantageously used this then-new medium. It bought significantly more air time on local television stations (some of which were owned by the networks) for its presidential nominee, Gen. Dwight D. Eisenhower, than the Democratic Party did for Adlai Stevenson, its nominee (Salmore & Salmore, 1989, pp. 43–47). This practice inaugurated a campaign strategy still used today of targeting ads to voters in specific counties in so-called "swing" states (West, 2009).

Candidates for the US presidency have always used available mass media to make persuasive appeals to the electorate (Friedenberg, 1997; Salmore & Salmore, 1989), going back to the voluminous number of printed pamphlets and handbills Andrew Jackson used in his 1828 campaign and extending to the use of radio and television in modern times (Friedenberg, 1997; Salmore & Salmore, 1989). But the 1970s reforms were a structural tipping point in the mediatization of the US presidential elections, for campaign organizations not political parties took charge of devising these appeals, and strategies to instrumentally use media technologies and interact with media organizations became paramount in their efforts to perform the genuinely political functions, such as coalition-building and taking issue stands, embedded in these appeals. On the surface, these developments would seem to have strengthened the political campaign logic over the media logic. However, precisely the opposite happened: candidate-centered campaigns morphed into mediatized campaigns the more campaign organizations came to *depend on* mediation and media organizations. In relation to Strömbäck's (2008) four-phase typology, 1970s-era campaign reforms, along with the diffusion of network and cable television, moved campaign organizations into a more sustained and embracing dependency on media technologies and media organizations than ever before. This, in turn, pushed mediatization into the third and fourth phases, heightening journalists' attention to the process of campaign forcing candidates to anticipate and react to news coverage, and bolstering the autonomy of the news media vis-à-vis campaign organizations.

In this light, the US presidential campaign offers a general lesson in the mediatization of electoral politics; namely, the news media cannot unilaterally co-opt the political campaign logic (Arterton, 1984; Blumler & Kavanagh, 1999). Rather, media independence is a function of the nature of reciprocal dependencies: the more campaign organizations rely on media organizations (including news), media formats and communications technologies to reach and persuade voters, the more they cede control to news (and other media) organizations. As Patterson (1993), a critic of media politics, stated, during the winnowing stage of the primary elections, candidates must "stand alone before the electorate", having "no choice but to filter their appeals through the lens of the news media" (p. 37). "If politics and the media were semi-independent and politics held the upper hand in the second phase," Strömbäck (2008) stated, "in the third phase, it is the media who hold the upper hand" (p. 238). By the fourth phase, which is where US media politics resides, "mediated realities replace the notion of a belief in objective realities" (p. 240). Or, as Arterton (1978) put it in his early work on US media politics, "[T]he political contest is shaped primarily by the perceptual environment within which campaigns compete," adding that, "because of the sequential nature of the process, the perceptual environment established by campaign reporting is seen [by campaign organizations] as a meaningful substitute for political reality" (pp. 10–11).

Interestingly, an embracing dependency on news organizations has impelled campaign organizations to develop strategies designed to bypass the news media (Lieber & Golan, 2011; Tedesco, 2011). Strategies to circumvent journalistic interference still rely on mediation but do not require campaign organizations to relinquish control to journalists. For example, campaign consultants have long viewed television ads – television now being an "old" medium – as a direct route to political persuasion. Many observers felt that Campaign 2008 was decisively swayed by Barack Obama's ad campaign, which ran over 190,000 ads, mostly in local television markets, during the general election phase, far more than the McCain campaign ran (West, 2009).[2] Emerging "new" media are also used to bypass the press. Indeed, the story of Barack Obama's successful 2008 presidential campaign is often told in terms of a strong campaign organization that expertly employed Web 2.0 features and tools to communicate his image to potential voters (e.g., Hendricks & Denton, 2010). For example, by Labor Day of Campaign 2008, members of Obama's online operation shot over 2,000 hours worth of video and posted 1,100 videos on his home site and his YouTube channel (Vargas, 2008). "We had essentially created our own television network, only better," noted David Plouffe, Obama's campaign manager, "because we communicated directly *with no filter* to what would amount to 20 percent of the total number of votes we would need to win" (2010, p. 364, emphasis added).

Yet determined efforts to manage and bypass the news media are in fact a sign that an advanced phase of mediatization is taking place within an election system. The reason why goes back to the notion that a strong media strategy on the part of a campaign organization links dependency with control. As Brants and Voltmer (2011) pointed out: "Mediatization comes at a price, because the struggle for control forces political actors to accept the terms and conditions of 'media logic'" (p. 5). Forecasting our interest in "metacoverage", a political logic that depends on mediation presents journalists with innumerable opportunities to frame a candidate's campaign activities – indeed, his or her political viability – in terms of his or her organization's ability to effectively use communications technologies and instrumentally interact with media organizations. Once storylines like this occur – indeed, once news coverage takes a heightened interest in mediation at all – an advanced stage of mediatization is taking place in an election system, for news stories that depict political functions in terms of media use and media interactions become important real-world cues that potentially shape a campaign's intertwined media and political strategies (see Esser & D'Angelo, 2006; Esser et al., 2001).

Weakened political parties and image campaigns; technological channel abundance and widespread media use by campaign organizations and voters; journalistic autonomy fostered by an institutional vacuum; a political logic that requires campaigns to use and manage (news) media; a press corps eager to tell stories about a political logic bound to mediation – these and other characteristics signal that the commercial imperatives, production routines, message formats and narrative interpretations of mass media organizations have moved to the center of the contemporary US presidential election, becoming threaded into the operations of political campaigns and transforming party-based elections into mediatized elections. As noted, the literature on US campaigns has discussed this transformation in terms of "media politics" (Arterton, 1984), the "mass media election" (Patterson, 1980) and "candidate-centered elections" (Wattenberg, 1994), rarely if ever mentioning "mediatization", a concept traditionally favored by scholars from continental Europe (see Schrott, 2009, pp. 43–44; Strömbäck, 2011, pp. 367–368). This chapter steps off from an exception, a comparative study by Esser and D'Angelo (2006) which suggested that the amount of metacoverage in a country's campaign news is a barometer of the level of mediatization in its election system.

Metacoverage as a logical outgrowth of mediatized politics

Metacoverage is a variation of "process" news – stories about campaign strategy and the "horserace" – that researchers have observed since the beginning of the mass media election (Aalberg et al., 2012; Carey, 1976; Patterson, 1980). By the 1988 US presidential campaign, scholars began to observe process news with a discernible media or publicity angle (see Bennett, 1992, p. 191; Diamond, 1991, pp. 173–181; Entman, 1989, p. 113). The term "metacoverage" was coined in an essay by Gitlin (1991) on the

1988 campaign and was used later in a set of content analyses by Esser and D'Angelo (2003, 2006). It forms part of a family of concepts, including *self-referential process news* (Kerbel, 1998), *media process news* (Kerbel et al., 2000), *media narcissism* (Lichter et al., 1999), *coverage of coverage* (Bennett, 1992), *stories about the media* (Johnson & Boudreau, 1996), *media stories* (Stempel & Windhauser, 1991), *stories about spin* (Esser et al., 2001) and *meta journalism* (Neveu, 2002), that researchers in the United States and Europe have used in order to observe how often news covers aspects of mediation and understand what this sort of coverage means for electoral politics.

Collectively, this area of research has found that mainstream US newspapers and television networks have no qualms about covering the working routines, attitudes and behaviors of members of the news media, particularly after candidates themselves criticize the amount or quality of their coverage. Also, this work has observed that mainstream news readily covers election-related content on "soft" news and in the so-called "shadow" campaign (Jones, 2005). Candidates use these non-news formats, which range from web-only platforms to entertainment programs (e.g., *Oprah*) to political comedy shows (e.g., *The Daily Show*), as a means to campaign. Moreover, these formats generate their own sort of subsequent coverage. However, because the content of soft news typically draws directly from reportage on mainstream news, most studies, with some exceptions (e.g., Wise & Brewer, 2010), consider mainstream news coverage *of* soft news to be metacoverage rather than soft news itself, even though soft news may be used more frequently than mainstream news as a source of campaign information by some segments of the electorate (Baum, 2003; cf. Prior, 2003). Finally, work on metacoverage has found that journalists are eager to cover, evaluate and monitor the mediated publicity efforts of campaign organizations. For example, perched above convention activities and roaming the convention floor, journalists routinely inform viewers that there is no news to report because the convention is scripted and staged for (television) news. Publicity-oriented metacoverage also covers political ads – not just the facts of their content but also the veracity of their claims and strategies behind their timing and placement.

In linking metacoverage to mediatization, this chapter follows the operational procedures of Esser and D'Angelo (2003, 2006). Observing metacoverage in campaign stories begins at the topic level, requiring salience rules and coding rules to determine how much, if any, of a particular story contains a "media" or "publicity" angle (or both). But the subtext of topic-level analysis is that metacoverage does more than simply document or describe mediation; rather, metacoverage can impact campaign organizations. "If the press is intent on reporting that the press is keeping a candidate from getting out his message, then the candidate is not getting out his message," Kerbel stated (1998, p. 38). Although it does not mention "mediatization", Kerbel's content analysis of television network coverage of 1992 US presidential campaign dovetails with contemporary normative debate about the potential pitfalls of mediatization (see Esser, 2013). He argues that every self-referential utterance in a broadcast news story contributes to the "strategic haze" that envelops presidential campaigns in cynical portrayals of the manipulative behaviors of campaign organizations. As a result, Kerbel argues, metacoverage side-tracks campaign organizations from presenting and debating the merits of their campaign agenda during the competition for their party's nomination or during the race for the presidency itself.

We agree with Kerbel that metacoverage can powerfully influence the operations of a campaign organization. In that sense, his critique under-scores the thesis of this chapter – that metacoverage is a molding force in the mediatization of electoral politics. But our theoretical framework stands Kerbel's critique on its head: primed by the political campaign logic that depends on mediation, journalists view a candidate's media strategy as being consequential to campaign outcomes. Inevitably, therefore, journalists meta-cover the political campaign logic. As Kerbel (1997, 1998) reminds us, these stories are not neutral depictions of mediation; rather, they can shape the political campaign logic.

Following Esser and D'Angelo (2003, 2006), we hold that observing "media" and "publicity" topics is the first step in demonstrating how metacoverage is a molding force of mediatization. However, we go a step further here and hold that media-driven influence happens by virtue of the framing devices that journalists use to contextualize "media" and "public-ity" topics. In practice, these framing devices, called "scripts", pertain to the roles that journalists, news organizations and communications technol-ogy play in the media politics environment. Like Esser and D'Angelo (2003, 2006), we conceptualize metacoverage frames in terms of scripts about con-nectivity, strategy and accountability. These scripts result in metacoverage that provides a rich set of process-oriented cues that campaign organiza-tions use in order to adjust to the media logic. Whereas metacoverage *topics* document media dependency in the political campaign logic, metacoverage *frames* – conduit, strategy and accountability – are discourses that influence the media-attentive political campaign logic.

The next two sections discuss how metacoverage covers and influences the political campaign logic (as defined in Note 1) in two US presidential elections. Each section utilizes the same two original datasets. Both are con-tent analyses of broadcast news aired during the campaign's general election period (Labor Day to Election Day). Our first dataset examined Campaign 2000 stories that aired on the flagship newscasts of two of the three major American over-the-air television networks: the ABC *World News Tonight* and the NBC *Nightly News* (see Esser & D'Angelo, 2003, 2006). Both newscasts aired from 6:30 to 7 p.m. EST. Our second dataset, from Campaign 2008, matches the eight-week sampling frame of the first dataset (Labor Day to Election Day) but also includes data for the flagship programs of two cable networks: CNN's *AC360* with Anderson Cooper, a 60-minute newscast that aired from 9 to 10 p.m., and Fox News Channel's *Special Report* with Brit Hume, a 60-minute newscast that aired from 6 to 7 p.m. EST.[3]

Covering political campaign logic: The topics of metacoverage

Figure 9.1 illustrates how we derived the two main metacoverage topics – "media" and "publicity" – from previous work, principally that of Kerbel and his colleagues. Two highlights of the model are as follows.

First, the topics (or "miniseries") that Kerbel observed in Campaign 1992 news were later conceived as frames in his analysis of Campaign 1996 news (see Kerbel et al., 2000). Hence, in the later content analysis, he and his colleagues observed the "media process" frame along with the other frames. In our typology, "media" and "publicity" topics are conceived as being overlaid onto one or more campaign topics within a news story. Although our typology of topics is obviously deeply indebted to Kerbel's work, we hold that metacoverage is "meta-" because it layers mediation topics *on top* of non-mediation topics (e.g., combines a media topic with substantive Issues/Plans). This typology allows us to observe more clearly the political logic demanding that campaign organizations skillfully use mediation to carry out functions, such as image-building and image-maintenance, associated with the political campaign logic.

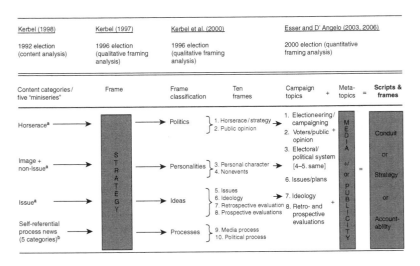

Figure 9.1   Derivation of metacoverage topics and frames from previous literature

[a] Topics also measured by Johnson and Boudreau (1996). [b] Kerbel's five categories were: (1) general references; (2) campaign behavior; (3) candidate motivation; (4) candidate-press relations; and (5) technical matters. Johnson and Boudreau's four categories were: (1) media performance/impact; (2) media coverage of policy issues and campaign issues; (3) candidate media strategy/performance; and (4) general media stories.

Whereas a *media* topic is about a media organization, format, technology or source that is "transmitting" a message or one that is being covered by a media organization, format or source as transmitting or depicting a message, a *publicity* topic is about the instrumental use of media organizations, formats, technologies and/or sources by some member of a campaign organization. Thus, the basic coding rules for distinguishing a *media* topic from a *publicity* topic are as follows: if the story is about how, when, why or by whom a topic or event *is being covered or was covered* in a news or hybrid or non-news format, or if it is about the actual environment in which news making, newsgathering or news coverage takes place, then it has a *media* topic. Thus, (a) a story does not have to be solely about *news* media to be coded as having a *media* topic (it can be about bloggers or blogging not affiliated with a news organization, for example); and (b) a story can be a *media* story even when it covers a publicity-oriented topic, such as a political advertisement (though the angle would be how mainstream news or soft news is covering the erstwhile publicity topic). Following Kerbel et al. (2000), a media topic was determined on the basis of salience rules applied to utterances and visual sequences: if enough of those context units (> 15% or > 50%) were about "media" or "publicity", then the topic had a secondary or a primary salience, respectively, in the story.[4] Only those stories were coded for metacoverage frames.

Second, for both data collections, we observed frames *after* topical observations were completed. The all-important scripts we used, discussed in the next section, were derived inductively in the 2000 data collection and subsequently codified for the second data-gathering effort on Campaign 2008 news. Kerbel et al. (2000) do not employ this step.

A content analysis of metacoverage topics provides a vivid portrait of the level of media dependency that drives the political campaign logic in US presidential campaigns. In terms of Strömbäck's (2008) typology, content analyses of metacoverage topics provide a Phase One baseline to assess if mediation has infused an election system enough to warrant the conclusion that mediatization is taking place. Not surprisingly, in our judgment US presidential elections have already passed that baseline (perhaps long ago, but that is a separate empirical question). Looking at the data for both the 2000 and 2008 presidential elections (Table 9.1), it is evident that the number of media metacoverage topics found within the broadcast channels ABC and NBC rises slightly from 19% to 28% of all stories, while the number of publicity metacoverage topics drops on a small scale, from 27% to 22% of all election stories. Stories explaining the slight increase in media meta-topics in 2008 included reports on an alleged pro-Obama bias among journalists (downplaying weaknesses in his and Biden's record) and a supposed "gotcha" journalism against Palin (fact-checking her statements and scrutinizing her record in office). Overall, however, Table 9.1 shows a steady amount of any metacoverage topic (i.e., media or publicity or both) throughout the two election years (41% in 2000 and 44% in 2008). The fact that, in

Table 9.1   Amount of metacoverage on ABC and NBC News during two presidential election campaigns

	Election year					
	2000			2008		
	Channel			Channel		
	ABC	NBC	Total	ABC	NBC	Total
	%	%	%	%	%	%
Stories[a] with media topic	19	20	19	33	25	28
Stories with publicity topic	27	27	27	17	25	22
Stories with overlapping media and publicity topics	8	2	5	7	5	6
Total share of stories with metacoverage topic[b]	38	45	41	43	45	44

Notes: (a) Only stories with "primary" or "secondary" salience are included. Stories aired on ABC World News and NBC Nightly News in last eight weeks before polling day.

(b) Designates all stories that contain either a media or publicity topic, or both. This means that these totals are calculated by summing up the percentages of stories "with media topics" and "with publicity topics", and then subtracting the stories "with overlapping topics" (i.e., stories that contain both topics; because they are counted twice in the first two rows of the table).

both these election years, roughly two out of five stories include one or the other metacoverage topic (or both) indicates not only that these topics are important themes in election campaign coverage, but also that mediation plays an important role in the political logic. In other words, frequent and salient metacoverage suggests a highly mediatized news environment (Esser & D'Angelo, 2006).

Admittedly, distinguishing a "media" topic from a "publicity" topic is not always straightforward, particularly when considering the fact that the political logic of electioneering forces a campaign organization to manage and attempt to manipulate the news media as a means to communicate their candidate's image. For example, NBC News ran stories on what it labeled a "Truth Squad". These stories dealt with the veracity of statements uttered by candidates during the three televised presidential debates and the single vice-presidential debate. For the *campaign* topic, these stories were typically coded as "Issues/Plans". But at times a metacoverage topic was prominent in these stories. In one example, NBC reported that facts were altered or even mendacious in spite of the fact that the media were scrutinizing the candidates' every statement. This story had a "media" topic, as the metacoverage dealt with how and by whom a topic or event was covered in a news environment.

In another "Truth Squad" story, aired on 10 October 2000, it was reported that the candidates were cautious and staying away from exaggerations, knowing that such exaggerations would be reported in the media. In fact, the misstatements they found were minor detail errors. For instance, Bush accused a former Russian prime minister of corrupting IMF money, and while it was true that Viktor Chernomyrdin was accused of corruption, there was no proof that this happened to IMF money. Even so, this is an example of a publicity topic (overlaid onto an Issues/Plan topic) because the mediation angle centered on an effort to manage news rather than on the news environment itself.

Although the foregoing examples distinguish a "media" topic from a "publicity" topic, our coding rules do not preclude that both topics can be observed in the same story. These stories are relatively rare compared to single-topic stories, occurring only in 5% (2000) to 6% (2008) of all stories. As noted, this finding is in part an artifact of our coding rules, which are designed to discriminate between the two metacoverage topics in news stories. An example of a dual-topic story was aired on ABC on 7th October 2000, a particularly bad day for the Bush campaign. The story began with polling data showing that the race was very close in July but had since turned in favor of Al Gore. Apparently "Bush woke up that morning to a spate of damaging comments on the news media" and Republicans were quoted as saying that the Bush campaign needed some tactical changes to get rolling again. This story covered both failures in campaign communication efforts (publicity metacoverage) as well as media reports about panic and loss of confidence among GOP voters (media metacoverage).

Observing campaign topics in conjunction with metacoverage topics shows the precise topical settings in which media logic has become integrated into the political campaign logic. Table 9.2 shows that metacoverage topics (re: the documentary evidence of mediation) tend to be combined with campaign topics from the Process and Personality sphere (mostly the topic Electioneering/Campaigning) rather than topics from the Polity and Policy sphere. However, when metacoverage is overlaid onto a Polity and Policy topic, it is likely to be a story about a particular substantive issue or policy matter. For example, on 4 October 2000, ABC ran a story discussing the debate tactics as well as the issue stances of the main candidates (hence combining publicity metacoverage with the Issues/Plans topic).

We turn next to specific contextual factors that influence the likelihood of metacoverage. One such factor is the type of broadcasting channel: cable vs. broadcast television (coded only during Campaign 2008). One could reasonably argue that the specialized cable news channels (such as CNN and Fox News) are in campaign mode 24/7 and offer a comprehensive approach (reflected in a program length of a full hour as opposed to a half hour on ABC and NBC) that makes metacoverage more likely to occur. Comparing ABC and NBC in 2008 with the results of Fox and CNN (see Table 9.3), we see that cable news channels air a much higher amount of metacoverage (54% media metacoverage topics, 31% publicity metacoverage topics) than the broadcast channels (28% media metacoverage topics and 22% publicity metacoverage

Table 9.2 Combinations of campaign topics and metacoverage topics in US election news

Campaign topics		Election year			
		2000		2008	
		Metacoverage topic		Metacoverage topic	
		Media topic	Publicity topic	Media topic	Publicity topic
		%	%	%	%
Polity & policy sphere	Electoral system/Political institutions	2	2	0	0
	Ideological positions/ political worldviews	0	0	3	0
	Pro- and retrospective evaluations of candidates	4	2	3	0
	Issues/policy matters/plans	5	11	10	14
Process & personality sphere	Non-issues/revelations/ exaggerations/gaffes	10	3	3	0
	Personality/character traits/	12	22	5	0
	Voters/polls/public opinion	41	11	15	14
	Electioneering/ campaigning	27	49	62	72

Note: Basis for percentages is the number of topics. Reading example: In 2000, 10% of all *media* "metacoverage topics" were combined with a *non-issue* "campaign topic" in the same story. Only those topics coded with primary or secondary salience are included in the analysis.

topics).[5] Fox and CNN ran reflective program segments (called Strategy Session or The Grapevine) as well as panel discussions with journalists and former consultants (such as Bill Kristol, Charles Krauthammer or Fred Barnes at Fox; and Ed Rollins, Peggy Noonan, Paul Begala or David Gergen at CNN) in which the role of the media and the publicity was debated as a matter of course. We are led to conclude that the broader and more specialized approach of the cable news shows, together with their interpretation-heavy and talking head-based delivery style, provides a more favorable opportunity structure for metacoverage than is found on the compact newscasts of the generalist broadcast channels. In sum, metacoverage seems to thrive especially under certain contextual conditions, including a particular topic environment (see Table 9.2) and a particular media type with a specific style of reporting (see Table 9.3).

Table 9.3 Metacoverage on broadcast and cable news programs during 2008 presidential campaign

	Channel				Channel type	
	ABC	NBC	CNN	Fox	Broadcast channels	Cable news channels
	%	%	%	%	%	%
Stories with media topics	33	25	55	53	28	54
Stories with publicity topics	17	25	35	29	22	31

Note: Basis for percentages is the number of topics. Reading example: of all election stories on ABC in the 2008 election, 33% contain a media topic. Programs coded in last eight weeks of campaign were ABC World News, NBC Nightly News, CNN AC360 with A. Cooper and Fox News Special Report with B. Hume.

Influencing political campaign logic: The frames of metacoverage

As Schrott (2009) explains, mediatization effects are indirect, second-order effects at the meso-level of organizations or the macro-level of systems. Our theoretical framework posits that the effects of metacoverage can be inferred when we move the analysis past observing mediation angles and consider the frames in these stories. With this point in mind, this section has three goals: (a) explain how the three metacoverage frames are observed; (b) present a demographic picture of metacoverage frames for Campaign 2008 and make brief comparisons with frames observed in Campaign 2000 news; and (c) discuss the effects of metacoverage frames on the office-seeking political campaign logic.

Conduit metacoverage frames

Various media organizations, formats, products and personnel are depicted in metacoverage, ranging from news organization to those outlets that produce "softer" media formats, such as political comedy and entertainment programs. Adapting Esser and D'Angelo's (2003, 2006) theoretical argument, even though any number of media organizations can depict mediation – e.g., political comedy programs regularly discuss how candidates are covered in the news or poke fun at their television ads – we reserve the function of framing "media" and "publicity" topics to the news media, owing to their commitment to original reporting, their market penetration and their professional autonomy from politics. Admittedly, this analytical decision may foreclose on other important avenues of mediatization of electoral politics.

Still, it is not an arbitrary decision, for news media still occupy a central place in candidates' media strategies, which range from courting news coverage to skirting it via other mediation routes. In other words, news media are still at the center of media politics, and hence a primary means by which politics is mediatized.

A conduit frame of a "publicity" topic depicts proactive mediation on the part of a campaign organization; a conduit frame of a "media" topic focuses on the transmission role of a media outlet, product or actor. In Esser's (2013) typology, these frames represent the "technical" side of mediatization. In both cases, the overarching mediatization effect reinforces dependency on mediation on the part of campaign organizations as they carry out the political logic of constructing and communicating a candidate's image. In other words, in monitoring metacoverage with a conduit frame, campaign organizations are led to think that publicity messages are "getting through" to voters and other constituents (e.g., "the advertisement of candidate 'x' appeared in market 'y' a total of 'z' times last week"). Also, they are treated to a sounding board of their non-mediated communication, which is depicted in terms of interactions with media organizations (e.g., "candidate 'x' spoke to reporters yesterday ... "), and offered a neutral reflection of their mediated communication, which is depicted as being "picked up" in news stories or presented in other mediated formats (e.g., "candidate 'x' appeared on the David Letterman Show last night").

During the 2008 presidential election, the *media conduit frame* was used in 26% of election stories on the broadcast channels and 44% of stories on the cable channel (see Table 9.4). The scripts that build a media conduit frame

Table 9.4 Distribution of metacoverage frames during 2008 presidential campaign

	Channel				Channel type	
	ABC	NBC	CNN	Fox	Broadcast channels	Cable news channels
	%	%	%	%	%	%
Media conduit Frame	33	22	47	42	26	44
Media strategy Frame	0	3	7	8	2	8
Media accountability frame	0	0	1	3	0	2
Publicity conduit Frame	2	3	10	11	3	10
Publicity strategy Frame	14	22	23	18	19	20
Publicity accountability frame	0	0	2	1	0	1

Note: Basis for percentages is the number of topics. Reading example: of all election stories on ABC in the 2008 election, 33% contain a media conduit frame.

can be verbal, visual or format-based.[6] They include, as Table 9.5 shows, references in election stories to other media outlets as sources of news, the tendency to conduct formal interviews with journalists as experts (rather than collecting viewpoints from outside the media bubble), or images showing the presence of reporters and cameras at events (thus reminding viewers of the mediated nature of modern campaigns; see Table 9.5 for additional details).

Turning to the "publicity" topic, it is striking that the four news programs used the conduit frame much less often with regard to political publicity than with regard to the media. *Publicity conduit frames* were used in only 3% of broadcast stories and 10% of cable stories (see Table 9.4), with the underlying script always being the neutral dissemination of publicity acts and actors (see Table 9.6).

Strategy and accountability metacoverage frames

As noted, conduit frames depict the technical transmission aspects of media organizations and mediated political publicity. However, as Esser (2013) has argued, media logic consists of two further elements in addition to "technical" aspects: "professional" and "commercial" imperatives of media logic. Professional and commercial imperatives of media logic operate in the *Accountability Frame* for both topics and the *Strategy Frame* for both topics, more so than in the conduit frames.

The *Strategy* frame places a "publicity" topic in a climate of reaction and a "media" topic in a climate of proactive influence. The power of a *Strategy* frame (for both topics) ensues from a professional imperative that pits news media in conflict with political logic – for example, ads can be depicted as too strident or too savvy in pursuit of presenting a policy; media organizations (including but not limited to news) can be depicted as being obstructionist to campaign organizations or distracting to voters. Further, how *Strategy* frames for both topics incorporate the commercial dimension of media logic also seems to be at odds with the political logic – for example, by allowing confrontainment, dramatization and personalization to filter into news stories (see Esser, 2013, pp. 171–172). In all, this means that *Strategy* frames provide a set of cues that, from the perspective of campaign organizations, present obstacles to carrying out the political logic. In both cases, the *Strategy* frame spurs campaign organizations to accede to the media logic, prompting adjustments along the mediation routes that a campaign organization feels will be a "better" (re: a more instrumental) approach to fulfilling campaign functions.

The *Accountability* frame contextualizes both metacoverage topics in terms of democratic norms and professional standards. The mediatization effect here is twofold. First, it prompts campaign organizations to adjust their media logic on the basis of professional standards and moral principles when

Table 9.5 Media-related scripts as building blocks of metacoverage frames in the 2008 campaign

Media conduit scripts		Media strategy scripts		Media accountability scripts	
Script type	Percent	Script type	Percent	Script type	Percent
Election stories…		Election stories referring to media as…		Election stories offering…	
– Citing other media as source of news; or reporting media-sponsored polls	55	– Watchdog	35	– Self-criticism: Self-policing the profession through media criticism	58
		– Biased	28		
		– Attack dog	13		
– Conducting interviews with journalists as pundits	29	– Influential	10	– Media education: enlightening the audience about media's role	42
		– Agenda setter	6		
– Showing presence of media at political events	6	– Dramatizing, negative	5		
		– Kingmaker	4		
– Self-promoting programs or website of own channel	4				
– Emphasizing the magnitude of a news story	4				
– Indulging in media insiderism, internal matters	4				
	100%		100%		100%
	N=713		N=116		N=33

Notes: All percentages are based on the number of media metacoverage topics. To interpret the totals in the bottom row, it is important to know that we coded only 50% of broadcast stories and only 25% of cable news stories. The true number of scripts used in the last eight weeks before Election Day 2008 was thus much higher on ABC, NBC, CNN and Fox.

Table 9.6 Publicity-related scripts as building blocks of metacoverage frames in the 2008 campaign

Publicity conduit scripts		Publicity strategy scripts		Publicity accountability scripts	
Script type	Percent	Script type	Percent	Script type	Percent
Election stories… – Disseminating publicity measures, messages and personnel in neutral fashion	100	Election stories addressing publicity as a strategic means to… – Build or sell a positive image – Launch a public attack on opponent – Communicate policy better – Influence the public or media – Defend against or rebut accusations – Discuss or evaluate it in general terms	 23 11 8 8 7 44	Election stories offering… – Publicity criticism: policing the campaigns through ad watches, debate fact checks, truth patrols – Publicity education: enlightening the audience about the role of political publicity in campaigns	55 45
	100% N = 182		100% N = 254		100% N = 20

Notes: All percentages are based on the number of publicity metacoverage topics. To interpret the totals in the bottom row, it is important to know that we coded only 50% of broadcast stories and only 25% of cable news stories. The true number of scripts used in the last eight weeks before Election Day 2008 was thus much higher on ABC, NBC, CNN and Fox.

carrying out the political logic of image construction. Second, it spurs media organizations to adjust how they portray politics along these same lines. Accountability frames thus show that journalists are "pushing" campaign organizations and media organizations to comply with normative standards. These standards derive from sources that have, to one extent or another, filtered into the scripts journalists use to contextualize mediation. For example, the professional imperative of media logic assigns democratic functions to the news media such as contributing to an enlightened understanding from an independent point of view (Dahl, 2000, p. 37). Such an understanding, while discordant with the rough and tumble of political campaigns, can lead to scripts that depict mediation in terms of "account holding, creating transparency, demanding answerability, [and] critical professionalism" (Esser, 2013, p. 170).

Somewhat surprisingly, given the concern in the political communication literature with strategy framing (e.g., Patterson, 1993), during the 2008 campaign we observed *Media Strategy Frames* in just 2% of broadcast stories and 8% of cable stories (see Table 9.4). As noted, the *Media Strategy Frame* characterizes media organizations pursuing their own professional and commercial interests (i.e., demonstrating independence and distance from political logic, relying on news values rather than political values, striving for public attention and economic success), presenting a media logic in which media organizations appear to confront campaign organizations. The scripts used to construct *Media Strategy Frames* are listed in Table 9.5 in terms of time-honored journalistic roles. However, we interpreted these roles in terms of an "intrusive" media logic. For example, media as *agenda-setter* was observed in terms of "intrusion through give too much or too little emphasis to a campaign topic"; media as *watchdog* was observed in terms of "intrusion through creating or perpetuating a media frenzy". It seems reasonable to suppose that campaign organizations would be especially attuned to these frames, particularly as they depict media practices and products as blocking nuanced discussion of issues on the part of candidates (see Kerbel, 1998; Patterson, 1993).

Publicity Strategy Frames were more numerous than *Media Strategy Frames*, observed in 19% of broadcast and 20% of cable stories (see Table 9.4). Scripts emphasize the tactical considerations and strategic purposes behind image management and news management, launching public attacks and defending against public attacks, as well as communicating policy more effectively (see Table 9.6). While the effect on the public may be increased cynicism, the effects on the campaigns themselves may be more varied. At best, campaign teams may use this kind of metacoverage as a sounding board for self-mirroring and fine-tuning the effectiveness of their publicity strategies. At worst, it may contribute to further the arms race in the mediatization process: candidates and their publicity experts may feel prompted to professionalize their self-presentational skills even more in order to regain control over the political communication process.

We move now to the *Accountability* frames. *Media Accountability Frames* aimed at self-policing the journalistic profession through media criticism or enlightening the audience with standards that guide decision-making in media organizations were never used on broadcast channels (0%) and only very rarely on cable channels (2%) (see Tables 9.4 and 9.5 for details). Likewise, the *Publicity Accountability Frame* was almost never used in 2008 campaign coverage (0% on broadcast and 1% on cable channels) (see Table 9.4). These results are disappointing, for stories with Accountability frames could have a self-correcting effect on manipulative publicity strategies and further contribute to an enlightened understanding of modern day political communication (see Table 9.6 for details on publicity accountability scripts). In 2000, the broadcast channels aired at least a few stories with accountability frames, mostly analyzing claims made in televised debates or TV ads, or examining new strategies of political marketing (see Esser & D'Angelo, 2003).

Stories with combined frames

Our analysis of metacoverage reveals that strategy frames are heavily dependent on the assistance of conduit scripts. As Table 9.7 (column B) shows, stories coded as having a *Media Strategy Frame* contain a substantial amount of media conduit scripts (39%) and publicity conduit scripts (10%). In our view, these conduit scripts serve as a foundation on which the more active, interventionist strategy discourse is based.

Because strategy scripts are located at a higher interpretive level than more simplistic conduit scripts, 37% of meaningful media strategy scripts in an average election story are sufficient to establish a media strategy frame in that story. Media Strategy Frames are particularly heavily imbued with conduit scripts, but they serve only as supporting acts. The situation is similar to *Publicity Strategy Frames* (Table 9.7, column E), which are also heavily dependent on conduit scripts to further their main message. Thus, the conduit scripts lose some of their supposed innocence or harmlessness, because they are used by journalists as a popular accessory for establishing strategy frames.

The most sophisticated and highly developed frames (in terms of journalistic reflection and analysis) are the *Accountability* frames (for both topics). They are, interestingly enough, highly dependent on the underpinning of strategy frames. Stories with *Media Accountability Frames* co-occur with 30% of media strategy scripts (see Table 9.7, column C) and stories with *Publicity Accountability Frames* co-occur with 25% of publicity strategy scripts (Table 9.7, column F) in the same story. This makes sense, for without strategy-based discourse there would be little foundation for having a reasonable and responsible accountability-based debate.[7] That also

Table 9.7 Story-level heterogeneity of frames: the contribution of diverse scripts to individual frames

		A	B	C	D	E	F
			Media frames			Publicity frames	
		Conduit	Strategy	Accountability	Conduit	Strategy	Accountability
		%	%	%	%	%	%
Media scripts	Conduit	66	39	40	37	39	28
	Strategy	5	37	30	7	5	0
	Accountability	1	5	27	1	1	0
Publicity scripts	Conduit	11	10	3	45	14	13
	Strategy	15	8	0	9	39	25
	Accountability	2	1	0	1	2	34

Note: Percentages are based on all scripts contained in the respective metacoverage frame. Reading example: of all scripts coded in stories with a media conduit frame (column A), 66% are scripts belonging to the media conduit frame, while roughly 34% are scripts belonging to other frames.

means that questionable strategy scripts can be turned around, defused and communicatively deconstructed by higher-level accountability discourse.

Conclusion

In foregrounding the news media and publicity processes, metacoverage presents both a descriptive account of mediation in campaigns and an interpretive layer of discourse that campaign organizations must attend to in order to carry out the political logic of image-building. Even in media formats in which candidates exercise some measure of control – for example, appearances on talk shows, political ads on radio or television or political websites – effectively carrying out campaign functions depends on monitoring metacoverage. The reciprocal dependency between campaign organizations and news organizations in the media politics environment gives rise to the notion that candidate-centered elections are not simply mediated – candidates using communications channels to do their job; the news media using communications channels to do theirs – but *mediatized* (Blumler & Kavanagh, 1999; Strömbäck, 2008; Strömbäck & Dimitrova, 2011). Campaign organizations depend upon communications technologies and media organizations in order to carry out the office-seeking part of political logic. In turn, their dependencies prime news media to metacover politics. Metacoverage becomes a sounding board in a reflexive cycle in which campaign organizations adjust to the media logic in order to campaign effectively. In all, as Arterton (1984) noted, "The behavior of campaigners is directly affected by the behavior of journalists" (p. 2).

In media politics, as Gurevitch and Blumler (1990) pointed out, mediated political messages "are a subtly composite product, reflecting the contributions and interactions of two different types of communicators, advocates and journalists" (p. 278). This chapter reports on our ongoing research program, which looks at how this subtly composite product is depicted in metacoverage, and at how metacoverage turns back and shapes the very political logic it depicts. In the process, we have aimed to clarify further how framing analysis is an invaluable tool to observe the surface and deeper layers – the manifest and latent layers – of a type of news that gauges the level of mediatization in a country's election system.

The study of metacoverage presents news researchers with a unique opportunity and a distinct challenge. The opportunity is there to take the pulse of the mediatization in a country's election system through an analysis of texts that delve into the media-infused process of an election. Given the normative alignments in political communication research, some scholars would seem to dismiss this endeavor as looking in the wrong place to answer the right questions about the health of a democracy (e.g., Kerbel, 1998; Patterson, 1993). In a discussion of journalistic autonomy, for example, Bennett and Livingston (2003) went so far as to state that, "The strategic management of the flow of information invites journalists to create news about nothing – or to report meta-news about the game of political communication and news management" (p. 360). By contrast, we feel that it is imprudent to dismiss outright news that focuses on the mediated process of modern elections. Rather, the challenge should be to continue to develop a conceptual framework and measurement tools that illuminate the role metacoverage plays in the inter-organizational dependencies of electoral politics. For only then will one of the molding forces of mediatization come into view.

Notes

1. This chapter utilizes Esser's (2013) definitions of media logic and political logic. A brief summary of these definitions is also given in the introductory chapter by Strömbäck and Esser of this volume. Note that of the three facets of political logic (a "politics-oriented self-presentational side" during elections, a "policy-and decision-based making of politics" that dominates the stages of policy making and policy implementation and the "institutional framework conditions of politics" that refer to the regulatory context), the present chapter only deals with the first facet. We refer to this first facet in this chapter as political *campaign* logic. It is particularly prevalent in phases "when politicians seek to gain office in election campaigns or when they, once in office, approach governing as a permanent campaign" (Esser, 2013, p. 165).
2. The total number of ads aired and the money spent on ads were surpassed during the 2012 election (from 1 June forward). President Obama aired more ads and outspent Gov. Romney; however, the gap between the two in both statistics narrowed considerably when factoring in the ads aired by political support groups, which spent more on ads for Gov. Romney.
3. Of all election-related stories on ABC and NBC News, we coded 100% in 2000 (N = 284) and 50% in 2008 (N = 106). In 2008, we added 25% of stories from CNN's AC 360 (N = 113) and Fox's Special Report (N = 200). Sampling was done according to a rolling rotation ensuring even representation of stories across channels and days.
4. The same salience rules were used to observe the eight "campaign" topics.
5. The difference between the two types of channels is significant (t-test, $p < .01$) for media metacoverage topics.
6. Coders were instructed to tote up scripts in order to determine at least one, but possibly two, dominant metacoverage frames in a story. However, for both election years, two frames were observed in less than 10% of the metacoverage stories.
7. Note that stories with accountability frames also contain a hefty dose of conduit-based mediation scripts, which stress the transmission role of mediation in the US presidential campaigns.

References

Aalberg, T., Strömbäck, J., & de Vreese, C. H. (2012). The Framing of Politics as Strategy and Game: A Review of Concepts, Operationalizations and Key Findings. *Journalism*, 13(2), 162–178.

Arterton, C. F. (1978). Campaign Organizations Confront the Media-political Environment. In J. Barber (Ed.), *Race for the Presidency: The Media and the Nominating Process* (pp. 3–25). Englewood Cliffs, NJ: Prentice Hall.

Arterton, C. F. (1984). *Media Politics: The News Strategies of Presidential Campaigns.* Lexington, MA: Lexington Books.

Baum, M. A. (2003). *Soft News Goes to War: Public Opinion and American Foreign Policy in the New Media Age.* Princeton, NJ: Princeton University Press.

Bennett, W. L. (1992). *The Governing Crisis: Media, Money, and Marketing in American Elections.* New York, NY: St. Martin's Press.

Bennett, W. L., & Livingston, S. (2003). The Semi-independent Press: Government Control and Journalistic Autonomy in the Political Construction of News. *Political Communication,* 20(4), 359–362.

Blumler, J. G., & Gurevitch, M. (2001). Americanization Reconsidered: US-UK Campaign Communication Comparisons across Time. In W. L. Bennett & R. M. Entman (Eds.), *Mediated Politics: Communication in the Future of Democracy* (pp. 380–403). Cambridge, UK: Cambridge University Press.

Blumler, J. G., & Kavanagh, D. (1999). The Third Age of Political Communication: Influences and Features. *Political Communication,* 16(3), 209–230.

Brants, K., & Voltmer, K. (2011). Introduction: Mediatization and Decentralization of Political Communication. In K. Brants & V. Voltmer (Eds.), *Political Communication in Postmodern Democracy. Challenging the Primacy of Politics* (pp. 1–16). Basingstoke: Palgrave Macmillan.

Carey, J. (1976). How Media Shape Campaigns. *Journal of Communication,* 26, 50–57.

Dahl, R. A. (2000). *On Democracy.* New Haven: Yale University Press.

Davis, R. (1992). *The Press and American Politics: The New Mediator.* New York: Longman.

Diamond, E. (1991). *The Media Show.* Cambridge, MA: MIT Press.

Entman, R. M. (1989). *Democracy without Citizens.* New York, NY: Oxford University Press.

Esser, F. (2013). Mediatization as a Challenge: Media Logic versus Political Logic. In H. Kriesi, S. Lavenex, F. Esser, J. Matthes, M. Bühlmann & D. Bochsler (Eds), *Democracy in the Age of Globalization and Mediatization* (pp. 155–176). New York: Palgrave Macmillan.

Esser, F., & D'Angelo, P. (2003). Framing the Press and the Publicity Process: A Content Analysis of Meta-coverage in Campaign 2000 Network News. *American Behavioral Scientist,* 46, 617–641.

Esser, F., & D'Angelo, P. (2006). Framing the Press and the Publicity Process in U.S., British, and German General Election Campaigns: A Comparative Study of Metacoverage. *Harvard International Journal of Press/Politics,* 11, 44–66.

Esser, F., Reinemann, C., & Fan, D. (2001). Spin Doctors in the United States, Great Britain, and Germany: Metacommunication about Media Manipulation. *Harvard International Journal of Press/Politics,* 6, 16–45.

Friedenberg, R. V. (1997). *Communication Consultants in Political Campaigns: Ballot Box Warriors.* Westport, CT: Praeger.

Gitlin, T. (1991). Blips, Bytes and Savvy Talk: Television's Impact on American Politics. In P. Dahlgren & C. Sparks (Eds.), *Communication and Citizenship* (pp. 119–136). London: Routledge.

Gurevitch, M., & Blumler, J. G. (1990). Political Communication Systems and Democratic Values. In J. Lichtenberg (Ed.), *Democracy and the Mass Media* (pp. 269–289). Cambridge: Cambridge University Press.

Hendricks, J. A., & Denton, R. E., Jr. (Eds.) (2010). *Communicator-in-Chief: How Barack Obama Used New Media Technology to Win the White House*. Lanham, MD: Lexington Books.

Hepp, A. (2012). Mediatization and the "Molding Force" of the Media. *Communications*, 37, 1–28.

Hjarvard, S. (2008). The Mediatization of Society: A Theory of the Media as Agents of Social and Cultural Change. *Nordicom Review*, 29(2), 105–134.

Johnson, T. J., & Boudreau, T. (1996). Turning the Spotlight Inward: How Leading News Organizations Covered the Media in the 1992 Presidential Election. *Journalism & Mass Communication Quarterly*, 73, 657–671.

Jones, J. P. (2005). The Shadow Campaign in Popular Culture. In R. E. Denton, Jr. (Ed.), *The 2004 Presidential Campaign: A Communication Perspective* (pp. 195–216). New York: Rowman & Littlefield.

Kerbel, M. R. (1997). The Media: Viewing the Campaign through a Strategic Haze. In M. Nelson (Ed.), *The Elections of 1996* (pp. 81–105). Washington, DC: CQ Press.

Kerbel, M. R. (1998). *Edited for Television: CNN, ABC, and American Presidential Politics*. 2nd Edition. Boulder, CO: Westview Press.

Kerbel, M. R., Apee, S., & Ross, M. (2000). PBS Ain't So Different: Public Broadcasting, Election Frames, and Democratic Empowerment. *Harvard International Journal of Press/Politics*, 5, 8–32.

Krotz, F. (2008). Media Connectivity: Concepts, Conditions, and Consequences. In A. Hepp, F. Krotz, S. Moores, & C. Winter (Eds.), *Connectivity, Networks and Flows* (pp. 13–32). Cresskill, NJ: Hampton Press.

Lichter, R. S., Noyes, R. E., & Kaid, L. L. (1999). Negative News or No News: How the Networks Nixed the '96 Campaign. In L. L. Kaid & D. G. Bystrom (Eds.), *The Electronic Election: Perspectives on the 1996 Campaign Communication* (pp. 3–13). Mahwah, NJ: Lawrence Erlbaum Publishers.

Lieber, P. S., & Golan, G. J. (2011). Political Public Relations, News Management, and Agenda Indexing. In J. Strömbäck & S. Kiousis (Eds.), *Political Public Relations: Principles and Applications* (pp. 54–74). New York: Routledge.

Mazzoleni, G., & Schulz, W. (1999). Mediatization of Politics: A Challenge for Democracy? *Political Communication*, 16(3), 247–262.

Neveu, E. (2002). Four Generations of Political Journalism. In R. Kuhn & E. Neveu (Eds.), *Political Journalism – New Challenges, New Practices* (pp. 22–43). London: Routledge.

Patterson, T. E. (1980). *The Mass Media Election: How Americans Choose Their President*. New York: Praeger.

Patterson, T. E. (1993). *Out of Order*. New York: Knopf.

Plouffe, D. (2010). *The Audacity to Win: The Inside Story and Lessons of Barack Obama's Historic Victory*. New York: Penguin.

Polsby, N. W. (1983). *Consequences of Party Reform*. Oxford, UK: Oxford University Press.

Prior, M. (2003). Any Good News in Soft News? The Impact of Soft News Preference on Political Knowledge. *Political Communication*, 20(2), 149–171.

Salmore, B. G., & Salmore, S. A. (1989). *Candidates, Parties, and Campaigns: Electoral Politics in America*. 2nd Edition. Washington, DC: Congressional Quarterly Press.

Schrott, A. (2009). Dimensions: Catch-all Label or Technical Term. In K. Lundby (Ed.), *Mediatization: Concept, Changes, Consequences* (pp. 41–61). New York: Peter Lang.

Stempel, G. H., & Windhauser, J. W. (1991). Newspaper Coverage of the 1984 and 1988 Campaigns. In G. H. Stempel, III & J. W. Windhauser (Eds.), *The Media in* the *1984 and 1988 Presidential Campaigns* (pp. 13–66). Westport, CT: Greenwood Press.

Strömbäck, J. (2008). Four Phases of Mediatization: An Analysis of the Mediatization of Politics. *International Journal of Press Politics*, 13(3): 228–246.

Strömbäck, J. (2011). Mediatization and Perceptions of the Media's Political Influence. *Journalism Studies*, 12, 423–439.

Strömbäck, J., & Esser, F. (2009). Shaping Politics: Mediatization and Media Interventionism. In K. Lundby (Ed.), *Mediatization. Concept, Changes, Consequences* (pp. 205–223). New York: Peter Lang.

Tedesco, J. C. (2011). Political Public Relations and Agenda Building. In J. Strömbäck & S. Kiousis (Eds.), *Political Public Relations: Principles and Applications* (pp. 75–94). New York: Routledge.

Vargas, J. A. (20 August 2008). Obama's Wide Web. *The Washington Post.* Retrieved from http://washingtonpost.com/wp-dyn/content/article/2008/08/19/ARC2008081903186_pf.html

Wattenberg, M. P. (1994). *The Decline of American Political Parties 1952–1992.* Cambridge: Harvard University Press.

West, D. M. (2009). *Air Wars: Television Advertising in Election Campaigns, 1952–2008.* 5th Edition. Washington, DC: CQ Press.

Wise, D., & Brewer, P. R. (2010). News about News in a Presidential Primary Campaign: Press Metacoverage on Evening News, Political Talk, and Political Comedy Programs. *Atlantic Journal of Communication*, 18, 127–143.

10
Mediatization of Political Organizations: Changing Parties and Interest Groups?

Patrick Donges and Otfried Jarren

This chapter analyzes the mediatization of politics at the meso level of political organizations. According to the theoretical framework of this book, our issue is located on the fourth dimension of mediatization, "the degree to which political actors are governed by a political logic or by media logic" (Strömbäck, 2008, p. 234; see also Strömbäck & Dimitrova, 2011). Our theoretical argument will challenge the idea of a single and homogenous media logic and of a clear dichotomy of political "versus" media logic. Instead, we want to argue that political organizations are influenced by a diversity of political as well as media logics. To develop our argument, we will first discuss what kind of actors political organizations like parties and interest groups are and what we can learn about them from organizational theories. Secondly, we will propose that we should broaden our scope by natural and open system views of organizations. Thirdly, we will reformulate the concept of mediatization at an organizational and institutional level. Fourthly, we will present some empirical results from surveys of party and interest-group organizations to illustrate our theoretical argumentation.

Missing theoretical concepts of political organizations

In the debate on mediatization of politics, there are quite a few implicit assumptions about the nature of political organizations, but no explicit concept of how the diverse forms of political organizations are affected by the media. In the literature, most authors speak of political actors, and not explicitly of organizations. The equation of organizations with actors is not unproblematic: organizations are not only actors that are capable of acting, which means they have goals, a strategy, resources, etc. They are also structures in which individual actors act. This duality of organizations, being "both micro and macro" (Taylor et al., 1996, p. 1), underlies their important role within our society as a whole and political communication in particular: (political) organizations act as agents or bridges – others say inter-mediaries (Habermas, 2006) – between citizens in their "lebenswelt" and the political system. Therefore we have to distinguish between organizations as actors and structures of political communication.

When equating actors with organizations, scholars commit themselves to a *rational paradigm* in organizational theory. Following Scott (2003), the rational paradigm considers organizations as systems of formalized struc-tures designed to attain specific goals with maximum (or at least satisfactory) efficiency. In such a paradigm, communication is regarded as an instrument of the organization to attain its goals. In other words: party organizations want to win elections, and therefore they communicate in a specific way. But Scott also specifies two other paradigms within organizational theory. In a *natural system view*, organizations may be regarded as "collectivities whose participants are pursuing multiple interests, both desperate and com-mon, but who recognize the value of perpetuating the organization as an important resource" (Scott, 2003, p. 28). In corresponding theories, e.g., the process-oriented approach of "organizing" by Weick (1979) or the "resource dependence perspective" by Pfeffer and Salancik (1978), it is not assumed to be a necessity for actors in organizations to share common goals. The main focus is their interaction and the result of their interaction, which we call organization. Therefore, communication is not regarded as an organizational instrument, but the organization itself is constituted by communication (CCO-Approach, see, e.g., Cooren et al., 2011; Putnam et al., 2009). Thirdly, in an *open system view*, organizations may be regarded as "congeries of interdependent flows and activities linking shifting coalitions of partici-pants embedded in wider material-resource and institutional environments" (Scott, 2003, p. 29). Some of these activities are connected by formal struc-tures, others are loosely coupled (Orton & Weick, 1990; Weick, 1976). The most important open system view is sociological institutionalism.

The missing theoretical concept of what a political organization is and how it works can be exemplarily understood when we look at the litera-ture on the mechanisms of mediatization. An integral part in definitions and descriptions of mediatization is the notion of *adaption* or *adoption* of political actors. Mediatization is characterized as "the adaption of politics to the needs of the mass media" (Kepplinger, 2002, p. 973) or as politi-cal actors who "adapt to the rules of the media system trying to increase their publicity and at the same time accepting a loss of autonomy" (Schulz, 2004, p. 89). Strömbäck (2008, p. 240) distinguishes between a third phase of mediatization where political actors "*adapt* to the media logic" from a fourth phase where they "*adopt* the same media logic [...], perhaps not even recognizing the distinction between a political and a media logic". Follow-ing Strömbäck and van Aelst (2013), "the question is not if political parties adapt to the media. They do. Hardly any political actor today would seri-ously claim that they do not take the media into consideration, either as presenting opportunities or threats" (p. 353). But is it justifiable (and reasonable) to equate "taking into consideration" with the concept of adaption? Originally based in biology, adaption refers to evolutionary processes that guide natural selection and lead to a "survival of the fittest". And while biologists are interested in the evolution and survival of species as a result of processes of adaption, social scientists are interested in the mechanisms of the processes itself. Following Giddens (1984), it may be argued that the term "adaption" often remains imprecisely defined in social sciences because it contains all possible sources of influence on social phenomena. Concerning the relationship between political organizations and the media, the problem for organizations is not to adapt to the needs of the mass media. The problem is that these needs are unclear, ambiguous or contradictory and may change rapidly. From an organizational viewpoint, there is no clear and stable environment called "the media" to which the organization can adapt, especially since the organization loses something in the process, namely, its adaptability in the event of environmental changes (Kurke, 1988). The challenge for the organization is its ability to cope with unclear, ambiguous or contradictory needs. The main challenge for (political) organizations, therefore, is not adaption per se but the capacity to adapt to multiple or conflicting environments (Staber & Sydow, 2002).

The dichotomy of (one) media vs. (one) political or party logic

The notion that environments of political organizations may be multiple or conflicting leads to another important argument in the debate on mediatization of politics: the dichotomy of (one) media vs. (one) political or party logic. The dichotomy was introduced by Mazzoleni in his classical article on "media logic and party logic" (1987). In this he defines media logic with reference to Altheide and Snow as

> the set of values and formats through which campaign events and issues are focused on, treated, and given meaning [by news workers and news organizations] in order to promote a particular kind of presentation and understanding that [is] compatible with, for example, scheduling and time considerations, entertainment values, and images of the audience.
> (Mazzoleni, 1987, p. 85)

Mazzoleni's juxtaposition of party logic vs. media logic inspired many follow-up studies and led to a further differentiation. Brants and van Praag (2006) use the term "media logic" to mark a phase of development in political communication in the Netherlands from 1990 onwards that they separate from a "partisan logic" (until 1970) and a "public logic" (1970–1990). Brants and van Praag characterized the phase of media logic as the public being mainly addressed as consumers but not as citizens. Journalism in the phase of media logic is described by Brants and van Praag as dominant, entertaining and cynical, and the style of coverage as interpretative and of less substance than in the preceding period of "public logic". The agenda of politics in media logic is no longer set by parties but by media, which is why audience democracy and no longer party democracy is the corresponding model of democracy (Brants & van Praag, 2006, p. 31). Van Aelst et al. (2008) distinguish a "partisan logic", "party logic" and "media logic" in a study on media attention. A media logic is characterized by the fact that the attention of politicians is supposedly defined by journalistic criteria, the "working rules of the media and elements that might attract and hold the attention of the public" (Van Aelst et al., 2008, p. 197). However, such media logic is difficult to operationalize empirically because there are almost no measurable indicators for media logic. The authors take a shortcut by describing media logic as absence of party logic (Van Aelst et al., 2008, p. 198).

Besides the differentiation of media logic from other logics in other subsystems of society, we also find differentiations within media logic. Mazzoleni (2008b, p. 445) distinguishes commercial logic (that he sees as the most important part) from industrial, technological, cultural and political logic. Characteristics of media logic are the accentuation of persons, the simplification of complex issues, the focus on confrontation instead of compromise, and a perspective on politics that is characterized by winners and losers. Media logic thus stands for processes "that eventually shape and frame media content" (Mazzoleni, 2008a, p. 2931). Esser (2013) specifies media logic towards a concept of news media logic and distinguishes between professional aspects (production following journalistic norms and criteria) and commercial and technological aspects: "Professionalization, commercialization, and technological change are the independent variables that explain (or drive) media logic but it is important to recognize that these processes have developed differently in different countries and across time" (Esser, 2013, p. 175).

But despite these attempts of differentiation, media logic is used as a very successful metaphor or catch-all term for several different perceived and actual forms of communication. It is not clear whether media logic is a form or a style of communication or (perhaps simultaneously) the rule of the process through which this form is created. This leads to the current situation wherein it is difficult to operationalize and to measure media logic(s).

A first step towards a more differentiated understanding of the logics of various media becomes possible with the definition of media by Ulrich Saxer. According to him, media are complex institutionalized systems around organized communication channels of specific capability (Saxer, 1999, p. 6). Saxer's definition points out that media are at the same time technical communication channels, organizations, institutions and social systems that have functional and dysfunctional effects on other parts or subsystems of society.

As *technical channels*, media are instruments and technologies that enable communication across space, time and social collectives. They transport visual, auditive or audiovisual signs with different capacities (cf. Jensen, 2008). In this aspect, the term media logic denotes the characteristics of communication channels as well as the used sign systems. First and foremost, it is of relevance which sign systems can be transported via which media. Print media like newspapers allow for a greater density of information than audiovisual media like television. They allow the recipients greater freedom, for example in their choice of speed of reception and thoroughness, by allowing them to "scan" or "flick" through texts or even pause the reception. Currently, text-based media also have a greater storage capacity than audiovisual media because they can be more easily tag-labeled or archived. Audiovisual media like television receive their genuine media logic through the combination of language and moving pictures, which has since the beginning led to the ascription of higher effects. From this technological perspective, the differentiation between pushes and pull forms of media also becomes relevant. Push media produce a hierarchy of messages and make them visible to a wider public, for example as headlines in daily newspapers. Pull media offer their content for recipients (now called users) to pick up. The communication process is then more strongly controlled by the recipient and less controllable for the communicator.

Media communication is secondly characterized as *being organized*. As organizations, media pursue their own aims and interests that may contain, depending on the type of organization, different logics. According to Altmeppen (2006), media can be differentiated as journalistic organizations (for example as editorial staff) or as economic organizations (as publishers or business enterprises). Journalistic organizations are more strongly bound to logics of selection that are induced by news values. As economic organizations, they are bound by a commercial logic. Besides this, media organizations may also follow a political logic, for instance the political orientation of the editors and publishers. Particularly in broadcasting, the organizational form is of importance. Private and public broadcasting corporations differ in their normative orientation, their style of addressing audiences as customers or as citizens, as well as the internally practiced procedures of quality control and diversity management (Kiefer, 1996). Many different studies point out that there are differences in the programming of both types of broadcasting corporations: political news coverage is mainly a responsibility of public service, whereas private media have marginalized political news coverage and instead concentrate on more "boulevardesque" elements and on visualization of emotions (Daschmann, 2009). These studies highlight the fact that we can clearly separate a logic of public television from a logic of private television. With the term "media logic", these differences in the provision of services by both types of organizations in broadcasting are neglected and ignored.

Furthermore, media can be characterized as *institutions*. They are systems of rules that create normative expectations, contain mechanisms for their realization, constitute actors, and influence the perception, preference formation, and structures in existing organizations (Cook, 1998, 2006; Donges, 2006; Ryfe, 2006a, 2006b; Sparrow, 2006). For other actors in society who depend on their intermediation, media are one of many relevant institutional environments; in other words, environments which place demands on actors and secure legitimacy if they follow these rules. The institutional demands of the media do not necessarily need to be homogeneous and crystallize into a form of media logic. In particular, normative expectations of media towards societal actors can be different. One only needs to think of the different demands of media geared to delivering information or entertainment. It is of further relevance that we distinguish between quality and popular media. Quality media are the result of an individual and social construction process, an expression of an audience's expectation of a certain quality of intermediation as well as knowledge (Jarren & Vogel, 2011). Quality media are characterized by their own logic that distinguishes them from other media.

Another important, but often neglected, differentiation in the media system is that of general and sectoral media. This differentiation becomes relevant for the question of media logics because sectoral media tend to address expert rather than lay audiences. Media and communication studies tend to overlook these media types. We know little about the content, usage and influence of sectoral media and their role in political communication. But it can be assumed that they are influential within certain political networks and therefore show their own "logic" with repercussions for the political process.

Another crucial problem of the notion of one media logic is the uncertainty of whether it includes *online media* or not. The specific rules by which online media provide orientation and generate attention are less well known than the traditional news values of old media. For example, there are news and messages that disseminate rapidly over the net and find many "followers", but as they are characterized by other properties than just traditional news values, it is less clear why exactly these and not other messages become viral. Online media have a higher speed of transmission, and content can be modified more quickly. The character of online media as an archive (storage media) is therefore ambivalent: a discussion of the characteristics of the "online media logic" is yet to come.

To conclude, there are good reasons to deny the existence of one single media logic and to accept that the logics of different media types such as tabloids, the quality press, public service broadcasting or online media differ. According to Lundby (2009, p. 117), it is "not viable to speak of an overall media logic; it is necessary to specify how various capabilities are applied in various patterns of social interactions". Furthermore, because the media are influenced by other social institutions or system logics such as commercialization, we cannot always be certain that observed media influences imply submission to media logic alone (Hjarvard, 2008). Like other social phenomenon, media logics do not exist naturally but are socially constructed. Therefore, as Altheide and Snow (1979) have already indicated, "the entire process is best understood as an interaction among the various participants rather than as a one-way form in which media dictate definitions of reality" (p. 236).

An institutional approach to mediatization at an organizational level

In our own theoretical approach, we reject the mainstream view of political organizations as rational or professional actors, but consider them as loosely coupled and open systems of action (see above). Secondly, we consider the media as one important institutional environment of political organizations and use the background of sociological institutionalism to elaborate our definition of mediatization at an organizational level.

In a general sense, an institution can be defined as a relatively stable collection or system of practices and rules defining appropriate behavior for specific groups of actors in specific situations (March & Olson, 1998, p. 948). Following Scott (1994), four different types of rules may be distinguished and assigned to the media as institutions: "Institutions are symbolic and behavioral systems containing representational, constitutive, and normative rules together with regulatory mechanisms that define a common meaning system and give rise to distinctive actors and action routines" (p. 68). *Firstly, institutions include normative rules in terms of expectations of how actors should behave in specific situations.* Media define such expectations since all political actors observe that the media observe them. All kinds of political actors must be prepared to be an object of media coverage at any time. In other words: the starting point of mediatization is the question "how will it play in the media?" (Blumler & Kavanagh, 1999, p. 214). *Secondly, institutions include representational rules that help to create shared understandings of reality that are taken for granted.* Media as institutions include many such "taken-for-granted accounts". The source of media power is the fact that everyone in society – including politicians, spokespersons or consultants – has learned to adjust and adapt to the different media logics as the "normal" way of perceiving and interpreting the world (Altheide & Snow, 1979, pp. 236–237). The logics of the different media are themselves socially constructed and have evolved from earlier practices and relations between the media and other spheres of society. Actors take them for granted as the "normal" or "rational" way to behave in a certain situation. Thereby, the institutional rules of the media are continually reproduced. *Thirdly, institutions include constitutive rules that create social phenomena.* Media are institutions because they structure both the actor's perception, especially in those fields where they constitute the most important or dominant source of information, and his or her preferences. They are not only mediators, but also creators of meaning. Finally, a wide range of actors, including spokespersons, consultants and agencies for communication, has been constituted because of institutional requirements. In other words, the process of mediatization creates its own driving forces, especially in the shape of actors with an interest in the process that is going on. *Finally, institutions include regulatory mechanisms for enforcement reasons.* One of these is the forfeiting of attention: whenever political actors do not follow the rules that indicate the newsworthiness of an event, they do not get the media's attention.

Therefore, media are one institutional environment characterized by rules and requirements to which these organizations must conform "if they are to receive support and legitimacy" (Scott & Meyer, 1991, p. 123). The notion of "one environment" is important, since organizations usually act within a variety of institutional environments. This is important since institutions "may abrade or even clash with each other", which may lead to fundamental conflicts within organizations. Actors still have the possibility, and sometimes are forced, to choose between several options on dealing with institutional requirements (Oliver, 1991; Scott, 2001; Suchman, 1995). One main assumption of sociological institutionalism is that organizations generally do not choose the most effective option, but rather the most legitimate one. Legitimacy may be defined as a "generalized perception or assumption that the actions of an entity are desirable, proper, or appropriate within some socially constructed system of norms, values, beliefs, and definitions" (Suchman, 1995, p. 574). While seeking legitimacy, organizations transfer and incorporate the requirements of their institutional environment in forms of "highly rationalized myths" (Meyer & Rowan, 1977, p. 343). One main mechanism of this incorporation is imitation or mimetic isomorphism: "When organizational technologies are poorly understood [...], when goals are ambiguous, or when the environment creates symbolic uncertainty, organizations may model themselves on other organizations" (DiMaggio & Powell, 1983, p. 151).

We are now able to transfer the institutional argument on our issue mediatization of political organizations and to develop – in three steps – a definition of mediatization and its indicators: *mediatization of politics at an organizational level may be defined as a reaction of political organizations.* As argued above, mediatization is neither a strategic option nor an enforcement of adaptation. Mediatization has to be treated as a reaction where some decisions are more probable than others, but not determined. *This reaction is the consequence of perceiving the media and mediated communication as gaining in importance in their environment.* This condition requires that organizations are able to perceive change in their environment, to decide that they are relevant and to act accordingly. *Finally, the reaction implies (and becomes visible through) changes in organizational structure (rules and resources for communication) and behavior (degree and form of communication output).*

Thus, the first aspect of mediatization is *perception*, which should not be taken for granted (see Table 10.1). Political organizations may misinterpret their social environment, or may follow some overdrawn assumptions of the effect of mediated communication. As on an individual level, it is plausible that there is an "influence of presumed influence" (Cohen et al., 2008; Gunter & Storey, 2003), which means that political organizations which presume a high media influence will act accordingly. One relevant indicator on this dimension of perception may be the assessment of the media and their role for the organization through their leaders. But it is also of importance that political organizations gain their information about the relevance of the media through the media. Therefore, another relevant indicator is how organizations organize their perception of the media, for instance through media monitoring. If organizations use clippings, the guiding rules of selection may give hints for changing modes of perception. It can also be analyzed how the outcomes of media monitoring are processed within the organization or how often and at what level general issues regarding the relationship between the organization and the media are discussed.

A special case of perception is the *orientation towards other organizations*, a prerequisite for processes of mimetic isomorphism. One relevant indicator is the question about which other organizations are monitored constantly, or to which organization personal contacts exist. Also the question of whether there is an ideal of a "best practice model" concerning organizational communication could be raised with organizational decision-makers. Finally, the modality with respect to whether and how the organization defines its target groups for communication could be relevant to finding out how the organization perceives its environment with regard to which sections are treated as important.

Mediatization at an organizational level becomes manifest in two general ways, namely, changes in organizational structure and behavior (Table 10.1; see also Strömbäck & van Aelst, 2013). Following the terminology of Giddens, *organizational structures* may generally be defined as rules and resources that constrain and enable the organization's activities (Giddens, 1984, p. 17; McPhee & Canary, 2008, p. 3471). *Rules* are generally accepted and formalized instructions relating to which actions should be taken by whom, in which situation and in which manner. Rules constitute behavior by permitting actors to speak for the organization or to decide, for instance, on the choice of press releases or longer-term strategies. Also of importance is the position of the communication unit within the organizational chart, and its competences and responsibilities. One important aspect is the question as to whether change within the media system leads to a centralization of competences at the highest organizational level. Further organizational rules refer to the communication culture or an elaborated

Table 10.1   Mediatization on an organizational level

Aspect	Characteristics	Possible indicators
Perception	Changes in perception of environment	– Increase of media monitoring – Diversification of guiding rules to select articles to monitor – Perception of a growing importance and relevance of mass media for the organization – Existence of a clipping report/transmission of information within the organization – Increase of news agency services
	Orientation to other organizations	– Existence of an ideal or "best practice" model concerning communication – Systematic observation of other parties/"observation of the enemy"
Structure	Increase and/or shift in resources	– Increase of human resources within the communication unit – Increase of financial resources for communication tasks
	Changes in rules	– Changes of organizational charts and position of the communication unit – Existence of a corporate identity – Existence of corporate communication – Changes of responsibilities concerning communication tasks
	Externalization	– Increase of cooperation with external consulters – Increase of media training and consulting services
Behavior	Increase and diversification in communication output	– Increase of press releases and press conferences – Diversification of channels or utilization of new channels and technologies – (podcast, Internet streaming, etc.) – Diversification of target group communication

identity of the organizations, manifested in rules of behavior, regulations for the use of logos and so forth. Such rules regulate social practices and constitute meaning, and their changes are important indicators for the process of mediatization.

The second component of organizational structures is the *resources*. The most obvious are financial and human resources; in other words, people and money invested in the organization's communication. Specific knowledge and access to media actors are also important resources from an organizational point of view, but not easy to measure. A special feature of the organizational resources is *externalization*, that is to say the question of whether the organization outsources certain tasks or cooperates with consultants or external coaches. The emergence of such actors outside political organizations and increased cooperation are indicators for mediatization processes.

Organizational *behavior* like communication always takes place within the organizational structure with its describable set of rules and resources (Table 10.1). Secondly, and this is the main idea of Giddens' theory of structuration, organizational structure is reproduced by organizational behavior. For the purpose of analyzing mediatization, the amount and the diversification of communication are of special interest. Possible indicators for an increase in communication are the number of press releases or press conferences, the diversification of target groups and special offers for them, or the diversification of channels of communication.

The distinction of the dimensions and its characteristics may be useful for empirical studies on mediatization. The listed indicators are of course context-dependent (e.g., concerning countries or types of political organizations) and time-dependent (e.g., concerning the intrusion of online media in political communication).

Empirical findings

To illustrate our theoretical argument, we will present some key findings on the mediatization of political parties (2005–2007) and interest groups (2009–2013) (Donges, 2008; Jentges, Brändli, Donges, & Jarren, 2012, 2013)[1] taken from two research projects within the National Center of Competence in Research Challenges to Democracy in the 21st Century (NCCR Democracy) at the University of Zurich.

Mediatization of political parties

The sample of our first study consists of traditional and large party organizations, both from the conservative or Christian democratic end and from the social democratic end of the political spectrum. Two parties were sampled for Germany (SPD, CDU), the United Kingdom (Labour, Conservatives) and Austria (SPOE, OEVP), and four in Switzerland (SPS, FDP, SVP, CVP). We chose traditional organizations because we are interested in change within organizations, not in the adjustment of newly founded organizations. We examined party central offices in non-election periods, analyzed party documents and interviewed party representatives such as the head of communication and the general secretary.

The results generally support the assumption that there are structural changes within party organizations as a consequence of processes of mediatization, but the data also support the qualification put forward by

Mazzoleni and Schulz (1999) that these changes take different forms and develop at different speeds depending on contextual conditions.

With respect to the first aspect of mediatization – the perception of the environment and the role of mediated communication for parties – it is hardly surprising that the interviewees perceive an increasing importance of the media. They use the term "professionalization" as a code for various changes of communication, most of all an increase of speed and the need for permanent availability. What is more interesting is that the respondents also pointed out that the importance of other forms of communication grows. Party organizations not only enlarge their mediated communication, but also the interpersonal and online communication – the latter mainly for the purpose of internal communication.

A second point is the question of whether there is a monitoring of other forms of organizations in terms of "best practice" models for the parties. These are mainly their direct competitors and other forms of member-based political organizations within the same country. This means the perception of party organizations is mainly national. There are some examples of transnational diffusion, for instance the successful implementation of an external campaign office by Labour in the United Kingdom in 1997, but most of the monitoring is nationally oriented.

A third point is more of a detail, albeit an interesting one. We found a very strong conservatism in how the party organizations monitor the media. The typical case is a long-serving member of staff going through the press clippings early on in the day and just using his or her intuition rather than following any formal rules. Delegating the task to trainees is also common. Only one organization used an electronic form of press observation, and it was interesting to see that this organization has difficulties defining catchwords in such a way as not to repeatedly get the same news from several sources.

Mediatization can be seen in the expansion of organizational structures and in the assignment of human resources. Two models of internal structures of communication became apparent: the integration of all communication within one unit and the differentiation of internal and external communication in different units. A bundling of competencies, tasks and resources in terms of centralization could not be validated. In particular, parties with a highly federalized organizational structure find it difficult to change their internal structures and instead have to balance the requirements of media communication (for instance on speed) and internal factions (for instance on participation or at a minimum consultation). Party organizations are investing more and more resources in communication, especially staff, but these developments must be considered against the background of declining membership and its financial impact. Concerning the amount of financial resources for communication, a general trend for an increase is not observable.

Table 10.2   Organizational chart of the SPS

1992	2000	2005
• Secretaries • Research associates • Administration, translation, information technology	• Politics • **Communication** • Campaigns/ • Cantons/women • Finance/administration	• Politics • **Campaigns & communication** • Board support unit • Finance/staff/ administration
Staff for communication: 0	3	9

To point out an example, Table 10.2 shows the development of the Social Democratic Party of Switzerland (SPS), which is typical for the development of Swiss party organizations. In 1992, the party had no clear responsibilities for communication and used none of its own staff for this purpose, while since 2005 campaigns and communication is the largest organizational unit of the party central office, with nine staff members.

Another point with respect to structural changes is the growing importance of the communication unit within the organization. An example of this is the German Social Democratic Party (SPD). In the 1990s, it had a small press office, affiliated to the party manager, and a public relations office, affiliated to the "Organization, Party Work" department. Seventeen years later, the press office has been upgraded to a department with more staff, while a second department dealing with planning and communication, with units for mediated, online and interpersonal communication, has also been established.

We do not want to suggest that all indicators on mediatization show a clear development towards increased importance for mediated communication. While the expenditure on staff mostly grows, there are some indicators that suggest that party organizations have difficulties maintaining the level of expenditure in times of decreasing membership.

The third aspect of mediatization focuses on the behavior of party organizations. With respect to the use of "old media" or traditional forms of communication, such as press releases, we found a general increase, with big differences between parties. For instance, the most successful party in Switzerland, the right-wing Swiss People's Party (SVP), produced the fewest press releases among the governing parties in Switzerland.

A second point is the Internet, which today is the most important medium for internal communication. But there is a link between mediated and online communication: the Internet is used not only because it is cheaper, but also to inform the party's membership or functionaries before the media do. In this sense, the Internet in our sample is mainly used for top-down communication; we found no references indicating that online communication leads to new forms of participation or bottom-up-communication, as is sometimes expected.

All new forms of communication (the Internet, podcasts, Internet streaming, etc.) are used in addition to traditional forms of mediated communication without replacing them. Nevertheless, parties do not have a clear strategy for the use of these new forms of communication. They use them because others do so, because consultants have told them to do so, and to give supporters the impression of a "modern" and "innovative" party.

Mediatization of political interest groups

The sample of our second study consists of 1,142 political interest groups in Germany and 862 in Switzerland. We drew this sample through a compilation of different data sources (handbooks, parliamentarian registries, etc.), eliminated the duplicate entries and collected the email addresses. Finally, a link to an online questionnaire was sent to the person in charge of communication. The response rate for this survey was 23% in Germany and 40% in Switzerland.

Concerning the aspect of mediatization that deals with *perception*, we found that *an interest group's own members are clearly its most important addressees* with respect to communication and that this is so irrespective of country or political area. The second most important addressees are government and administration, with the media following in third position. In other words, media are important, but not as important as expected. Citizens appear to have rather low relevance in the communication of interest groups, including in Switzerland with its direct democracy.

Concerning the question of which media are important addressees for political interest groups, we have been surprised by the fact that special interest publications (print as well as online) are perceived as the most important form of media, followed by newspapers and public service television. The least important media in Germany are private television, private radio and blogs/Twitter, and in Switzerland political weeklies, social networks on the Internet and blogs/Twitter.

With respect to the resources for communication, we found a clear correlation between instruments used for communication purposes and the organizational resources in the shape of the annual budget. Not surprisingly, the finding was the higher the budget, the higher the degree of communication output. We also found correlations between the communication repertoires and political areas: the output of media-related communication is higher in interest groups that belong to the areas "politics", "environment" and "business and work". Finally, there is a higher communication output in Germany than in Switzerland.

Not only does the general media-oriented communication output of political interest groups depend on organizational resources: the same holds true for their activity in the online world. The greater the size and budget of a political interest group, the more tools it uses for online communication (social network sites, Twitter, blogs, etc.). We expected a link between the age of an interest group and its online communication in the sense that younger organizations would use more tools, but there is no significant correlation. This suggests that the possibility of online communication does not bring about an equalization of weaker political interest groups, but that instead a normalization takes place (Ward & Gibson, 2009; Wright, 2012). Generally speaking, online communication tools are mostly perceived to have gained most in importance, even though they are still used by comparatively few organizations.

In contrast to the idea of a general professionalization of political communication, we also found that very few interest groups outsourced communication activities. This suggests that communication is a task that most organizations want to keep "in house". Only for research do political interest groups tend to draw on external support.

Conclusion

This chapter started with the assumption that "mediatization of politics" could be a valuable and profitable concept if it were more precisely defined and if its theoretical fundaments and implicit suppositions were to be more exposed. Following Mazzoleni and Schulz (1999), the main idea of mediatization is that it represents the media's growing incursion into the political process and not the outcome of an intended form of behavior or even control. Mediatization is the outcome of interdependence and interaction between and within political organizations and the media. For the elaboration of the theoretical concept of mediatization as well as for its empirical appliance, it is thus necessary to clarify what "the media" and "media logic" actually mean. We therefore proposed to reconsider the media and their effects on other social systems from an institutional perspective, and to focus on political organizations both as objects and as actors of mediatization processes. Theories like sociological institutionalism seem to be appropriate for translating the idea of an intrusion in theoretically evident and empirically observable mechanisms, such as in the form of coercive isomorphism, mimetic processes, and normative pressures. Following this approach, mediatization at an organizational level may be defined as a reaction of political organizations following their perception that media and mediated communication gain importance in their environment, and implies change in organizational structure (rules and resources for mediated communication) and behavior (amount and form of mediated communication). This definition of mediatization at an organizational level allows the development of indicators for empirical research and seems to be more appropriate than concepts of a simple adaptation of political actors to the needs of the mass media.

The case study on party organizations gives evidence that mediatization takes place, but we also have reason to believe that transformations within the intermediary system are very complex, uneven and highly conditional: different national contexts, media structures and institutional media arrangements will create different conditions in which mediatization takes place. The theoretical reflection as well as empirical findings point out that it is not adequate to speak about a full adaption of party organizations to one media logic. This assumption is confirmed by the general fact that political parties are very conservative organizations, although – and especially after election defeats – they are able to adjust certain developments and to change structures. Thus, we believe that it is as inappropriate to speak about a single party logic as it is to speak about a single media logic. Therefore, it is necessary to redefine the logics and to substantiate them (see also Esser, 2013; Landerer, 2013; Lundby, 2009).

The degree of the media's impact on political organizations is also dependent on the country-specific context. The perceived media logics lead parties and interest groups to structural changes, but since their organizations are loosely coupled systems of action with a high degree of path dependency, they are not able to simply adjust or subordinate to a media logic, as the literature sometimes suggests. Especially parties with a high degree of internal federalism have to balance the requirements of a "professional" media communication (for instance on speed) and internal factions (for instance on participation or at least consultation). The history of the party organization is also of importance, since parties are very path dependent or conservative organizations.

Finally, the issue of resources should not be neglected. Changes in organizational structures and behavior are not for free, and for the internal differentiation of party organizations it is important which part gets the money. In particular for political interest groups, we must keep in mind that there is not always a structured form of organization, and that direct and interpersonal forms of communication are still of importance. Altogether, this suggests that mediatization as defined as being the structural reactions of organizations to different media logics does take place, but not to the expected degree. For interest groups in particular, interpersonal and closed forms of political communication are still of importance. Generally speaking, we thus follow Marcinkowski's (2005) notion that political organizations as well as political systems will never be completely mediatized, but will rather be characterized by islands of greater or lesser mediatization (p. 364).

Note

1. This publication was created under the auspices of NCCR Democracy, which is funded by the Swiss National Science Foundation (SNF) and the University of

Zurich, and of the research unit "Political Communication in the Online World", subproject "Political Organizations in the Online-World", which is funded by the German Research Foundation (DFG).

References

Altheide, D. L., & Snow, R. P. (1979). *Media Logic.* Beverly Hills, CA: Sage.

Altmeppen, K.-D. (2006). *Journalismus und Medien als Organisation: Leistungen, Strukturen und Management.* Wiesbaden, Germany: VS Verlag für Sozialwissenschaften.

Blumler, J. G., & Kavanagh, D. (1999). The Third Age of Political Communication: Influences and Features. *Political Communication,* 16(3), 209–230.

Brants, K., & van Praag, P. (2006). Signs of Media Logic: Half a Century of Political Communication in the Netherlands. *Javnost – The Public,* 13(1), 25–40.

Cohen, J., Tsfati, Y., & Sheafer, T. (2008). The Influence of Presumed Media Influence in Politics: Do Politician's Perceptions of Media Power Matter? *Public Opinion Quarterly,* 72, 331–344.

Cook, T. E. (1998). *Governing with the News: The News Media as a Political Institution.* Chicago, IL: University of Chicago Press.

Cook, T. E. (2006). The News Media as a Political Institution: Looking Backward and Looking Forward. *Political Communication,* 23(2), 159–171.

Cooren, F., Kuhn, T., Cornelissen, J. P., & Clark, T. (2011). Introduction to the Special Issue: Communication, Organizing and Organization: An Overview. *Organization Studies,* 32(9), 1149–1170.

Daschmann, G. (2009). Qualität von Fernsehnachrichten: Dimensionen und Befunde. Eine Forschungsübersicht. *Media Perspektiven,* 5, 257–266.

DiMaggio, P. J., & Powell, W. W. (1983). The Iron Cage Revisited: Institutional Isomorphism and Collective Rationality in Organizational Fields. *American Sociological Review,* 48(2), 147–160.

Donges, P. (2006). Medien als Institutionen und ihre Auswirkungen auf Organisationen: Perspektiven des soziologischen Neo-Institutionalismus für die Kommunikationswissenschaft. *Medien & Kommunikationswissenschaft,* 54(4), 563–578.

Donges, P. (2008). *Medialisierung politischer Organisationen: Parteien in der Mediengesellschaft.* Wiesbaden, Germany: VS Verlag für Sozialwissenschaften.

Esser, F. (2013). Mediatization as a Challenge: Media Logic Versus Political Logic. In H. Kriesi, S. Lavanex, F. Esser, J. Matthes, M. Bühlmann & D. Bochsler (Eds.), *Democracy in the Age of Globalization and Mediatization* (pp. 155–176). Basingstoke, UK: Palgrave Macmillan.

Giddens, A. (1984). *The Constitution of Society: Outline of the Theory of Structuration.* Cambridge, UK: Polity Press.

Gunter, A. C., & Storey, J. D. (2003). The Influence of Presumed Influence. *Journal of Communication,* 53(2), 199–215.

Habermas, J. (2006). Political Communication in Media Society: Does Democracy Still Enjoy an Epistemic Dimension? The Impact of Normative Theory on Empirical Research. *Communication Theory,* 16(4), 411–426.

Hjarvard, S. (2008). The Mediatization of Society: A Theory of the Media as Agents of Social and Cultural Change. *Nordicom Review,* 29(2), 105–134.

Jarren, O., & Vogel, M. (2011). Leitmedien als Qualitätsmedien: Theoretisches Konzept und Indikatoren. In R. Blum, H. Bonfadelli, K. Imhof & O. Jarren

(Eds.), *Krise der Leuchttürme öffentlicher Kommunikation. Vergangenheit und Zukunft der Qualitätsmedien* (pp. 17–29). Wiesbaden, Germany: VS Verlag für Sozialwissenschaften.

Jensen, K. B. (2008). Media. In W. Donsbach (Ed.), *The International Encyclopedia of Communication* (pp. 2811–2817). Oxford, UK: Wiley-Blackwell.

Jentges, E., Brändli, M., Donges, P., & Jarren, O. (2012). Die Kommunikation politischer Interessengruppen in Deutschland: Adressaten, Instrumente und Logiken. *SCM*, 1(3–4), 381–409.

Jentges, E., Brändli, M., Donges, P., & Jarren, O. (2013). Communication of Political Interest Groups in Switzerland: Addressees, Channels and Instruments. *SCOMS*, 13(1), 33–40.

Kepplinger, H. M. (2002). Mediatization of Politics: Theory and Data. *Journal of Communication*, 52(4), 972–986.

Kiefer, M.-L. (1996). Unverzichtbar oder überflüssig? Öffentlich-rechtlicher Rundfunk in der Multimedia-Welt. *Rundfunk und Fernsehen*, 44(1), 7–26.

Kurke, L. B. (1988). Does Adaptation Preclude Adaptability? Strategy and Performance. In L. G. Zucker (Ed.), *Institutional Patterns and Organizations. Culture and Environment* (pp. 199–222). Cambridge, MA: Ballinger.

Landerer, N. (2013). Rethinking the Logics: A Conceptual Framework for the Mediatization of Politics. *Communication Theory*, 23(3), 239–258. doi: 10.1111/comt.12013

Lundby, K. (2009). Media Logic: Looking for Social Interaction. In K. Lundby (Ed.), *Mediatization: Concept, Changes, Consequences* (pp. 101–119). New York: Peter Lang.

March, J. G., & Olson, J. P. (1998). The Institutional Dynamics of International Political Orders. *International Organization*, 52(4), 943–969.

Marcinkowski, F. (2005). Die "Medialisierbarkeit" politischer Institutionen. In P. Rössler & F. Krotz (Eds.), *Mythen der Mediengesellschaft – the Media Society and its Myths* (pp. 341–369). Konstanz, Germany: UVK.

Mazzoleni, G. (1987). Media Logic and Party Logic in Campaign Coverage: The Italian General Election of 1983. *European Journal of Communication*, 2(1), 81–103.

Mazzoleni, G. (2008a). Media Logic. In W. Donsbach (Ed.), *The International Encyclopedia of Communication* (pp. 2930–2932). Oxford: Wiley-Blackwell.

Mazzoleni, G. (2008b). Media Logic. In L. L. Kaid & C. Holtz-Bacha (Eds.), *Encyclopedia of Political Communication* (Vol. 2, pp. 445–446). Los Angeles, CA: Sage.

Mazzoleni, G., & Schulz, W. (1999). "Mediatization" of Politics: A Challenge for Democracy? *Political Communication*, 16(3), 247–261.

McPhee, R. D., & Canary, H. (2008). Organizational Structure. In W. Donsbach (Ed.), *The International Encyclopedia of Communication* (pp. 3471–3476). Oxford, Malden: Wiley-Blackwell.

Meyer, J. W., & Rowan, B. (1977). Institutionalized Organizations: Formal Structure as Myth and Ceremony. *American Journal of Sociology*, 83(2), 340–363.

Oliver, C. (1991). Strategic Responses to Institutional Processes. *The Academy of Management Review*, 16(1), 145–179.

Orton, D. J., & Weick, K. E. (1990). Loosely Coupled Systems: A Reconceptualization. *Academy of Management Review*, 15(2), 202–223.

Pfeffer, J., & Salancik, G. R. (1978). *The External Control of Organizations: A Resource Dependence Perspective*. Stanford, CA: Stanford University Press.

Putnam, L. L., Nicotera, A. M., & McPhee, R. D. (2009). Introduction: Communication Constitutes Organization. In L. L. Putnam & A. M. Nicotera (Eds.), *Building Theories of Organization: The Constitutive Role of Communication* (pp. 1–20). London, UK: Routledge.

Ryfe, D. M. (2006a). Guest Editor's Introduction: New Institutionalism and the News. *Political Communication*, 23(2), 135–144.

Ryfe, D. M. (2006b). The Nature of News Rules. *Political Communication*, 23(2), 203–214.

Saxer, U. (1999). Der Forschungsgegenstand der Medienwissenschaft. In J.-F. Leonhard, H.-W. Ludwig, D. Schwarze & E. Straßner (Eds.), *Medienwissenschaft: Ein Handbuch zur Entwicklung der Medien und Kommunikationsformen. 1. Teilband* (pp. 1–14). Berlin, New York: Walter de Gruyter.

Schulz, W. (2004). Reconstructing Mediatization as an Analytical Concept. *European Journal of Communication*, 19(1), 87–101.

Scott, W. R. (1994). Institutions and Organizations: Toward a Theoretical Synthesis. In W. R. Scott & J. W. Meyer (Eds.), *Institutional Environments and Organizations. Structural Complexity and Individualism* (pp. 55–80). Thousand Oaks, CA: Sage.

Scott, W. R. (2001). *Institutions and Organizations*. 2nd Edition. Thousand Oaks, CA: Sage.

Scott, W. R. (2003). *Organizations: Rational, Natural, and Open Systems*. 5th Edition. Upper Saddle River, NJ: Prentice Hall.

Scott, W. R., & Meyer, J. W. (1991). The Organization of Societal Sectors: Propositions and Early Evidence. In P. J. DiMaggio & W. W. Powell (Eds.), *The New Institutionalism in Organizational Analysis* (pp. 108–140). Chicago, IL: University of Chicago Press.

Sparrow, B. H. (2006). A Research Agenda for an Institutional Media. *Political Communication*, 23(2), 145–157.

Staber, U., & Sydow, J. (2002). Organizational Adaptive Capacity: A Structuration Perspective. *Journal of Management Inquiry*, 11(4), 408–424.

Strömbäck, J. (2008). Four Phases of Mediatization: An Analysis of the Mediatization of Politics. *The International Journal of Press/Politics*, 13(3), 228–246.

Strömbäck, J., & Dimitrova, D. V. (2011). Mediatization and Media Interventionism: A Comparative Analysis of Sweden and the United States. *International Journal of Press/Politics*, 16(1), 30–49.

Strömbäck, J., & van Aelst, P. (2013). Why Political Parties Adapt to the Media: Exploring the Fourth Dimension of Mediatization. *International Communication Gazette*, 75(4), 341–358. doi: 10.1177/1748048513482266

Suchman, M. C. (1995). Managing Legitimacy: Strategic and Institutional Approaches. *Academy of Management Review*, 20(3), 571–610.

Taylor, J. R., Cooren, F., Giroux, N., & Robichaud, D. (1996). The Communicational Basis of Organization: Between the Conversation and the Text. *Communication Theory*, 6(1), 1–39.

Van Aelst, P., Maddens, B., Noppe, J., & Fiers, S. (2008). Politicians in the News: Media or Party Logic? Media Attention and Electoral Success in the Belgian Election Campaign of 2003. *European Journal of Communication*, 23(2), 193–210.

Ward, S., & Gibson, R. (2009). European Political Organizations and the Internet. In A. Chadwick & P. N. Howard (Eds.), *Routledge Handbook of Internet Politics* (pp. 25–39). London, UK: Routledge.

Weick, K. E. (1976). Educational Organizations as Loosely Coupled Systems. *Administrative Science Quarterly*, 21(1), 1–19.

Weick, K. E. (1979). *The Social Psychology of Organizing*. 2nd Edition. Reading, MA: Addison-Wesley.

Wright, S. (2012). Politics as Usual? Revolution, Normalization and a New Agenda for Online Deliberation. *New Media & Society*, 14(2), 244–261.

11
Mediatization and Political Agenda-Setting: Changing Issue Priorities?

Peter Van Aelst, Gunnar Thesen, Stefaan Walgrave and Rens Vliegenthart

Agenda-setting is one of the most influential theories on the media's political influence (Graber, 2005). While often focusing on the media's impact on *public* opinion, another equally important facet of agenda-setting theory has the media's influence over the agendas of *political* actors and policy makers as its central object of investigation. Scholars use the term "political agenda-setting" and in some instances "agenda-building" to refer to the transfer of media priorities to political priorities. Despite the growing popularity and importance of political agenda-setting research, it has seldom been conceptualized as part of or related to the mediatization of politics.

Political agenda-setting and mediatization as distinct worlds

For several reasons, political agenda-setting studies and mediatization studies have developed as almost completely distinct research schools (but see Van Noije et al., 2008). Political agenda-setting studies share a strong empirical focus. They deal mainly with testing the effect of the media agenda on the political agenda in different contexts and circumstances. The basic question underlying most of the research reads: does more journalistic attention for an issue subsequently lead to more attention for that issue from politicians? With the help of sophisticated methods such as time-series analyses, researchers have been able to provide a nuanced and detailed answer to this question, identifying a set of contingent factors that determine the size and strength of the effect. While being empirically strong and analytically sophisticated, political agenda-setting work has, until recently, remained somewhat undertheorized. In particular, insights on why and how politicians adapt to the agenda of the media are still in need of elaboration. Furthermore, agenda-setting focuses only on thematic priorities and it remains unclear how the impact of the media on issue agendas relates to other types of influence.

The literature on mediatization, on the other hand, has been character-ized by a broader theoretical input and goals (see Strömbäck & Esser, in this volume), as well as by a broader scope covering media influence on sev-eral areas outside politics. The thesis on mediatization of *politics* provides an overarching view on the role of the media in the political system, and is in this volume defined as a long-term process through which the importance and influence of media in political processes and over political institutions and actors has increased (Strömbäck & Esser, in this volume). While being strong on conceptual discussions and theoretical perspectives, the media-tization literature is lacking in empirical research. Admittedly, some recent studies explore mediatization empirically. For instance, related to the third dimension of mediatization, Strömbäck and Nord (2006) find that journal-ists retain the most power over the content and framing of news while other studies document how mediatization of news content is stronger in the United States compared to Europe (Strömbäck & Dimitrova, 2011; Esser, 2008). Furthermore, analyses indicate that mediatization has affected the organization of European political parties (Donges, 2008) and the (media) behavior of Members of Parliament (Elmelund-Præstekær et al., 2011). Nev-ertheless, there is still "a remarkable dearth of systematic empirical research on the mediatization of politics" (Strömbäck, 2011, p. 423). One reason might be that there is little consensus on how this meta-theory should be translated into operationizable phenomena and concrete hypotheses. Some scholars even claim that mediatization partly transcends media effects and is therefore hard to measure by traditional empirical research (Schulz, 2004). Finally, the mediatization literature often addresses the implications for democracy of growing media influence (Esser & Matthes, 2013; Landerer, 2013; Mazzoleni & Schulz, 1999). These normative considerations are mostly ignored in the empirically driven agenda-setting work. Table 11.1 contrasts – in a slightly simplified manner – the research associated with the two media-and-politics theories.

Against this background, this chapter discusses and compares both con-cepts and streams of research with a focus on what they can learn from

Table 11.1 Comparison of concepts

Political agenda-setting	Mediatization of politics
Middle range theory	General theory
Mainly empirical focus	Mainly theoretical focus
Focus on political content, issues	All aspects of politics
Media influence is contingent and often modest	Media influence is often large and growing (process)
Media influence can be measured	Mediatization of politics goes partly beyond media effects and is difficult to measure

each other. On the one hand, we argue that political agenda-setting research can be used to make at least a part of the fourth dimension of the mediatization theory empirically testable. On the other hand, mediatization can provide a broader theoretical framework embedding the role of the media in political agenda-setting. We point to challenges and limitations when trying to integrate the two bodies of literature. But first, we give an overview of the central ideas and main findings of studies that focused on the political agenda-setting influence of the media.

Political agenda-setting and the media

The origins of a popular concept

In both communication and political science, agenda-setting has become one of the dominating paradigms. The same concept, however, means quite different things in the two domains. In communication science, agenda-setting is largely a theory about media effects on citizens: media coverage of issues influences the issue priorities of the public, and indirectly their voting preferences. Since the study of McCombs and Shaw (1972), the popularity of the agenda-setting approach among media scholars has grown steadily and is now one of the most cited media effects concepts (Bennett & Iyengar, 2008; Dearing & Rogers, 1996).

In political science, the political agenda-setting approach deals mainly with the limited attention of political actors to a wide range of political issues. Building on the insights of Schattschneider (1960), Cobb and Elder (1972) were among the first who investigated why some issues managed to get the attention of decision-makers, while others failed. The media was seen as one of the possible factors that could influence the agenda of policy makers, but not a very important one. Gradually the media got more attention in the study of political agendas, but it was seldom the main focus of attention (Baumgartner & Jones, 1993; Kingdon, 1984; but see Linsky, 1986).

A more recent stream of research tries to combine both traditions and focuses on the effect of mass media coverage on the political agenda (Rogers & Dearing, 1988; Walgrave & Van Aelst, 2006). For these scholars, the central question is to what extent mass media coverage affects the issue priorities of politicians. Although some prefer the term *policy* agenda-setting (Rogers & Dearing, 1988) or agenda-*building* (Denham, 2010), we refer to this research as political agenda-setting.[1] This does not mean that we believe that the political agenda-setting process is highly similar to the process of public agenda-setting. Although both processes deal with the relative importance or salience of issues, we agree with Pritchard (1992) that the agenda of policy-makers is different from the agenda of the public. The agenda of politicians is hardly ever operationalized by asking them to list the issues uppermost in their minds, but rather by looking at their words or deeds (see below). It is not what politicians think (cognitive) but what they do (behavior) that matters. Furthermore, using the term "agenda-setting" does not imply that the agenda of politicians is simply "set" by the media but rather that the media is one potential source of influence among many others.

Political agenda-setting can be considered as an early stage of the larger policy process. This process has generally been conceptualized in terms of a sequence of different phases[2]: problem identification, policy formulation, policy adoption, implementation and evaluation (Cobb & Elder, 1981, p. 394). Agenda-setting overlaps with this first phase. Due to its ability to focus attention, media influence is typically seen as relatively high in this phase of the policy process[3] (Baumgartner & Jones, 1993; Esser & Pfetsch, 2004, p. 388). This does not mean that journalists entirely autonomously initiate new issues, but rather that they play a role in strengthening and structuring the initiatives taken by political actors (Reich, 2006; Wolfsfeld & Sheafer, 2006). Mostly this role is defined positively: issues that are high on the media agenda can obtain, in turn, a more prominent position on the political agenda. However, the media also influence the political agenda by filtering and selecting issues that do not appear on the agenda. Or, as Van Praag and Brants (1999, p. 199) conclude on the basis of their campaign study, "The agenda-setting power of journalists seems to lie more in denying access and in forcing politicians to react on issues than in actually initiating them." Some have called this negative agenda-setting effect "agenda-constraining" (Walgrave et al., 2010); it is closely related to the well known gatekeeping process (Shoemaker, 1991) in communication science: only a minority of the many issue messages generated by political actors pass the media gates and receive news coverage. From a policy perspective, the media contribute to limiting the scope of decision-making to some issues (Bachrach & Baratz, 1962, p. 952).

Defining and operationalizing the political agenda

Agenda-setting scholars never study "the" political agenda, but rather choose to focus on one or more distinct political agendas (Dearing & Rogers, 1996, p. 18). Actually, there is no such thing as the political agenda (Walgrave & Van Aelst, 2006, p. 95). Political agenda-setting scholars have studied (a combination of) the following agendas: of parliament or Congress (Soroka, 2002b; Trumbo, 1995; Van Noije et al., 2008; Jones & Wolfe, 2010), political parties (Brandenburg, 2002; Green-Pedersen & Stubager, 2010; Kleinnijenhuis & Rietberg, 1995), government (Walgrave et al., 2008; Thesen, 2013a), the president (Gilberg et al., 1980; Wanta & Foote, 1994; Edwards & Wood, 1999) or public spending (Cook & Skogan, 1991; Pritchard & Berkowitz, 1993).

Each political actor has his or her own semi-independent agenda that is composed according to its own logic and dynamic. Furthermore, most agendas can be operationalized in different ways. For instance, the agenda of a political party can be measured by coding its manifesto, an extensive document that can be considered as a list of issue priorities (Walgrave & Lefevere, 2010). The same party agenda, however, can also be operationalized by using a much shorter time span, as Brandenburg (2002) did by using daily press releases during a British election campaign. Both ways of measuring the party agenda are valid, but not identical as both agendas, manifestos and press releases, play different roles and are ruled by diverging, short- or long-term dynamics.

Not every political agenda has the same relevance for actual policy. Walgrave and Van Aelst (2006) suggest that agendas can be placed on a continuum ranging from symbolic to substantial. Symbolic agendas are primarily rhetorical: they contain the talk of politicians but have limited tangible political consequences. Substantial agendas, on the other hand, do have a direct impact on, or *are*, policy (e.g., legislation, budgets). In their overview of political agenda-setting studies, Walgrave and Van Aelst (2006) showed that all studies that actually found strong media impact on the political agenda defined the political agenda symbolically rather than substantially; they found effects of media coverage on parliamentary debates or presidential speeches (e.g., Bartels, 1996; Edwards & Wood, 1999). However, when more substantial political agendas like legislation and budgets were subjects of study, researchers found much less media impact. Probably the most substantial political agenda is the state's budget or what Pritchard and Berkowitz (1993) call the "resource agenda". The allocation of money and resources to different issues or policy domains has the most far-reaching, tangible consequences. However, since this agenda is highly incremental and stable over time it is no surprise that hardly any media impact has been found (Landry et al., 1997; Pritchard & Berkowitz, 1993; but see Van Belle, 2003).

In sum, findings on the agenda-setting impact of the media depend to a large extent on how scholars define and operationalize the political agenda. Media influence is strongly associated with which type of political agenda we are looking at. Although probably the most important factor explaining variation in media impact, it is certainly not the only one.

The contingency of political agenda-setting by the media

Most agenda-setting studies cited above rely on a time-series design testing to what extent the actual behavior of political actors regarding specific issues is preceded in time by media coverage about the same issues. A majority of these studies have concluded that "the media matter", but at the same time stressed the conditionality of the media's influence on the political agenda (Van Aelst & Walgrave, 2011). Besides the type of political agenda (see above) we distinguish between, and briefly discuss, four contingent factors: types of issues, characteristics of the media agenda, party characteristics and system-level characteristics.

First, the influence of the mass media varies considerably across issues. According to Soroka (2002a, p. 16), "difference in agenda-setting dynamics are most often products of differences in the issues themselves". Soroka has introduced a typology distinguishing between prominent (e.g., unemployment), sensational (e.g., environment) and governmental (e.g., national deficit) issue types. Media influence on the political agenda is most plausible for sensational issues that are not obtrusive (little direct experience) and that lend themselves to dramatic events. Differences in the agenda-setting impact of the media can also be related to the structure, constellation of actors and dynamics of a policy field in which an issue is embedded. Also, some issues are simply not newsworthy and therefore lack the basic premise for media impact (Koch-Baumgarten & Voltmer, 2010).

Second, we mostly talk about "the" media, but that does not mean that all media outlets and types of media coverage have the same agenda-setting potential. Previous studies have shown that newspapers have a higher agenda-setting impact but that this influence only becomes effective via TV news (e.g., Bartels, 1996). Some types of coverage such as investigative journalism clearly have a higher impact on politics than routine coverage (Protess et al., 1987). Coverage exerts more influence if it is congruent across outlets (Eilders, 2000). The more homogenous the media, the more difficult it is for politicians to ignore it. Also the tone of the news is relevant: positive and negative news lead to different public and political reactions (Soroka, 2006; Baumgartner & Jones, 1993; Thesen, 2011).

Third, Green-Pedersen and Stubager (2010) and Vliegenthart and Walgrave (2011b) found party characteristics in multi-party systems to be a third set of contingency factors. They showed that the political influence of the media depends on parties' institutional position (opposition versus government) and the parties' own issue agendas. Opposition parties react more to media cues than government parties and parties in general tend to embrace mediatized issues to a larger extent when they "own" these issues. In a recent study, Thesen (2011) has linked the tone of the news and party positions showing that opposition parties mainly react to negative news as it offers them the opportunity to attack government policy, while government parties prefer to use positive news to defend their policy record.

A fourth and final set of contingent factors is related to the country level, being the political and media system at stake. Despite increased attention to the contingencies of political agenda-setting, we still know relatively little about how the responsiveness of politicians to the media agenda varies across countries. The literature about political agenda-setting is overwhelmingly based on single-country studies and mainly comes from the United States (see Green-Pedersen & Stubager, 2010, p. 663). Only a few studies looked at the agenda-setting role of the media from a comparative perspective. For instance, Van Noije et al. (2008) compared press coverage and parliamentary debates in the Netherlands and the United Kingdom while Vliegenthart and Walgrave (2011a) focused on parliamentary questions and news coverage in Denmark and Belgium. Both studies stress the similarities rather than the differences in the media–politics dynamic between the two countries. However, studies that included more different countries found differences in media impact across institutional systems. Van Dalen and Van Aelst (2014) compared the perceptions of political journalists on the political agenda-setting power of different actors including the mass media in eight West-European countries. Spanish journalists perceive the role of the media in the agenda-setting process as much weaker. This could be related to the higher degree of political control over the media in Spain and to the degree of political concentration of power. In political systems that lack strong centralized power, such as Sweden and Norway, politicians are more responsive to the agenda of the media, journalists contend.

Towards an integration of agenda-setting and mediatization

We believe political agenda-setting studies may complement mediatization theory in different ways. This implies, however, that we specify what agenda-setting can and cannot contribute to. In this section, we sketch some ideas about how both streams could enter into a dialog and profit from each other. As mediatization is a broad theory that stretches across all aspects of politics it is important to define where political agenda-setting can be helpful. Therefore, we use the conceptualization of Strömbäck (2008; see also Strömbäck & Esser, 2009; Strömbäck & Van Aelst, 2013; see also Chapter 1 of this volume). Strömbäck distinguishes four distinct but highly related dimensions in the process towards a complete mediatization of politics. The first dimension relates to the extent to which the news media have become the most important source of information and channel of communication between citizens and political actors. The second dimension is the degree of independence of the media vis-à-vis political institutions. The third dimension of mediatization refers to the extent to which media content is determined independently by the media's own news values and by their need to attract a large audience. It is clear that these three dimensions or trends have an influence on the behavior of politicians, which is conceptualized as the fourth dimension of mediatization:

> The fourth dimension of mediatization thus refers to the extent to which political actors adjust their perceptions and behavior to the news media logic rather than political logic. This might affect not only their communication efforts, but also the actual political output and the way political actors are organized.
>
> (Strömbäck & Van Aelst, 2013, p. 344)

Political agenda-setting makes one aspect in particular of the fourth phase testable: the ability of the media to co-determine the thematic agenda of politicians. To the extent that media coverage influences the issue priorities of political actors, politics is mediatized since political actors are affected in their behavior. A growing body of political agenda-setting literature shows that this is actually the case. Not only the US studies (Trumbo, 1995; Baumgartner et al., 1997; Edwards & Wood, 1999; Yanovitsky, 2002), but more recently also European studies proved that the media matter. For instance, Bonafont and Baumgartner (2013) show in the Spanish case that when newspaper attention to an issue spikes, parliament tends to follow.

While the current strand of political agenda-setting research seems to confirm the idea that the media matter for politics, thereby supporting the main idea of the fourth dimension of mediatization that political actors tend to follow the media logic, a good deal of the available evidence nuances the media's power. Indeed, most studies found that the media seem to exert some power but that this power is by and large limited and almost always highly contingent (see above). The media has an influence on some issues but not on others, and in some political contexts but not in others. For example, the fact that studies found most influence of the media on symbolic and not on substantial agendas challenges the claim of mediatization scholars that mediatization affects the (policy) output of politics. The media logic definitely affects what politicians *talk* about, but there is much less proof that it influences what politicians actually *do*.

The nuanced findings of political agenda-setting studies seem to be at odds with politicians' perceptions. Elite surveys in several European countries have shown that a large majority of politicians perceive the media as an undisputed agenda-setter and reckon that the behavior of politicians is highly mediatized (Strömbäck, 2011; Van Aelst et al., 2008). These media power perceptions, however, might be related to other aspects of political life such as the media's influence on the personal careers of politicians (Van Aelst & Walgrave, 2011). Political agenda-setting work can say little on these other aspects of politics. Added to that, the contradiction between empirical political agenda-setting studies and the perceptions of elites may be due to the fact that elites, even if they appear to have taken the initiative unaffected by the media agenda, may still have been affected by the media – and thus mediatized. In fact, political agenda studies are unable to assess the anticipatory behavior of political actors. Political actors may act by devoting attention to an issue not because the media have acted before but because they think the media will act (or not). Cook (2005) noted that the negotiation of newsworthiness between journalists and politicians is partly indirect and implicit because political actors (attempt) to anticipate how journalists will react to their communication messages. According to Davis (2009), there is an all-permeating "media reflexivity" (politicians invariably think about possible media coverage when they undertake something) that has become part of every single decision a politician takes. This pre-emptive behavior can be considered as proof of mediatization but is very difficult, if not impossible, to capture with classic political agenda-setting designs.

In the remainder of this section, we discuss three specific aspects of the political agenda-setting literature that directly speak to the central claim of mediatization scholars. First, we show that the media not only affect the political agenda but that there are good reasons to believe that the opposite is the case as well. Next, we discuss the fact that political elites use the media agenda strategically and are not taking over media cues blindly. And finally, we highlight some longitudinal political agenda-setting studies that test whether the media's impact on the political agenda increases over time, a key claim in the mediatization debate.

Media and politics: A reciprocal relationship

The mediatization literature is based on the idea that media influence politics, and claims that political actors need to adapt to the media and its logic. This premise, however, is not uncontested. Probably the best-known theory claiming that politics affects the media (and not the opposite) is Bennett's (1990) indexing theory. The gist of this is that journalists monitor the range of ideas and opinions present among the political elites and focus their coverage on these political cues only. They have no interest in devoting attention to novel ideas that fall outside of the scope of elite attention. While Bennett's theory is not particularly focused on issue salience transfer, it has clear agenda-setting implications: issues are initiated by elites and only afterwards picked up by the mass media, not the other way around. Other theorists of media–politics relations have formulated similar accounts. Wolfsfeld (2011), for example, speaks of the PMP-model with "PMP" standing for Politics-Media-Politics. He claims that almost everything, so also attention for new issues, starts with politics, that it then spills over to the media and that political actors then again react to this media coverage. Similarly, in his book *Cycles of Spin*, Sellers (2010) argues that strategic communication (by Congress members) and agenda-setting (by the media) should be studied together as both processes form an integrated whole. In short, this work suggests that "news construction is a negotiated process" (Bennett & Livingston, 2003, p. 359) and that, to fully understand the interaction of media and politics, we need to take into account the efforts of both sides.

A majority of agenda-setting studies acknowledge that the relationship between media and politics can only be described as a *reciprocal* one. Political actors adopt issues that have been mediatized but the opposite happens as well, of course: media start covering issues after, and because, they have received political attention. In a sense, it is no more than normal that media cover things that happen in politics. This is the news media's prime role: covering things that happen in the world and that may be relevant to their users. The mere fact that there is a transfer from politics to media that counterbalances the media-to-politics transfer puts the mediatization approach into perspective. Political actors are still independent and they even affect the agency that is affecting them. In other words, there is a process of "media agenda-setting" going on. Political agenda-setting work can bring to the mediatization debate a more explicit understanding of the complex, multidirectional battle between media and political actors.

It is clear that political actors have a keen interest in feeding the media with the issues they care about. For example, parliamentarians have an interest in devoting their attention to some issues and not to others. Some issues correspond to their own ideological preferences, or to the preferences of their constituency. Other issues may be directly damaging for their competitors, producing a competitive advantage. Following Fenno's (1973) typology of Congressmen's incentives, issue attention is a resource that can be employed by MPs to increase their chances of re-election, to generate policies reflecting their ideological preferences or to increase their power in parliament. Consequently, MPs also have an interest in drawing media attention to the issues they address in parliament. It increases their visibility regarding the issue and, more generally, increases the salience of the issue among the public and among colleagues. Hence, there are good reasons to expect that issues on the political agenda would translate into media attention.

An example of a reciprocal approach to political agenda-setting is the paper by Edwards and Wood (1999) studying the US president and his agenda relationship with Congress and the mass media using time-series data. They find that the president sometimes reacts to the media but often also sets the agenda and makes the media cover his own preferred issues. Especially with regard to domestic issues, the president is able to act in an entrepreneurial fashion and to impose his agenda onto the media (and often also onto Congress). Van Noije and colleagues came to a similar nuanced conclusion after investigating agenda interactions between parliament and media in the United Kingdom and the Netherlands from the late 1980s to the early 2000s: influence goes in both directions (with more impact from media on politics than the other way around, though). Brandenburg (2002), studying election campaigns in the United Kingdom, found the politics-to-media influence to largely outweigh the opposite relationship. Parties select issues and the media follow. Kleinnijenhuis and Rietberg (1995) similarly found that politics was leading the media in the Netherlands regarding economic issues in the early 1980s.

This handful of studies looking at both directions of impact supports the idea that the agenda interactions between politics and media are essentially bidirectional. It must be acknowledged that most of these reciprocal studies date from a few years back, drawing on evidence that is at least ten years old. Things may have changed. In fact, as has been shown in one of the previous sections, there is evidence that the agenda influence of the media has risen over time, as the mediatization theory would predict. That the media matter more now to politics than they used to does not automatically imply that politics will matter less to the media and that the opposed, antipodal relation will have disappeared altogether. We rather expect that the mutual entanglement of media and politics has increased in both directions, but we do not have empirical proof for that contention.

Based on a survey among MPs in five countries, Walgrave and colleagues (2010) show that MPs who tend to take their cues *from* the media are also the ones who are the most successful in getting their issues *into* the media. This suggests that, at the individual level, when the impact in one direction is strong it tends to be strong in the other direction as well. When actors surf on the media waves and react to media coverage they, in turn, get their actions more easily into newspapers and on TV. This finding indicates that there is a feedback loop in which media power and political power reinforce each other, at least at the level of individual MPs. In a recent study, Midtbø and colleagues (Midtbø et al., 2014), drawing on similar evidence, find that this mutual reinforcing relationship also applies to the country level. In countries where MPs, in their legislative activities, take more media issues into account they also display higher success rates in getting media coverage for their initiatives.

In sum, theoretical and empirical research in political agenda-setting challenges what we perceive as an overemphasis on the strength and political influence of media logic in mediatization theory. Political agenda-setting studies suggest that reciprocal analyses offer a more nuanced picture. And even when political actors take over media issues, they do this on their own terms and with clear strategic goals. This argument will be developed next.

Mediatized politics as strategies of party and issue competition

As shown extensively in a large body of research, including political agenda-setting studies, the media influence the behavior of politicians. However, this should not be interpreted to mean that politicians are always forced to react and adapt. Political actors also proactively try to use the media to reach certain political goals (Strömbäck & Van Aelst, 2013). This constitutes a key finding in the many political agenda-setting studies reviewed above, where the political contingencies of media influence on politics are modeled (cf. Walgrave & Van Aelst, 2006).

Several examples seem relevant to explain how political actors react strategically to media coverage. For instance, Yanovitsky (2002) showed on the basis of his longitudinal study of the issue of drunk driving that legislative action only followed when it fitted the policymakers' agenda. Moreover, the studies finding that parties are more likely to respond to news on issues they "own" (cf. Green-Pedersen & Stubager, 2010; Vliegenthart & Walgrave, 2011b) highlight how parties act strategically when facing the media agenda. The theory of issue ownership argues that a party's history of political prioritization, competence and policy results on a specific issue generates an electoral advantage because the public comes to think of the party as more capable of handling it (Petrocik, 1996). Thus, when left-wing parties respond more often to news on (un)employment and the environment and right-wing parties concentrate on crime and immigration, they are actively trying to capitalize on their issue-specific electoral benefits. Finally, Thesen (2013a) finds that government and opposition parties have divergent preferences for news tone in political agenda-setting and that the attribution of policy responsibility by the media is crucial to understand how and why political agendas are set by the media. Opposition parties respond to bad news that (implicitly or explicitly) attributes blame to the government, because this will help politicize government incompetence. The government prefers to respond to good news that reflects positive developments in social problems because this could politicize policy success.

In these examples, media attention to issues offers opportunities for politicization to political actors (Green-Pedersen, 2011, p. 143). Thus, even though a media logic shapes the way in which political actors communicate their messages (Esser & Mathes, 2013, p. 177), a distinct political logic of party and issue competition is crucial to explain when and how politicians react to media coverage. If the media offer a means to politicizing preferable issues, own competence or the incompetence of opponents, then news attention often turns into politics. Consequently, mediatized politics should be considered as a more evenly matched contest between media and political logic. It is a process in which political actors actively use media attention to their advantage, thus behaving in accordance with a political logic of party competition. Put differently, politicians react to the media because they want to, not only because they have to. To be sure, recent mediatization contributions acknowledge this, as in for instance the (somewhat negative) concept of "self-mediatization" (Esser, 2013). However, our contention is that much of the literature still implicitly portrays political actors as forced and somehow helpless when faced with media logic. This is perhaps best illustrated by Cook's (2005, p. 163) widely supported and cited claim that politicians might win the daily battles but end up losing the war "as they apply standards of newsworthiness to evaluate issues and policies". The implication is that even though political actors do use the media to their own ends, a loss of power and influence is still unavoidable (see also Esser & Matthes, 2013, p. 186). We prefer the concept of "strategic adaptation" (Landerer, 2013, p. 253), because it captures both the force of the media (necessitating adaptation) and the strategic motives of politicians, without a preconceived idea about the outcome in terms of the media–politics power balance.

The idea that mediatization involves increasing media influence in society and politics is common to the mediatization literature (cf. Mazzoleni, 2008; Hjarvard, 2008). Most often, this influence is said to decrease the importance of political logic and influence (cf. Meyer, 2002; Strömbäck, 2008). Besides raising the status of political logics in the media–politics relationship, we believe that political agenda-setting could challenge or at least supplement the prevailing zero-sum game interpretation where gains for some actors come at the expense of others (Strömbäck & Dimitrova, 2011,

p. 32). The combination of political actors that adapt to or master media communication and the media's increased societal importance at least questions an a-priori conclusion of a loss of influence of political actors. From an agenda-setting perspective, what facilitates such an argument is the strong emphasis on form/format in mediatization research. Effectively, the questions of which issues and problems are on the agenda and who benefits from the political attention these problems are receiving are more or less ignored. Rather than just assuming decreasing political influence, the effect of mediatization should be treated as an empirical question; some political actors might lose, but others might just as well win.

Recent mediatization perspectives do offer a theoretical account of this, at least at an institutional level. The idea is that political institutions vary in their need for publicity, and this variation in turn explains why institutions or processes that are "characterized by the power- and publicity-gaining self-presentational aspects of political logic" are more mediatized than those "characterized by the policy- and decision-based production aspects" (Esser & Matthes, 2013, p. 177). This fits nicely with political agenda-setting findings on the differences between substantial and symbolical agendas (see above). However, a political agenda-setting perspective could draw attention to a supplementary view focusing on actor-level variation in mediatized politics and, most importantly, its effects. For instance, Thesen (2013b) argues that opposition politics is more mediatized than government politics. Both opposition and government parties would like to maximize attention to advantageous issues and avoid the less favorable issues from the media agenda, but the nature of the media agenda, and of party competition, skews the outcome of political agenda-setting processes in favor of opposition parties. First, opposition parties have more opportunities to politicize favorable issues from the media agenda due to a negativity bias in news coverage. Second, the increasing frequency of political scandals in the media (Thompson, 2000), their effect on the vote shares of political parties (Clark, 2009), together with the fact that such events constitute the strongest predictor of opposition responses to news, make them a strong opposition asset in media-based party competition.

In sum, we argue that mediatization does not necessarily equal a zero-sum game between media and politics. Rather, there is a need, in both political agenda-setting and the mediatization literature, to differentiate between political actors or institutions, and to study how the media affect the distribution of power between them. We will elaborate on this point in the conclusion.

Mediatization: The influence of the media is growing?

A final key assumption in mediatization literature is that the impact of media on society, and the political process in particular, is growing. The theory does not claim that media influence was absent in the past, but rather that it has grown over time. Strangely enough, this claim is seldom backed up by longitudinal data that actually show that media impact is on the rise (but see Zeh & Hopmann, 2013; Elmelund-Præstekær et al., 2011).

In the agenda-setting literature, time is a central concept. The idea of media impact is mainly based on the fact that the issue was on the media agenda first and on the political agenda later. In that respect the assumption of mediatization as a process can be rephrased in terms of contingent political agenda-setting: *time* is a variable that moderates the effect of the media agenda on the political agenda. As time progresses, the impact increases. Since agenda-setting studies often rely on longitudinal time-series designs that cover considerable periods in time, this hypothesis can be tested straightforwardly by including an interaction term between time and issue attention in the models. If this interaction term is positive and significant, it signals a confirmation of an increasing agenda-setting power of media. While this test is rather straightforward and agenda-setting data are suitable to conduct it, remarkably enough, very few scholars have incorporated this idea of (linearly) changing influences in their models. This is mainly a consequence of the high costs, in terms of resources and time, of gathering longitudinal data on different agendas.

In a study covering ten years (1993–2000) of agenda-setting in Belgium, Vliegenthart and Walgrave (2011b) did incorporate this test in their models and they found a confirmation. Over a time period of eight years, the reactivity of MPs to media coverage increased. In their study of agenda-setting patterns in the United Kingdom and the Netherlands, Van Noije and colleagues (2008) divided their research period (1988–2003 for the United Kingdom and 1995–2003) into, respectively, three (the UK) and two (the Netherlands) sub-periods. In the United Kingdom, they found that the impact of media was stronger in the later periods. In the Netherlands, results show that the media's agenda-setting influence was absent in the first period, but present in the last period. From these findings, we can tentatively conclude that agenda-setting studies provide cautious support for the claim of mediatization scholars that the media's power over the political process has indeed increased in the past two decades.

Conclusion and discussion

In recent decades, both mediatization and political agenda-setting have become central concepts in political communication. Although both deal with the influence of the media on politics, they have largely developed as distinct fields. In this chapter we tried to integrate the two traditions, or at least start a dialog about how political agenda-setting could be integrated in the more comprehensive theoretical story of the mediatization of politics. We suggested three aspects that have been used in political agenda-setting studies that could be useful to adjust or complement mediatization research.

First, agenda-setting work suggests that the power relationship between politics and media is reciprocal. The media influence the work of political elites but the opposite is the case as well. This nuanced image of media-politics agenda interactions complements the more one-sided and crude account offered by mediatization scholars (e.g., Mazzoleni & Schulz, 1999) claiming that politicians cannot but adapt to a powerful media logic that threatens to reduce their power and autonomy. Empirical research in political agenda-setting that includes reciprocal design challenges this claim.

Second, even when political actors take over media issues, they do this often on their own terms and with clear strategic goals. In a sense, rather than to a general decline of power of political actors, mediatization probably leads to a *redistribution* of power in politics, with some actors profiting and other paying a higher price. In a more general way, political agenda-setting studies, through their attention to the dynamics of party competition, may nuance the distinction between media and party logic that is key in the mediatization literature. From a mediatization perspective, opposition parties that respond frequently to negative news reflect an adaption to or adoption of a media logic where conflict and negativity are important. However, such a pattern of behavior is also undoubtedly inherent to political competition and party strategies for electoral success. From this perspective, strong agenda-setting effects or close interactions between media and politics take place as a result of *overlapping logics*, rather than one logic dominating the other.

Third, mediatization as a concept refers to social change over time, in this case a growing influence of the media on political actors. Most studies, however, deal with mediatized politics and don't study actual changes over time. In political agenda-setting, the temporal aspect is central and therefore offers an opportunity to actually test this. To be honest, as only a few agenda-setting studies have actually employed a longitudinal perspective, this is rather a suggestion for further research.

We don't claim that these three factors have been completely ignored by mediatization scholars so far. We rather argue that they should be placed more center stage in such a way that mediatization becomes a more nuanced and empirically testable theory. More in general, the idea of contingency that has gradually become an integrated part of agenda-setting research has too often been downplayed in mediatization studies. There are accounts that develop the notion of contingent mediatization, such as Esser and Matthes' (2013, p. 177) distinction between the "power- and publicity-gaining" and the "policy- and decision-based" aspects of politics, where the former induces stronger mediatization. This way of reasoning is in line with the distinction made in political agenda-setting between "symbolic" and "substantial" agendas. In our view, such perspectives deserve more research attention, both because they nuance the mediatization thesis and because they represent interesting opportunities for integration with similar conceptualizations in political agenda-setting. Furthermore, moving in the direction of a more empirically testable theory does not mean that the all-inclusive concept of mediatization should be reduced to a few simplistic stimulus–response hypotheses. For instance, the anticipatory behavior of politicians towards media coverage cannot easily be captured in a classical design that focuses on political and media agendas. At the moment political agenda-setting studies probably underestimate media influence as politicians incorporate beforehand how journalists will cover (or ignore) their actions. Still, we believe scholars of both traditions should try to come up with more innovative and advanced research designs that can tackle the media reflexivity of political actors. If this and other empirical and theoretical challenges are ignored, then mediatization and political agenda-setting will probably further develop as distinct fields that hardly speak with each other.

Finally, if both strands of literature could be integrated more, not only mediatization, but also political agenda-setting can profit. The big advantage of agenda-setting is its clear and undisputed focus on issue salience. However, this is also its weakness. Political agenda-setting studies talk about media influence on issue priorities, but have little or no idea how this impact relates to other types of media influence. Mediatization can be a useful concept with which to place the agenda-setting impact of the media in perspective.

Notes

1. "Agenda-setting" is preferred over "agenda-building" because it allows political media effect studies to connect with the large political agenda-setting research tradition in political science. Berkowitz (1992) tried to differentiate between agenda-setting and agenda-building as two related but different processes. We rather treat these terms as synonyms (see also McCombs, 2004, p. 143). The reason to prefer "political" agenda-setting over "policy" agenda-setting is mainly because the latter term is more narrow and focuses primarily on what governments say and do, while the first term is much broader and for instance also includes the agendas of ordinary MPs or political parties.
2. The idea that the policy process is a well-structured chronological process is highly contested by public policy scholars. Among others, Cobb and Elder (1981) claim that the classical idea of a policy process should be replaced by a more dynamic and flexible model (see also Kingdon, 1984).
3. Esser and Pfetsch (2004, p. 388) add that in the last phase of the policy process the role of the media becomes more important again.

References

Bachrach, P., & Baratz, M. (1962). Two Faces of Power. *American Political Science Review*, 56, 941–952.
Bartels, L. M. (1996, September 1996). *Politicians and the Press: Who Leads, Who Follows?* Paper presented at the APSA 1996, San Francisco.

Baumgartner, F. R., & Jones, B. D. (1993). *Agendas and Instability in American Politics.* Chicago: University of Chicago Press.

Baumgartner, F. R., Jones, B. D., & Leech, B. L. (1997). Media Attention and Congressional Agendas. In S. Iyengar & R. Reeves (Eds.), *Do the Media Govern? Politicians, Voters and Reporters in America* (pp. 349–363). Thousand Oaks: Sage.

Bennett, L. (1990). Toward a Theory of Press-State Relations in the United States. *Journal of Communication,* 40, 103–125.

Bennett, L., & Iyengar, S. (2008). A New Era of Minimal Effects? The Changing Foundations of Political Communication. *Journal of Communication,* 58, 707–731.

Bennett, L., & Livingston, S. (2003). A Semi-independent Press: Government Control and Journalistic Autonomy in the Political Construction of News. *Political Communication,* 20, 359–362.

Berkowitz, D. (1992). Who Sets the Media Agenda? The Ability of Policymakers to Determine News Decisions. In D. Kennamer (Ed.), *Public, Opinion, the Press and Public Policy* (pp. 81–103). Westport, CT: Praeger.

Bonafont, L. C., & Baumgartner, F. R. (2013). Newspaper Attention and Policy Activities in Spain. *Journal of Public Policy,* 33(01), 65–88. doi: doi:10.1017/S0143814X12000219

Brandenburg, H. (2002). Who Follows Whom? The Impact of Parties on Media Agenda Formation in the 1997 British General Elections Campaign. *Harvard Journal of Press and Politics,* 7(3), 34–54.

Clark, M. (2009). Valence and Electoral Outcomes in Western Europe, 1976–1998. *Electoral Studies,* 28(1), 111–122.

Cobb, R. W., & Elder, C. D. (1972). *Participation in American Politics: The Dynamics of Agenda Building.* Boston: Allyn and Bacon.

Cobb, R. W., & Elder, C. D. (1981). Communication and Public Policy. In D. D. Nimmo & K. R. Sanders (Eds.), *Handbook of Political Communication* (pp. 391–416). Beverly Hills: Sage.

Cook, F. L., & Skogan, W. G. (1991). Convergent and Divergent Voice Models of the Rise and Fall of Policy Issues. In D. L. Protess & M. E. McCombs (Eds.), *Agendasetting: Readings on Media, Public Opinion and Policymaking* (pp. 189–206). Hillsdale, NJ: Lawrence Erlbaum Associates.

Cook, T. E. (2005). *Governing with the News: The News Media as a Political Institution.* 2nd Edition. Chicago: University of Chicago Press.

Dearing, J. W., & Rogers, E. M. (1996). *Communication Concepts 6: Agenda-setting.* Thousand Oaks, CA: Sage.

Denham, B. E. (2010). Toward Conceptual Consistency in Studies of Agenda-building Processes: A Scholarly Review. *Review of Communication,* 10(4), 306–323. doi: 10.1080/15358593.2010.502593

Donges, P. (2008). *Medialisierung politischer Organisationen: Parteien in der Mediengesellschaft.* Wiesbaden: VS Verlag.

Edwards, G. C., & Wood, D. (1999). Who Influences Whom? The President, Congress and the Media. *American Political Science Review,* 93(2), 327–344.

Eilders, C. (2000). Media as Political Actors? Issue Focusing and Selective Emphasis in the German Quality Press. *German Politics,* 9(3), 181–206.

Elmelund-Præstekær, C., Hopmann, D. N., & Nørgaard, A. S. (2011). Does Mediatization Change MP-Media Interaction and MP Attitudes Toward the Media? Evidence from a Longitudinal Study of Danish MPs. *The International Journal of Press/Politics,* 16(3), 382–403. doi: 10.1177/1940161211400735

Esser, F. (2008). Dimensions of Political News Cultures: Sound Bite and Image Bites News in France, Germany, Great Britain and the United States. *International Journal of Press/Politics*, 13(4), 401–428.

Esser, F. (2013). Mediatization as a Challenge: Media Logic Versus Political Logic. In H. Kriesi, S. Lavenex, F. Esser, M. Bühlmann, J. Matthes & D. Bochsler (Eds.), *Democracy in the Age of Globalization and Mediatization* (pp. 155–176). Basingstoke: Palgrave Macmillan.

Esser, F., & Matthes, J. (2013). Mediatization Effects on Political News, Political Actors, Political Decisions, and Political Audiences. In H. Kriesi, S. Lavenex, F. Esser, M. Bühlmann, J. Matthes & D. Bochsler (Eds.), *Democracy in the Age of Globalization and Mediatization* (pp. 177–201). Basingstoke: Palgrave Macmillan.

Esser, F., & Pfetsch, B. (2004). *Comparing Political Communication: Theories, Cases and Challenges*. Cambridge: Cambridge University Press.

Fenno, R. F. (1973). *Congressmen in Committees*. Boston: Little, Brown.

Gilberg, S., Eyal, C., McCombs, M., & Nicholas, D. (1980). The State of the Union Address and the Press Agendas. *Journalism Quarterly*, 57, 584–588.

Graber, D. (2005). Political Communication Faces the 21st Century. *Journal of Communication*, 55(3), 479–507.

Green-Pedersen, C. (2011). *Partier i nye tider: Den politiske dagsorden i Danmark*. Aarhus University, School of Business and Social Sciences, Institut for Statskundskab, Department of Political Science and Government.

Green-Pedersen, C., & Stubager, R. (2010). The Political Conditionality of Mass Media Influence: When do Parties Follow Mass Media Attention? *British Journal of Political Science*, 40(3), 663–677.

Hjarvard, S. (2008). The Mediatization of Society. *Nordicom Review*, 29(2), 105–134.

Jones, B. D., & Wolfe, M. (2010). Public Policy and the Mass Media: An Information Processing Approach. In K. Voltmer & S. Koch-Baumgarten (Eds.), *Public Policy and Mass Media: The Interplay of Mass Communication and Political Decision Making* (pp. 17–43). London: Routledge.

Kingdon, J. W. (1984). *Agendas, Alternatives and Public Policies*. New York: Harper Collins.

Kleinnijenhuis, J., & Rietberg, E. (1995). Parties, Media, the Public and the Economy: Patterns of Societal Agenda-setting. *European Journal of Political Research*, 28, 95–118.

Koch-Baumgarten, S., & Voltmer, K. (2010). The Interplay of Mass Communication and Political Decision Making – Policy Matters! In K. Voltmer & S. Koch-Baumgarten (Eds.), *Public Policy and Mass Media: The Interplay of Mass Communication and Political Decision Making* (pp. 215–227). London: Routledge.

Landerer, N. (2013). Rethinking the Logics: A Conceptual Framework for the Mediatization of Politics. *Communication Theory*, 23(3), 239–258.

Landry, R., Varone, F., Laamary, M., & Pesant, M. (1997). *What Sets the Policy Agenda? The Media Agenda or the Party Agenda? Empirical Evidence on the Societal Agenda*. Unpublished paper, Université de Laval, Quebec.

Linsky, M. (1986). *Impact: How the Press Affects Federal Policymaking*. New York: W. W. Norton.

Mazzoleni, G. (2008). Mediatization of Politics. In W. Donsbach (Ed.), *The International Encyclopedia of Communication* (pp. 3047–3051). Malden, MA: Blackwell.

Mazzoleni, G., & Schulz, W. (1999). Mediatization of Politics: A Challenge for Democracy. *Political Communication*, 16, 247–261.

McCombs, M. E. (2004). *Setting the Agenda: The Mass Media and Public Opinion.* Cambridge: Polity Press.

McCombs, M. E., & Shaw, D. (1972). The Agenda-setting Function of the Mass Media. *Public Opinion Quarterly*, 69(4), 813–824.

Meyer, T. (2002). *Media Democracy: How the Media Colonize Politics.* Cambridge: Polity Press.

Midtbø, T., Walgrave, S., Van Aelst, P., & Christensen, D. A. (2014). Do the Media Set the Agenda of Parliament or Is It the Other Way Around? Agenda Interactions between MPs and Mass Media. In K. Deschouwer & S. Depauw (Eds.), *Political Representation in the Twenty-First Century.* Oxford: Oxford University Press.

Petrocik, J. R. (1996). Issue Ownership in Presidential Elections, with a 1980 Case Study. *American Journal of Political Science*, 40(3), 825–850.

Pritchard, D. (1992). The News Media and Public Policy Agendas. In D. Kennamer (Ed.), *Public Opinion, The Press and Public Policy* (pp. 103–112). Westport, CT: Praeger.

Pritchard, D., & Berkowitz, D. (1993). The Limits of Agenda-setting: The Press and Political Responses to Crime in the United States, 1950–1980. *International Journal of Public Opinion Research*, 5(1), 86–91.

Protess, D. L., Cook, F. L., Curtin, T. R., Gordon, M. T., Leff, D. R., McCombs, M. E., & Miller, P. (1987). The Impact of Investigative Reporting on Public Opinion and Policymaking: Targeting Toxic Waste. *Public Opinion Quarterly*, 51, 166–185.

Reich, Z. (2006). The Process Model of News Initiative: Sources Lead, Reporters Thereafter. *Journalism Studies*, 7(4), 497–514.

Rogers, E. M., & Dearing, J. W. (1988). Agenda Setting Research: Where Has It Been? Where Is It Going? In J. Anderson (Ed.), *Communication Yearbook* (Vol. 11, pp. 555–594). Thousand Oaks: Sage.

Schattschneider, E. E. (1960). *The Semi-Sovereign People.* New York: Holt.

Schulz, W. (2004). Reconstructing Mediatization as an Analytical Concept. *European Journal of Communication*, 19(1), 87–101. doi: 10.1177/0267323104040696

Sellers, P. (2010). *Cycles of Spin: Strategic Communication in the US Congress.* New York: Cambridge University Press.

Shoemaker, P. J. (1991). *Communication Concepts 3: Gatekeeping.* Newbury Park: Sage Publications.

Soroka, S. N. (2002a). *Agenda-settting Dynamics in Canada.* Vancouver: UBC Press.

Soroka, S. N. (2002b). Issue Attributes and Agenda-setting by Media, the Public, and Policymakers in Canada. *International Journal of Public Opinion Research*, 14(3), 264–285.

Soroka, S. N. (2006). Good News and Bad News: Asymmetric Responses to Economic Information. *Journal of Politics*, 68(2), 372–385. doi: 10.1111/j.1468-2508.2006.00413.x

Strömbäck, J. (2008). Four Phases of Mediatization: An Analysis of the Mediatization of Politics. *International Journal of Press Politics*, 13(3), 228–246.

Strömbäck, J. (2011). Mediatization and Perceptions of the Media's Political Influence. *Journalism Studies*, 12(4), 423–439.

Strömbäck, J., & Dimitrova, D. V. (2011). Mediatization and Media Interventionism: A Comparative Analysis of Sweden and the United States. *The International Journal of Press/Politics*, 16(1), 30–49.

Strömbäck, J., & Esser, F. (2009). Shaping Politics: Mediatization and Media Interventionism. In K. Lundby (Ed.), *Mediatization. Concept, Changes, Consequences* (pp. 205–224). New York: Peter Lang.

Strömbäck, J., & Nord, L. W. (2006). Do Politicians Lead the Tango? *European Journal of Communication*, 21(2), 147–164.

Strömbäck, J., & Van Aelst, P. (2013). Why Political Parties Adapt to the Media: Exploring the Fourth Dimension of Mediatization. *International Communication Gazette*, 75(4), 341–358.

Thesen, G. (2011). *Attack and Defend! Explaining Party Responses to News*. Phd thesis, Aarhus University, Forlaget Politica.

Thesen, G. (2012). *Political Agenda-setting and the Mediatization of Politics: How the Media Affect Political Issue Attention & Party Competition*. Paper presented at the Comparative Policy Agendas Conference, Reims, France.

Thesen, G. (2013a). When Good News Is Scarce and Bad News Is Good: Government Responsibilities and Opposition Possibilities in Political Agenda-setting. *European Journal of Political Research*, 52(3), 364–389. doi: 10.1111/j.1475-6765.2012.02075.x

Thesen, G. (2013b). Political Agenda Setting as Mediatized Politics? Media–Politics Interactions from a Party and Issue Competition Perspective. *The International Journal of Press/Politics*. doi: 10.1177/1940161213515756.

Thompson, J. B. (2000). *Political Scandal: Power and Visibility in the Media Age*. Cambridge: Polity Press.

Trumbo, C. W. (1995). Longitudinal Modelling of Public Issues: An Application of the Agenda-setting Process to the Issue of Global Warming. *Journalism and Mass Communication Monographs*, 152(2): 1–57.

Van Aelst, P., Brants, K., Van Praag, P., De Vreese, C., Nuytemans, M., & Van Dalen, A. (2008). The Fourth Estate as Superpower? An Empirical Study on Perceptions of Media Power in Belgium and the Netherlands. *Journalism Studies*, 9(4), 494–511.

Van Aelst, P., & Walgrave, S. (2011). Minimal or Massive? The Political Agenda Setting Power of the Mass Media According to Different Methods. *International Journal of Press Politics*, 16(3), 295–313.

Van Belle, D. A. (2003). Bureaucratic Responsiveness to the News Media: Comparing the Influence of the New York Times and Network Television News Coverage on US Foreign Aid Allocations. *Political Communication*, 20(3), 263–285. doi: 10.1080/10584600390218896

Van Dalen, A., & Van Aelst, P. (2014). The Media as Political Agenda-Setters: Journalists' Perceptions of Media Power in Eight West European Countries. *West European Politics*, 37(1), 42–64. doi: 10.1080/01402382.2013.814967.

Van Noije, L., Oegema, D., & Kleinnijenhuis, J. (2008). Loss of Parliamentary Control Due to Mediatization and Europeanization: A Longitudinal and Cross-sectional Analysis of Agenda Building in the United Kingdom and the Netherlands. *British Journal of Political Science*, 38(3), 455–478.

Van Praag, P., & Brants, K. (1999). The 1998 Campaign: An Interaction Approach. *Acta Politica*, 34(2–3), 179–199.

Vliegenthart, R., & Walgrave, S. (2011a). Content Matters: The Dynamic of Parliamentary Questioning in Belgium and Denmark. *Comparative Political Studies*, 44(8), 1031–1059.

Vliegenthart, R., & Walgrave, S. (2011b). When the Media Matter for Politics: Partisan Moderators of Mass Media Influence on Parliament in Belgium, 1993–2000. *Party Politics*, 17(3), 321–342. doi: doi:10.1177/1354068810366016

Walgrave, S., & Lefevere, J. (2010). Do the Media Shape Agenda Preferences? In K. Voltmer & S. Koch-Baumgarten (Eds.), *Public Policy and Mass Media: The Interplay of Mass Communication and Political Decision Making* (pp. 44–64). London: Routledge.

Walgrave, S., Soroka, S., & Nuytemans, M. (2008). The Mass Media's Political Agenda-setting Power: A Longitudinal Analysis of Media, Parliament and Government in Belgium (1993–2000). *Comparative Political Studies*, 41(6), 814–836.

Walgrave, S., & Van Aelst, P. (2006). The Contingency of the Mass Media's Political Agenda-setting Power: Towards a Preliminary Theory. *Journal of Communication*, 56(1), 88–109.

Walgrave, S., Van Aelst, P., & Bennett, L. (2010). *Beyond Agenda-setting: Towards a Broader Theory of Agenda Interactions between Individual Political Actors and the Mass Media*. Paper presented at the APSA Annual Meeting, Washington.

Wanta, W., & Foote, J. (1994). The President-news Media Relationship: A Time Series Analysis of Agenda-setting. *Journal of Broadcasting & Electronic Media*, 38(4), 437–451.

Wolfsfeld, G. (2011). *Making Sense of Media & Politics. Five Principles of Political Communication*. New York: Routledge.

Wolfsfeld, G., & Sheafer, T. (2006). Competing Actors and the Construction of Political News: The Contest over Waves in Israel. *Political Communication*, 23, 333–354.

Yanovitsky, I. (2002). Effects of News Coverage on Policy Attention and Actions: A Closer Look into the Media-policy Connection. *Communication Research*, 29, 422–451.

Zeh, R , & Hopmann, D. N. (2013). Indicating Mediatization? Two Decades of Election Campaign Television Coverage. *European Journal of Communication*, 28(3), 225–240. doi: 10.1177/0267323113475409

Part IV
Conclusion

12
A Paradigm in the Making: Lessons for the Future of Mediatization Research

Frank Esser and Jesper Strömbäck

As stated in the Introduction, the twofold purpose of this book is first to bring together state-of-the-art chapters on the mediatization of politics, thereby assessing what we know and providing a framework for further research; and second to move research on the mediatization of politics forward towards a more fully developed theory. For this reason, we invited leading scholars in this field to comment in their chapters on basic and more advanced questions and to develop various topics and perspectives. The scope in content and the depth of analysis of their contributions underscore the many different ways in which mediatization research can augment the literature of political communication and how stimulating the impulses are that it evokes.

This is not the place for summarizing the respective contents of each individual chapter one more time. Instead, we will investigate the way in which each individual chapter contributes to a superordinate theoretical framework. For this, we take up the organizing structure of the introductory chapter. In Chapter 1, we gave a brief overview of the current state of research. By using a very similar organizational structure, we highlight in this concluding chapter what our authors say about the core components of the mediatization paradigm. We are interested in tying the individual components together and detecting superordinate, pertinent connections that could serve as bigger theoretical building blocks for the consolidation and further development of the mediatization paradigm. The purpose of this closing chapter is thus to create a synthesizing whole that is more than the sum of its parts. We do not intend to end a process by presenting a definitive conclusion but rather to bring together and organize the splintering contributions to mediatization literature and make them again accessible to the research community for further discussion and development. Clearly, the mediatization of politics is still a concept under construction. But we

223

believe that the revelations presented here will enrich further theoretical and empirical work and pave the way towards a more fully developed theory.

Understanding mediatization and social change

With respect to the effects of mediatization on social change, our authors in essence hold two positions. Mazzoleni stands for its strong influence. He argues that the developmental stage to "mediatized society" has been reached because all spheres of society have been "penetrated so deeply" by aspects of media communication or mass self-communication "that it is impossible to imagine individuals and social groups existing outside the dense web of media influences" (Mazzoleni, in this volume). In the area of politics in particular, no actor in the public sphere can risk ignoring the media and its operating logic – "mediatized discourse has become the accepted way for politics to address the citizenry".

A more relativized position is that of Marcinkowski and Steiner. They argue that mediatization is not to be understood as "the" dominant meta-process of social change. They suggest that "it is wrong to understand mediatization as a 'meta-process,' in the sense of being the most important one, as the dominant or somehow superordinate process of social change, one which leads inevitably to a social formation dominated by mass media" (Marcinkowki & Steiner, in this volume). Therefore, they believe that to speak of "media society" would be going too far. It is always only subsystems that can be mediatized within society and not society as a whole. In addition, mediatization is only one of many interactive relationships between social subsystems. There are other powerful interactive relationships that occur at the same time, and their effects are denoted as, for instance, politicization (of the education system), legalization (of the political system) or economization (of the healthcare system). They also do not cancel each other out in the sense of a zero-sum game but overlap each other. Overall, according to Marcinkowski and Steiner (in this volume), it holds true that "mediatization does not stand alone and should thus not be understood as an all-encompassing primary phenomenon".

Blumler (in this volume), too, warns of inflating the mediatization paradigm. Even within the field of political communication, mediatization receives increasing competition. Blumler mentions for instance the increasing importance of rationalization, single-issue orientation, user-generated content, popularization and ideologization of political communication.

Understanding implications for democracy

No matter how one conceptualizes the transformational process, it is an undisputed fact that it is taking place and that politics are affected by it.

Marcinkowki and Steiner (in this volume) describe it as the multiplication of new channels, diversification of media types, acceleration of news cycles and above all the growing autonomy and assertiveness of how the news-media-covered politics pressurize political parties to adopt a "professionalized advocacy-model of political communication" that relies heavily on news management and attempts to "dominate political journalism" (Blumler, in this volume). Journalists have responded to these attempts to constrain their reporting options with a further emphasis on the "journalistic voice" as opposed to the "political voice" in their stories, which have led to counter-measures and, over time, spiraled into the struggle for communication control that has become so characteristic of highly mediatized election campaigns (see D'Angelo, Büchel & Esser, in this volume).

From the beginning, as Schulz (in this volume) notes, mediatization research took a rather "dismal view" of the effects on politics. The gloomy diagnosis, according to Mazzoleni (in this volume), is that mediatization has primarily led to "spectacularization", "personalization", "fragmentation" and "simplification" of the culture of political discourse. In particular, he stresses that mediatization of politics has helped create a widespread populism. Evidence for this, so Mazzoleni claims, is "that many leaders of established government parties do not recoil from striking sensitive popular chords and use populist slogans [...] to please and coax their traditional electorates". Under the conditions of a "media-saturated audience democracy", not only politicians but the media as well have become susceptible to populist strategies. The media find especially worth mentioning "what ordinary people find interesting, engaging, relevant, and accessible". In the political realm, more pressure is felt to address voters "in a more popular idiom and to court popular support more assiduously" (Mazzoleni, in this volume). Both trends occur at the expense of hard news and substantial policy debate. Populist movements and their often flamboyant leaders make effective use of "means of communication, of both the mass and social kinds", and they successfully tap "into the media's hunger for entertaining events, person-centered stories, caustic language, and [...] controversial performances" (Mazzoleni, in this volume). Giving a great many examples, Mazzoleni shows how media populism is spreading in Western democracies. It can be observed as "unintentional complicity" of commercial media logic and political populism, or as willful "ideological partnership" of partisan media-outlets and populist movements. In both varieties, media populism is however a brainchild of the mediatization of politics.

As Blumler (in this volume) notes, what is still missing beyond such case-by-case observations is a systematic, comprehensive explication of the highly charged relationship between mediatization and democracy. Because the media are crucial for making politicians responsive to public concerns and for holding them accountable for their actions, they are expected to fulfill certain normative expectations in serving the democratic system (such as providing transparent and reliable information, enlightened analysis, critical scrutiny and pluralist public-affairs coverage that also mobilizes participation; for more see Schulz's chapter in this volume). Often, however, the media seem to enjoy themselves in a different role – one that seeks "impact", triggers emotional responses of "outrage" and indulges in "confrontation" and "heating up" the atmosphere – all undermining the information value of news coverage. For citizens, this means a lack of access to substantive, undistorted and diverse information as well as a lack of opportunity to deliberate public issues; this poses serious challenges to a vibrant public sphere and thus, democratic life. A failing media market may also impair a citizen's capabilities to evaluate the inclusiveness and fairness of the policy-making process and properly evaluate political outcomes for their service to the public good (Esser, 2013).

In addition to these points, Blumler (in this volume) mentions further challenges for democracy. Under the condition of increased mediatization, political actors who possess many resources could much more easily manage to be heard whereas those with few resources could get drowned out (communication imbalances). Also, political decisions could increasingly be oriented towards short-term news cycles ("how well will it play in the media?") instead of making them subject to long-term, sustainable considerations ("what is good for the country?"). Reducing media discourses to the mainstream viewpoints of the big parties could limit citizens' ability to realize the full scope of possible actions (politics as cut-and-dried show-fights). The presumed compulsion to convey politics in the most attractive way could also diminish the willingness of citizens (and journalists!) to engage in in-depth discussions of substantial political issues. And Habermas' argument that open debates are of central importance to the advancement of knowledge could eventually be carried to absurd extremes if the media presented every political discourse as a "feud" or "crisis" (conflict-stylization).

However, it is a valid question whether these fears of mediatization's negative impact are in fact directed towards conditions of political communication that, in this sense, no longer exist. Both Blumler and Schulz emphasize in their contributions to this book the potentially positive democratizing effect of the Internet, which is becoming ever more influential. In the new media age, politicians have access to new communication channels to make administrative work more efficient, governing more effective and the political decision process increasingly participatory. Both established authorities and new challengers can reach their publicity goals more easily; in particular, weakly organized groups and ordinary people find lower access barriers to the public sphere on the Internet. Even the news media profit from that development: they have new ways to collect and disseminate information, and this in turn makes it easier for them to fulfill their democratic tasks (creating transparency, exposing misuse). In addition, as Schulz notes (in this volume), the position of the citizen is also strengthened: "Citizens are no longer confined to being passive consumers of standard political journalism, of statements by party and government officials but can react to official sources and voice alternative positions in various new media spaces."

However, as Blumler (in this volume) correctly notes, the all-decisive question is whether or not the "new" forms of communication will occur "mainly outside or inside" the mediatization paradigm. There are plausible reasons for thinking "inside": Schulz (in this volume) points out that many – if not all – online news providers continue to follow the logic of traditional media. Shehata and Strömbäck (in this volume) emphasize that citizens turn primarily to those political information sources that are online offshoots of traditional news organizations. And Blumler (in this volume) stresses that "most politicians will continue to act according to the mediatization rationale". The same is true, he says, for all others who are concerned about their public image.

This gives a lot of credence to the unbroken prevalence of the mediatization paradigm. Nevertheless, the challenge continues for researchers to further the development of the concept and to adapt it to changing conditions. Special consideration must be given to the *political actors* who have new ways of communicating at their disposal. This leads many of our authors to a differentiated understanding of the mediatization of politics.

Understanding the mediatization of politics

The increase in varieties of ways for political actors to communicate in the age of the Internet leads a few of our authors to propose a change from a *media-centric* to an *actor-centric* perspective on mediatization research. During the pre-Internet age, citizens depended a great deal on the services of the news media. These traditional news organizations can, says Schulz (in this volume), be easily understood as integrated, uniform institutions in which similar practices and consistently used news-reporting strategies are applied. But does that still hold true? A few are skeptical of the idea:

> In particular, the premise of an autonomous media institution committed to homogeneous media logic has become disputable. New digital media defy the institutional autonomy of mainstream news media. Hence, even proponents of an institutional approach to the news media have become critical of the "homogeneity hypothesis". The new media environment offers not only a wide variety of alternative information sources but also new ways of participating in public discourses. Political actors are becoming less dependent on the classical news media and their media logic. But this does not necessarily result in diminishing political media influence.
>
> (Schulz, in this volume)

For that reason, Schulz favors an actor-centric mediatization perspective that puts the political actor, not the media, at its core:

> The actor-centric perspective implies two propositions: first, political actors and organizations expect the media to operate in a specific way and adapt to the opportunities and constraints media usage entails; and second, political actors and organizations proactively take account of the media and try to capitalize on media performances for their political purposes.

(Schulz, in this volume)

Other authors can easily adopt this view. Blumler (in this volume) also places political actors in the center and defines mediatization as "a process whereby politicians (and by extension other opinion advocates) tailor their message offerings to the perceived news values, newsroom routines, and journalism cultures prevalent in their societies". His understanding of mediatization is consistent with what the introductory chapter denotes as "self-mediatization" (Strömbäck & Esser, in this volume).

Donges and Jarren (in this volume) also place actors – in their case political parties and interest groups – in the center of their analysis. They define mediatization of politics "as a reaction" of political organizations to "their perception" that media have become an influential factor in their environment. These "reactions", which by the way also include elements of evaluation and choice, are evident empirically in "changes in organizational structure" (expansion and prioritization of communication departments) and "changes in behavior" (intensification of communication output). According to this actor-centric understanding, it is not the media which cause changes in political organizations but it is the political organizations themselves that decide, on the basis of their own perception, to make changes. Effects of mediatization are the result of interactional relationships, not a one-way impact.

Van Aelst, Thesen, Walgrave and Vliegenthart (in this volume) follow this same path. They find the assumption wrong that "politicians are always forced to react and adapt". They propose instead that "politicians react to the media because they want to, not only because they have to". Thus, Van Aelst et al. (in this volume) also follow an actor-centric perspective, as it is widely used in political science literature with regard to the relationship between politics and media. They also suggest, as do Donges and Jarren, conceiving the relationship as an interactional one. Mediatization may force politicians to carry out "strategic adaptations" but does not lead to a "general decline of power of political actors" (Van Aelst et al., in this volume). Even if politicians adopt issues from the media, they do it on their own terms and in accordance with their own strategic motives. Overall, the actor-centric mediatization perspective presumes a primarily reflexive understanding of media impact. In principle, this is not at all new, as Van Aelst et al. (in this volume) admit, because in mediatization research it has long been discussed and theorized as "self-mediatization" and "anticipatory behavior of political actors" (see Strömbäck & Esser, Chapter 1). Van Aelst et al. advocate an increased dissemination of this kind of political science literature that places this perspective even more in the center.

The opposite position, a media-centric mediatization perspective, is not supported by any of the authors explicitly. But there are chapters in this book in which writers come close to the concepts of media interventionism or media interference. De Vreese (in this volume) links journalistic news framing – for him a key indicator of mediatization – to the media's discretionary power. Journalistic news frames, he argues, take their starting point in the "autonomy of journalists" as they focus on what news media organizations "actively do" to the topics they select and how they adapt and modify frames coming from political elites. Journalistic news frames, he continues, "can therefore be considered indicative of mediatization where journalism has the upper hand in determining not only what is covered but also how it is covered in the news" (De Vreese, in this volume).

Mazzoleni (in this volume) is also an emphatic proponent of media-induced effects on politics and of the "supremacy of media logic" over political logic. He defines mediatization as "the result of *media-driven* influences in the political domain". Even the proliferation of the Internet will not make him reverse his position. On the contrary, Mazzoleni believes that the increased interconnection between old and new media will "radicalize the mediatization of politics". Under the conditions of "Mediatization 2.0", where the logic of traditional media blends with interactive modes of communication, the political system will become "more dependent than ever" on the media, he argues. He sees the advent of a "new information environment" in which political communicators have forever "lost their central position in favor of a multiplicity of communicators who join the established players in the competition for power" (Mazzoleni, in this volume).

In their analysis of highly mediatized election campaigns in the United States, D'Angelo, Büchel and Esser also do not assume that in the online age the pressure put on political candidates "to adapt to and internalize media logic" has decreased. A strong reason for this is that, as Shehata and Strömbäck (in this volume) argue, the operating methods of the information sources relevant for political communication continue to be closely oriented towards the classical media logic – an aspect that has been grossly underestimated by other authors. Above all, however, the US case shows that under certain structural conditions the "reciprocal interdependencies" between politics and media can "over time tilt toward the media" (D'Angelo et al., in this volume).

All followers of an actor-centric mediatization perspective can find a complex theoretical foundation in the contributions by Marcinkowski and Steiner (in this volume). They deduce from a specifically system-theoretical perspective that not only the media but politics as well are autonomous, independent systems; however, politics is – in order to receive acceptance and legitimacy for its actions in the public sphere – dependent on the services of the media. This last point, a functional requirement under conditions of modern democracy, is assumed to be of central importance.

> [It] produces precisely the effects that we denote as the mediatization of the political sphere: the political system relies on mass-media performances and is orientated toward their selection and presentation criteria – in the sense of a reflexive mediatization – to be able to provide the kind of issues to which the mass media can easily relate.
>
> (Marcinkowski & Steiner, in this volume)

Marcinkowski and Steiner argue that "the term 'mediatization' denotes not so much the passive submission of other systems to media forces but the *active* utilization of media services". Mediatization also describes the circumstance when other systems – such as politics – absorb the capability of the media to focus public attention on issues in accordance with their own needs. They suggest differentiating among three types of mediatization: simple mediatization, reflexive mediatization and mediatization consequences.

"Simple" mediatization occurs when politics takes up media topics to discuss them and process them further. Van Aelst et al. (in this volume) point out that it is especially the "symbolic issues" that are often successfully transferred onto the political agenda whereas the political development of "substantial, policy-based issues" occurs mostly without any influence from the media.

"Reflexive" mediatization, according to Marcinkowski and Steiner, denotes everything that, in the political sphere, has to do with public relations, message control, strategic framing, proactive agenda-setting or news management. In this regard, Van Aelst et al. (in this volume) speak of "strategic adaptations" that combine "both the force of the media – necessitating adaptation – and the strategic motives of politicians", whereas Blumler (in this volume) describes it as "self-mediatization" of politicians. There are several different evaluations of this process. While Marcinkowski and Steiner as well as Van Aelst et al. emphasize that reflexive mediatization helps the political system better fulfill its own goals and functions in society, Blumler points to a number of dysfunctional implications which can take the form of an intensive orientation towards the selection and presentation criteria of the news media. He elaborates on these negative effects using catch phrases such as "increased complicity", "a here-today-gone-tomorrow attitude", "dramatization" or "ratcheted-up rhetoric". Some authors argue that reflexive mediatization goes hand in hand with losses in autonomy (e.g., D'Angelo et al.), while others do not see it in such a way (e.g., Marcinkowski & Steiner).

Marcinkowski and Steiner (in this volume) denote as "mediatization consequences" those structural and procedural changes that arise from interactions of other systems with the media system. Donges and Jarren emphasize
that generally many of these changes of the political system are *self-effected*
and not *forced upon* it by the media system. Consequently, they explain the
changes they examined in European political parties (for details, see Donges
and Jarren, in this volume) as internally initiated and not as externally
caused effects.

Understanding the difference between effects and consequences of mediatization

Schulz (in this volume) advocates understanding the mediatization of politics as a "pull process" and refers in this regard to the chapter written by
Marcinkowski and Steiner (in this volume). The concept of the pull process
is inferred directly from the assumptions of an actor-centric mediatization
perspective. It rejects the idea that mediatization consequences in politics
are to be understood as causally affected by the media ("externalizing" the
reasons for political changes) and supports the idea that they arise from
the needs of the mediatized system itself (internal reasons for borrowing
media performances to fulfill the political need for public attention and
acceptance). Marcinkowski and Steiner (in this volume) therefore understand mediatization "not in terms of a linear, media-induced influence".
They argue:

> To view it as a development process that is, as it were, "imposed" onto the
> political system from the outside is to get it wrong. Mass media cannot
> (and do not want to) force anything on politics, not even to media-savvy
> self-presentation. It is politics itself that realizes its dependence on media
> more than ever and is therefore reprogramming itself to appear more
> attractive.

Thus, mediatization of politics has little to do with external effects because
it is only possible in very rare cases to attribute observable consequences to
intentions and objectives of the media. But the assumption of a "causal"
effect would have to presuppose it. For this reason, some authors prefer
to speak of mediatization "consequences" instead of mediatization "effects"
(see Donges & Jarren; Marcinkowski & Steiner).

Many authors in this book (see Van Aelst et al.; Blumler; D'Angelo et al.)
emphasize that mediatization is a reflexive process. The permanent observation of the media as well as the readiness to carry out political course
adaptations in accordance with these perceptions are a central element of the
"reflexive cycle", as it has been discussed for many years in the US-American
political communication literature.

D'Angelo et al. (in this volume) point this out and argue further that, therefore, "meta-coverage" has a big impact on politics. Metacoverage refers to news stories with which journalists meta-cover mediatized events by addressing the role of the media and of political image management in these events. In the US election campaigns, campaign teams follow the metacoverage of the media very intently and use it "as a sounding board for self-mirroring and fine-tuning the effectiveness of their publicity strategies" (D'Angelo et al., in this volume).

Marcinkowski and Steiner point to additional differentiations of consequences, namely, that they include structural "adaptations" of mass media's criteria for the creation of attention as well as structural measures for "protection" against public attention. While Donges and Jarren (in this volume) focus mostly on examining the structural adaptations, protection plays a role in the contributions of D'Angelo et al. (in this volume). The growing use of strategies by the US candidates designed to *bypass* the news media and *circumvent* journalistic interference – often using "new" media – can indeed be interpreted as "a sign that an advanced phase of mediatization is taking place within an election system" (D'Angelo et al., in this volume). It is another example of a reflexive response to adapt to media logic. Adaptations to media logic, as even Marcinkowski and Steiner must admit, can "in selected political subsections such as government or administration" go so far that they "have inflationary [...] consequences that ultimately block political decision making processes" which – however caused – would be a substantial effect of mediatization.

Apart from consequences on politics there are also effects on the general public, which according to De Vreese are an interaction product, too. They are the outcome of the interplay of frames sponsored by political elites and those brought about by journalists. In terms of "framing power", it is obvious to him that "that there is considerable leeway and autonomy on the side of journalism when deciding how to frame issues" (De Vreese, in this volume).

Understanding media logic and political logic

The research concerned with mediatization of politics presupposes two systems that, respectively, fulfill different functions for society. According to Marcinkowski and Steiner (in this volume), in the case of politics it is "the production of collectively-binding decisions" and in the case of the media "the creation of a public space for issues and opinions".

In order to translate these abstract functions into concrete practices, systems need to put internal decision-making mechanisms in place that Marcinkowski and Steiner call "programs" and all others call "logics". In the case of mass media, they refer to the selection criteria and presentational formats used to provide descriptions of society and the world.

What fuels the hegemony of the media is – as Marcinkowski and Steiner (in this volume) argue – that no other institution can compete with the media's reality constructions in terms of social reach, relevance, binding character, diversity and timeliness. "The source of media power," state Donges and Jarren (in this volume), is the fact "that everyone in society – including politicians, spokespersons, and consultants – has learned to adjust and adapt to the different media logics as the 'normal' way of perceiving and interpreting the world." Another reason for the hegemonial position of the media is that all other systems in society depend on the scarce resource "public attention" and are therefore interested in adapting to the media logic or integrating elements thereof in their own action programs (see Marcinkowski & Steiner, in this volume). As De Vreese argues, media logic is also amply demonstrated in the process of journalistic frame-building and frame-setting in which "journalistic conventions and production processes translate political events into templates for news stories". Media logic refers here to "how journalists and news organizations select, possibly adopt or contrast these frames, or re-negotiate and re-frame them into a frame following the logics of journalism, the news organization, and the news genre" (De Vreese, in this volume).

Early mediatization research was based on the assumption that, as Schulz (in this volume) points out, all the various kinds of media organizations "are committed to a *unique and universal* media logic determining the media users' – and ultimately society's – definition of reality". With good reason, several authors in this book point once more to necessary (and often long-implemented) differentiations. Donges and Jarren (in this volume) argue that the ideas of a "single and homogenous media logic" and of a "clear dichotomy of media logic versus political logic" can hardly be sustained. This argument is taken up in many other chapters.

Donges and Jarren (in this volume) substantiate their doubts regarding a single, homogenous media logic by pointing to the different types of news media organizations (e.g., public vs. private, quality vs. tabloid). But research efforts have begun, and the authors do mention this, to take these differentiations into account. As described in the introductory chapter, Esser's (2013) concept of a multifaceted media logic, for example, presumes that in the case of public broadcasters and quality newspapers, the "professional aspects of media logic" are much more pronounced while in the case of private broadcasters and popular newspapers, the "commercial aspects of media logic" are a driving force.

Schulz (in this volume) also doubts the validity of the idea of a single, homogenous media logic. He argues that the properties of new media such as "networking, time-shifting, sharing content, co-creating media products, and mashing-up messages" are "hardly compatible with core assumptions of the media logic concept". Schulz's main argument – namely that "most new media operate on organizational principles, content production, and distribution procedures which have little in common with conventional mass media" – is however questioned by other authors. As mentioned above, Shehata and Strömbäck (in this volume) argue on the basis of representative data that online media relevant for political communication are those that are still associated with the operating logic of traditional media. Hence they conclude that "the rising importance of the Internet does not necessarily herald the demise of mediated politics, nor of the mediatization of politics" (Shehata & Strömbäck, in this volume).

Let us look at another point from the above comment by Donges and Jarren, namely, that the "clear dichotomy of media 'versus' political logic in the mediatization literature is misplaced". Van Aelst et al. (in this volume) use a very similar argumentation. They stress that political logic is multi-layered and that it can, under certain circumstances, correspond exactly to the premises of media logic. Those facets in particular that are dedicated to party competition and election campaigning are very much compatible with media logic. Behavior that looks as if it were an adaption to media logic – for example, that opposition parties react very strongly to negative coverage – is to be seen as "inherent to political competition and party strategies for elec-toral success", and this speaks in favor of assuming "*overlapping logics* rather than one logic dominating the other" (Van Aelst et al., in this volume).

D'Angelo et al. (in this volume) argue similarly, but reach different conclu-sions. Following previous work by Esser (2013), they distinguish three facets of political logic, and focus their chapter entirely on the one facet they call "political *campaign* logic". They also argue that the election-related politi-cal *campaign* logic is highly compatible with media logic. Diverging from Van Aelst et al., they point out that adjusting to the media logic may "on the surface" look as if it "strengthened the political campaign logic over the media logic". The reality of US presidential elections demonstrates, however, that it "moved campaign organizations into a more sustained and embrac-ing dependency on media technologies and media organizations than ever before" (D'Angelo et al., in this volume).

All these remarks confirm that it is necessary to distinguish carefully between the *different aspects and driving forces* of media logic and political logic because differing rationales for actions exist in various sectors of the heterogeneous fields of media and politics. We are convinced that, besides the all-encompassing abstract terms media and political logic, one has to distinguish between various subordinated facets which will, according to contextual conditions, sometimes carry more weight and sometimes less. The introductory chapter gives an example of what such a conceptualiza-tion of media and political logic may look like (see Strömbäck & Esser, in this volume).

Understanding the situational character of mediatization

As we also stated in our introductory chapter, "neither political logic nor news media logic is fixed and consistent across time, countries, or political or media institutions within countries" (Strömbäck & Esser, in this volume).

It is therefore necessary to specify the conditions that advance or obstruct mediatization processes. Marcinkowski and Steiner (in this volume) argue convincingly that not all political institutions are equally prone to being mediatized. Those institutions that depend on the active involvement of citizens and support of the sympathetic public (i.e., are dependent on inclusivity) are affected most strongly by the mediatization impact. The authors propose the following theorem:

> The greater the inclusivity of a social system is, the greater is the need for attention and acceptance for its issues of communication (its "mediatization needs"). Conversely, the more exclusive a system is, the lower is its receptivity to mediatization.
>
> (Marcinkowski and Steiner, in this volume)

As a prime example for political areas highly susceptible to mediatization, they mention election campaigns because the political sphere is dependent on involving as many citizens as possible in the political process. As prime examples for political areas unsusceptible to mediatization, they name actual decision-making in backstage negotiation networks or the administrative implementation of decisions in the bureaucratic apparatus. Whereas the first example follows a political *campaign* logic that depends on a close adaptation of media logics, the latter follows a political *bargaining and policy-making* logic. The all-decisive situational factor for the mediatization of politics, as one can deduce from Marcinkowski and Steiner's chapter, is the "degree of inclusivity" or "need for publicity". However, what this also implies is that studies regarding the mediatization of election campaigns cannot be subject to generalization for the mediatization of politics as a whole.

D'Angelo et al. are fully aware of that fact when they argue that the transformational quality of mediatization "is nowhere more evident than in contemporary election campaigns". They also emphasize clearly the specific systemic conditions of the political communication system of the United States:

> Weakened political parties and image campaigns; technological channel abundance and widespread media use by campaign organizations and voters; journalistic autonomy fostered by an institutional vacuum; a political logic that requires campaigns to use and manage (news) media; a press corps eager to tell stories about a political logic bound to mediation – these and other characteristics signal that the commercial imperatives, production routines, message formats, and narrative interpretations of mass media organizations have moved to the center of the contemporary U.S. presidential election, becoming threaded into the operations of political campaigns and transforming party-based elections into mediatized elections.
>
> (D'Angelo et al., in this volume)

What can be deduced for international research from their case study is that inclusive, direct-democratic elements (such as primary elections) – or any other attempts to "democratize" political processes – entail the risk of elevating the mass media into a powerful intermediary position. One could go even a step further and say that any structural changes aimed at making politics more transparent and policy-makers more responsive to public opinion are likely to trigger a push in mediatization as politicians become more dependent on the mass media. In the United States, the introduction of primary elections has helped diminish the power of the parties and helped create an institutional vacuum that has turned the news media into a consequential actor in electoral politics.

But even outside the election campaign phases, not all branches of politics are affected equally by mediatization, as Marcinkowski and Steiner (in this volume) emphasize. Van Aelst et al. (in this volume) also stress the need for such necessary differentiations. Oppositional politics have to be seen as being more susceptible to (and more dependent on) mediatization than is governmental politics, and the same is true for symbolic issues in comparison to substantial ones. After all, the findings of Donges and Jarren (in this volume) confirm that transformations of European party systems are highly conditional because "different national contexts, different media structures, and institutional media arrangements [...] create different conditions in which mediatization takes place".

However, on the side of the media are also situational factors that affect the degree of mediatization. De Vreese (in this volume) points out that the media's discretionary power is heavily influenced by "forces internal to the newsroom", such as editorial policies, news values, type of media organization and its political orientation, as well as role perceptions and job motivations of the producing journalists.

Understanding dimensions of the mediatization process

The introductory chapter explicates the mediatization of politics as a four-dimensional concept and process, and the authors of this book address all four dimensions. *The first dimension* refers to the degree to which media constitute the most important source of information about politics and society. Despite the assumption that modern politics is largely mediated politics, the review by Shehata and Strömbäck (in this volume) shows that it is not easy to determine the extent to which individuals rely on mass media for information about politics and society. While all evidence suggests that mass media are extremely important as a source of information about politics and society and that politics is indeed mediated, there is no obvious approach for examining exactly *how* important the media are as a source of political information. A systematic review of available empirical studies and a critical examination of indicators used shows that different approaches yield somewhat different albeit not contradictory results, and that the degree of media dependency might vary across not only individuals within or between countries but also depends on the nature of different issues and the availability of alternative sources of information.

The second dimension refers to the degree to which media have become independent from other political and social institutions. One of just a few studies that systematically explore this question comes from Udris and Lucht (in this volume). Their cross-nationally and cross-temporally comparative analysis presents empirical evidence that the emancipation of the press has progressed first and foremost in the liberal system (Great Britain), followed by the largest democratic-corporatist system (Germany) and the polarized pluralist system (France). In Austria, the process is still underway and the political parallelism of the press is still fairly noticeable. Interestingly, the study finds clear evidence that this growing independence from politics has coincided with a growing dependence on the market. In all countries examined, stock exchange-listed media now play a larger role than in the 1960s. And the authors point to yet another structural transformation in media systems: at the same time as press systems grow more dependent on the market, the share of tabloid and free papers offering lower-quality journalism increases also; furthermore, they find in several press markets a growing division between down-market papers and up-market papers, squeezing the market share for mid-market papers. Returning to the core of the second dimension of mediatization, the study finds that the intensity with which European media differentiate themselves from politics follows largely the assumptions of Hallin and Mancini's (2004) models of media–politics relationships.

The third dimension refers to the degree to which media content and the coverage of politics and current affairs is guided by media logic or political logic. A good illustration of news coverage guided by media logic is D'Angelo et al.'s (in this volume) study of metacoverage. This is a type of news that moves to the foreground mediational aspects of campaign events. When covering highly mediatized political events, journalists often feel prompted to cover the involvement of the media (e.g., the behaviors of members of the press corps) and the publicity efforts of campaign organizations to "use" the media for their own goals (e.g., the strategies to influence or bypass journalists). As D'Angelo et al. argue, the amount of metacoverage in a country's campaign news is a barometer of the level of mediatization in its election system (topical analysis). In terms of impact, it provides campaign organizations with a rich set of process-oriented cues (frame analysis) that they use to adjust to the media logic, doing so in order to help the candidate better construct and communicate his or her image in particular situations.

A broader approach to the third dimension is taken by De Vreese (in this volume). He focuses on the autonomy of journalists to actively select topics, highlight some aspects while downplaying others and promote their own frames while modifying those offered by others. Starting from the assumption that "the more journalistic news frames dominate the news, the higher the degree of mediatization", he explicates the role of four frames for mediatized portrayals of politics and their effect on the public. These are (i) episodic and human interest framing, (ii) conflict and competitive framing, (iii) economic consequences framing and (iv) strategy and game framing.

Finally, *the fourth dimension* refers to the extent to which political actors and institutions are guided by media logic or political logic. An example of operationalizing adaptive responses by political parties vis-à-vis a growing media environment is provided by Donges and Jarren (in this volume). Based on an empirical analysis of ten European parties, using 18 indicators of organizational change, they find broad support for the hypothesized reactions to mediatization albeit depending on contextual conditions. Another example is the chapter by Van Aelst et al. (in this volume) that examines the extent to which the issue-priorities of political actors are affected by media coverage. A close review of relevant empirical studies finds that the media's influence on the thematic agenda of politics is "relatively high" in the early phase of the policy process (stages of problem identification and issue framing) and when symbolic issues are concerned (that ignite emotions, passions or controversies). But because the process is highly conditional, it would be wrong to assume that the media were generally able to "set" the agenda for politicians. Like many other authors, they also come to the conclusion that the powerful relationship between politics and media is reciprocal (or interactional). "The media influence the work of political elites, but the opposite is the case as well" (Van Aelst et al., in this volume).

Cumulative theory-building

The chapters of this book are a significant contribution to theory-building. They confirm many basics of the mediatization concept, as described in the introductory chapter (Strömbäck & Esser, Chapter 1), but they also provide important additions and in-depth discussions. In individual cases, they point to readjustments that should be explored through further research.

Our contributors agree that the mediatization of politics describes a long-term process that should be studied with longitudinal designs (see the chapters by Strömbäck & Esser; Udris & Lucht; Van Aelst et al.). They also agree that mediatization does not compete with other political communication theories but rather has the potential to integrate different theoretical strands within one framework. Good illustrations are the chapters by Marcinkowski and Steiner, who link it to systems theory, Donges and Jarren, who link it to institutionalist and organizational theories, Van Aelst et al., who link it to political agenda-setting and De Vreese, who links it to framing. The fact that the theories just mentioned represent different levels of analysis illustrates another important feature of the mediatization concept, namely, that it combines micro-level with meso- and macro-level processes and phenomena.

At the macro level, the news media have reached their autonomy through the functional and structural differentiation of news media from other institutions. This process has so far been mostly studied from an institutionalist perspective (see Strömbäck & Esser, in this volume) but a systems-theory approach seems possible, too (see Marcinkowski & Steiner). The growing significance of the news media occurs, as we have argued in the introductory chapter, through a process in which elements of media logic become integrated into other institutions' operations. What this does to other institutions at the macro level has been described by some as a "meta-process" that ultimately leads to a "media society" or "media democracy". Some of our authors (for instance, Marcinkowski & Steiner) suggest, however, that we should be more careful with such grand statements because mediatization cannot claim an exclusive position in society and can never affect "the" society or "the" democracy as a whole but only certain elements of it.

A few of our authors seem to suggest avoiding some oft-cited generalizations from the early era of mediatization research. For example, Hjarvard's definition of mediatization as "a process whereby society to an increasing degree is *submitted* to the media and their logic" (as cited in our introductory chapter) is indeed all-inclusive. Mazzoleni is very similar in defining "mediatization of society" as the "extension of the influence of the media into *all* spheres of society and social life" (as cited in our introductory chapter). Of course, one can question the usefulness of such all-encompassing and unrestricted terminology. Some of our authors also seemingly want to relativize another famous statement that was made during the beginning stage of mediatization research. The statement made by Mazzoleni und Schulz (1999), whereby mediatization describes a process within which politics has increasingly "lost its autonomy" and "has become dependent in its central functions on mass media", is no longer something with which all the authors of our book can readily agree. Several of them emphasize that increased orientation towards media logic is not automatically synonymous with a loss of control or impact experienced by politics.

Based on current research, we ourselves have described mediatization of politics in our introductory chapter as "as a long-term process through which the importance of the media and their spill-over effects on political processes, institutions, organizations and actors have increased" (Strömbäck & Esser, Chapter 1). As with previous examples, it is very important to specify what this core statement means and embed it into a broader context. Indeed, we have done this in our introductory chapter. There, we write that our definition is "not to say that different political or social actors and institutions have lost all their autonomy and influence" and that the "exact nature, extent, and effects of media influence are always contextual and situational – and an empirical question" (Strömbäck & Esser, Chapter 1). And we add that "as a consequence, media influence should not be equated with media effects". The reasons we give for these restrictions are that "most media-effect theories largely fail to account for the interactions, inter-dependencies, and transactions" between media and politics at the meso and macro levels of analysis. This reciprocal character "makes it difficult to treat media as an exogenous and independent variable" (Strömbäck & Esser, Chapter 1 of this volume).

We are tempted to say that many of the additions and modifications that some of our authors have emphasized in this regard have been contemplated – if not explicitly expressed – in previous scholarship. On the other hand, the points made are too important to be ignored. Our authors have emphasized in clear language the necessary differentiations and clarifications for such terms as "media influence", "media autonomy" and "political autonomy" as well as "interactions" and reflexive "trans-actions". In particular, they have introduced farther-reaching theoretical reasons and empirical evidence than we have been able to find in current research. We expressly recommend a sensitive and receptive stance with regard to these points in further theory-building. A concrete conse-quence of this could be – following suggestions made by Marcinkowski and Steiner as well as Schulz – to speak in future mediatization research of "media pull" instead of "media power". To emphasize the (often indi-rect and reciprocal) impact media have on politics, we decided to use the terms "spill-over effects" or "ripple effects" in a number of places in our introductory chapter (Strömbäck & Esser, Chapter 1). In contrast to our ear-lier writings (Strömbäck, 2008; Strömbäck & Esser, 2009), and with respect to the third and fourth dimensions of mediatization, we now also find it more appropriate to distinguish between the extent to which media con-tent (third dimension) and political actors, organizations and institutions (fourth dimensions) are *guided* rather than *governed* by media logic vs. polit-ical logic (Strömbäck & Esser, Chapter 1). Although we never intended to say that there are media or political actors, organizations and institutions that are completely governed by media logic – this marks one of the extreme endpoints of the continuum in our earlier writings – some have read this as suggesting more widespread and undifferentiated media influence than we intended. "Governed" may thus be too strong a word, while "guided" better expresses how we conceptualize the mediatization of politics along the third and fourth dimensions.

Our authors wholeheartedly support many of the premises that we have summarized in our introductory chapter. They agree with the idea that the process of mediatization consists of "four distinct but highly inte-grated dimensions", and they provide ample evidence in their support, arguably with the exception of the fourth dimension – that political actors, organizations and institutions are "mainly guided by media logic". Important to note, though, is that we have always claimed that mediatization is a matter of degree and an empirical question. Hence, an important empirical question that remains is the degree to which political actors, organizations and institutions are guided by media logic.

There is also complete agreement throughout the book with the position – as we have phrased it in the introductory chapter – that mediatization is not "a linear or unidirectional process" nor have political institutions, organizations and actors "all become media slaves". There is also complete agreement that mediatization is "contingent on a host of factors at different levels of analysis that may vary both within and across countries" and that the "relationship between media and politics should always be understood as interactive" (Strömbäck & Esser, Chapter 1). Nevertheless, the in-depth statements made by our authors in this regard are of significant value for a better understanding of the entire paradigm and arguably one of the most important contributions this book makes to theory-building.

A great challenge for future theory-building lies in the increased fragmentation of the term "media" with regard to the empirically unanswered question of whether or not we can continue to conceive of the multitude of platforms providing news contents as an institution. Another question closely connected with this is to what extent a new conceptualization of "news media logic" under the influence of "new" communication platforms is required. Based in no small part on the collection of chapters in this book, it is our opinion that the definitions and differentiations of media logic (and political logic) that we have suggested in the introductory chapter are still justified and compatible with all of the relativizations and additions of our authors. We will not repeat our conceptualizations of political logic and media logic here. But we will say that they account for the fact that political logic varies across institutions and countries (as pointed out by Marcinkowski & Steiner, and Donges & Jarren) as well as for the fact that the various facets of political logic change depending on how closely an institution is involved in the battle for votes, offices or public support (as pointed out by Marcinkowski & Steiner, and D'Angelo et al.). Our conceptualization of media logic can explain the often found evidence (see Van Aelst et al.; D'Angelo et al.) that the front-stage part of political processes (called "politics") is mediatized more easily than the backstage part (called "policy"). It also accounts for often noticed differences (see Donges & Jarren; Schulz) in news organizations with regard to their commercial orientation (quality vs. tabloid) or their technological basis (offline vs. online). Nonetheless, and especially with regard to the last aspect, we are very eager to see what new facets of media logic will be suggested in future mediatization research to account for the specific modus operandi of online news media.

Another great challenge for future theory-building and research is to continue efforts at operationalizing mediatization along all four dimensions to allow systematic, empirical research on the mediatization of politics. We believe this is crucially important, because otherwise mediatization risks becoming "a matter of belief rather than a proper theory that can be tested, refined, and perhaps even refuted" (Strömbäck & Esser, Chapter 1). A key part of this is to continue efforts at exploring how mediatization could integrate other theories on the politics–media relationship and even borrow empirical indicators from those theories. The chapters by De Vreese on journalistic news framing, Van Aelst et al. on political agenda-setting and D'Angelo et al. on metacoverage, to take three examples from this volume, all convincingly show the potential of mediatization as an integrative theoretical framework and how fruitful such efforts can be.

While our authors do not suggest precise definitions for political logic and media logic, they have pointed to their situational character, which we regard as another significant contribution this book makes to theory-building. We have already stated in the introductory chapter that "those political institutions and actors dependent on public support must communicate through news media". With regard to the identification of contextual conditions, under which mediatization of politics takes place most strongly, D'Angelo et al., Van Aelst et al. and especially Marcinkowski and Steiner have delivered impressive contributions.

In conclusion, we can state that the combined contributions in this book add greatly to the establishment and contextualization of the theory of mediatization that we have outlined in the introductory chapter. We have enjoyed working on this volume and have learned a great deal from the collaboration with our authors. We are convinced that this volume will not only contribute to a deeper understanding of mediatization but also foster further research into the mediatization of politics.

References

Esser, F. (2013). Mediatization as a Challenge: Media Logic versus Political Logic. In H. Kriesi, S. Lavenex, F. Esser, J. Matthes, M. Bühlmann & D. Bochsler (Eds.), *Democracy in the Age of Globalization and Mediatization* (pp. 155–176). Basingstoke: Palgrave Macmillan.

Hallin, D. C., & Mancini, P. (2004). *Comparing Media Systems: Three Models of Media and Politics*. New York: Cambridge University Press.

Mazzoleni, G., & Schulz, W. (1999). Mediatization of Politics: A Challenge for Democracy? *Political Communication*, 16(3), 247–261.

Strömbäck, J. (2008). Four Phases of Mediatization: An Analysis of the Mediatization of Politics. *The International Journal of Press/Politics*, 13(3), 228–246.

Strömbäck, J., & Esser, F. (2009). Shaping Politics: Mediatization and Media Interventionism. In K. Lundby (Ed.), *Mediatization: Concept, Changes, Consequences* (pp. 205–224). New York: Peter Lang.

Index

Note: Page references to figures are indicated by an '*f*'; to tables by a '*t*'.

Printed and bound in the United States of America